MUSIC EDUCATION
PRINCIPLES AND PROGRAMS

I dedicate this book
to my associates

GLADYS TIPTON
BEATRICE LANDECK
HARRIET NORDHOLM
ROY E. FREEBURG
JACK M. WATSON

MUSIC EDUCATION
PRINCIPLES AND PROGRAMS

JAMES L. MURSELL
Teachers College
Columbia University

SILVER BURDETT COMPANY
MORRISTOWN, N.J. · NEW YORK · CHICAGO
SAN FRANCISCO · DALLAS · ATLANTA

45598

Copyright © 1956, by

SILVER BURDETT COMPANY

Printed in the United States of America

PREFACE

This book is the outcome of reflection on and study of music education extending throughout most of my professional career, brought to a head by intensive cooperative work on what I believe is a highly significant enterprise. As the years have passed, bringing many opportunities for discussion with able people and many challenges to thought, it has seemed to me that my understanding of the issues of music education has grown clearer, and that my convictions have defined themselves better. This fruition, for whatever it may be worth, is what I have to offer here. When I wrote my first book on music education, nearly thirty years ago, I thought that if, because of it, a few children here and there might be better taught, I would feel amply rewarded. I have the same feeling about this book.

I am indebted to so many people both for the evolution of my thinking in general and for the preparation of this book in particular, that I find myself quite at a loss. I have learned so much from so many that I cannot possibly thank them all here. But there are certain individuals whom it is both an obligation and a privilege to mention.

First of all must come my five associates to whom I have dedicated this book, so that their names need not be repeated here. I would like to tell them in this public and somewhat formal manner what I am sure they know—that working with them has been a great experience. Very much in this book has emerged from the meeting of our minds, but I accept full individual responsibility for all that I say in these pages.

Beyond this group there are a number who have been extraordinarily kind and helpful. Dr. Helen Heffernan, Chief, Bureau of Elementary Education of the California State Department of Education, has read the book in proof. Her extended, careful, and penetrating comments and criticisms have been most helpful. To Mr. William Hartshorn, Supervisor in Charge, Music Education, of the Los Angeles Public Schools I owe a debt of gratitude almost embarrassingly great. His lengthy, detailed, critical, yet encouraging review of the book, again in proof form, has been a professional favor so great that I can hardly hope to repay it. Furthermore, it is a heartening evidence of the friendship which exists between us. I also wish to tender my very warm thanks to Miss Eileen MacMillan of Western Washington College of Education, Bellingham, Washington, for her judicious and stimulating reactions to large sections of this book, which she read, and which we discussed together.

To all these individuals I wish to tender my sincerest thanks, while at the same time I remember not without genuine pain that I am indebted also to a multitude of others to whom I cannot so directly convey my gratitude here.

JAMES L. MURSELL

CONTENTS

PART ONE

THE FOUNDATIONS OF THE PROGRAM

How This Book Is Organized and What it Tries to Do

If you will glance through this book, perhaps referring to the table of contents, I am sure you will soon understand how it is organized. But I think that a word or two of explanation may be helpful.

In writing the book I have tried to live up to the title. I have set up thirteen principles, each of which is a brief, compact statement of what I think is the proper point of view on a fundamental issue in music education. Each principle is dealt with in a separate chapter, which begins with a statement of the principle itself, goes on to explain it in a general way, and to give the reasons for it, and then shows how it applies to the music program. Hence the title—*Music Education, Principles and Program*.

The book is divided into three parts. The first part deals with what I call the *Foundations of the Music Program*, namely, its aims, its orientation, and its general content. This takes up four chapters. Next come the *Special Areas of the Program*, by which I mean music reading, singing, playing instruments, rhythmic activities, and listening. The third part deals with the *Coordination of the Program*. Here I have in mind three factors which should not be considered special areas or special-type activities, because they run through and permeate the whole program, and hold it together as a unified whole. They are integration, creation, and administration.

In this book I have dealt mainly with the elementary-school music program. But the principles apply just as well to music teaching everywhere, in secondary schools, in music schools, and in private studios. For I believe that they point straight to fundamental issues, that all teachers of music, and everyone interested in the teaching of music, ought to understand.

Anyone is likely to get more out of a book if, when he reads it, he understands its general plan and the intentions of its writer. Then he can see the relationship of one part of it to other parts, and also to the book as a whole. This is why I have presented this short explanation. Now I invite your attention to chapter one!

The Aims of the Music Program:
Their Importance and Meaning

The Principle

As we plan and carry out our music program, we should give constant and earnest thought to its aims, always trying to see just what they are, and just what we should do if we are to fulfill them.

What is it that, in the widest sense, we are trying to do when we bring music to children? Why should we want to bring music to children at all? These are fundamental questions. We should think about them as hard, as seriously, and as well as we can. We should be willing to bring all our work into line with whatever answers seem right, and reasonable, and true. That is what our first principle tells us.

This first principle is a brief, compact statement; but there is a great deal in it. To help you see what is in it, I am going to consider four things:

1. *Why* should we think about aims?
2. *How* should we think about aims?
3. *When* should we think about aims?
4. *Who* should think about aims?

5

I. Why Think About Aims?

Probably you will agree that it is a good thing to think about our aims, and to ask ourselves what all our work is really for. Indeed, I hardly see how you can deny it. But I believe it is important to see just why thinking about aims is worth while, and what it can do for us.

As a matter of fact, there does not seem to be much good thinking about aims among music educators. Many books and articles have been written on music education; but there is remarkably little in them about aims. Hundreds of courses of study in music start off with a statement of aims. But quite often the aims that are formulated seem rather unreal, and are quite unrelated to the working plan that follows. One has to suspect that they were put in to satisfy the curriculum committee or the curriculum director, rather than because they flowed from the constant and serious thinking of the people who made the course of study. This suggests what is probably the case, namely, that working music educators do not put in much time on hard thinking or serious discussions about their basic aims.

Now this raises a doubt. If large numbers of serious, able, and devoted persons give little attention to the question of aims, the reason may be that the question is not worth serious consideration. Such certainly might be the conclusion. But I do not think it is the correct conclusion; for there are two excellent reasons why music educators tend to neglect this kind of thinking.

First, the average working music educator is far busier than he has any business to be. He has to plan, give, and supervise lessons, to look after music, recordings, instruments, and equipment, to organize rehearsals, to arrange programs, to complete official paper work, to help out here and there with many kinds of odd jobs. All this is taken for granted, so he is apt to find himself treated as a sort of musical chore boy, rather than as a serious educator with a well-defined and respected function. He has to work from hand to mouth; and to ask him to think hard and long about basic issues is to expect something above and beyond the call of duty. If he omits to do such thinking, this does not prove that he considers it useless, for he has to work under conditions that discourage it; and those who unthinkingly impose such conditions have a large share of the blame.

Again, the music educator is a specialist. Some general educators instantly say that this is really why he does not do more fundamental thinking; for they intimate that he sees nothing but his specialty. Of course this is always possible; but there is quite another side to the matter. Every specialist ought to be enthusiastic about his specialty. As for the music educator, he is the trustee of a great art, with vast potentialities, and with problems peculiar to it. It is his bounden duty to defend his work, for in so doing, he is defending the true interests of the children. He can see better than anyone else the things that music can do for children; and so is able to make a unique contribution to the common thinking, if he is encouraged to do so. But often he is not encouraged. Quite the contrary, indeed! Often his general-educator associates regale him with tirades about his narrowness, and brush off his suggestions as interested special pleading. General educators who take such an attitude do well to bethink themselves that they too are specialists—specialists in general ideas, plans, practices, and techniques—and that they have plenty of blind spots, and are by no means endowed *ex officio* with universal omniscience. They should be willing to learn with and from their fellow specialists, for the enrichment of the common thinking. If they are not willing, they are not merely specialists, which they ought to be, but narrow specialists, which they ought not to be. When, as not seldom happens, music educators find themselves treated by narrowly specialized general educators as though their ideas were worthless and annoying, they are naturally discouraged from cultivating any ideas. Incidentally, anyone who imagines that to call a general educator a narrow specialist is a contradiction, has much to learn about the facts of educational life.

So I am sure that the reason why music educators do comparatively little serious thinking about aims is not that they consider it useless. The reason is that they are hustled and bustled to excess, and get little positive encouragement, and even positive discouragement. Music educators as I have come to know them are outstandingly eager to make their work count for all that it has in it, which is a great deal. And one of the best ways for them to set about doing that very thing is to think long and hard about aims. Why this is so I shall now try to point out.

1. The clarification of basic aims is the way to bring about that widespread cooperative understanding needed for a good music program today.

The place of music in the educational scheme is changing because the scheme is changing. Classroom teachers are being urged to handle their own music, or most of it. Integrated or comprehensive units such as Our Community, Indians, or Our South American Friends, and the like, are being used, with music introduced into them.* Also various forms of activity curriculum are in operation, though much less widely. And on higher levels there are many programs of general education.

Many music educators are concerned about these developments. They fear that the sequential music program, with its recognized place in the schedule, is being undermined, and that the schools may be on the way to offering nothing but sporadic, superficial, incidental musical activities and experiences. And they regard this as a great threat to their work.

This puts music educators in a very difficult position. They instinctively feel that, if the sequential music program were destroyed, it would be a great misfortune. They are moved to

---

* For reasons that will appear later, I prefer to call such units "comprehensive units" rather than "integrated units," and I use the latter term only because of its familiarity.

protest. Yet they seem to be going against the tide of modern developments. And they resent being considered merely as a pressure group, fighting for its own interests.

What is the solution? It is to do some basic educational thinking about basic aims.

Music can do certain very desirable things for people. It can achieve certain great life-values, or human values. Moreover, these values are to some extent unique. They are unique at least in the sense that music can realize them better than anything else, in the setting of our school life and work. Music can do certain things for people, young and old, that nothing else can do as readily. These are our aims.

Yet these aims are completely harmonious with modern educational trends. Classroom teachers who live and work with their children and know them well as persons, guidance workers concerned with the personal growth of individuals, curriculum workers and administrators who think in terms of the over-all aims of education, can understand very clearly the values that music can realize, and can sympathize with them whole-heartedly. So it is very important for music educators to clarify and formulate these aims. And of course classroom teachers, guidance workers, curriculum workers, and administrators should share in this business of clarification and formulation. For it should be a cooperative business which points hopefully to basic agreements.

Then comes the question of application. At once certain conclusions appear. The values of music cannot be realized by sporadic, superficial, incidental experiences. But the wide use of music in comprehensive or integrated units, in general education programs, and above all the contribution of the classroom teacher are of the utmost value, *so long as they are parts of a planned, sequential, coordinated whole.* If a program made up of nothing but haphazard, superficial experiences cannot do what it ought to do, neither can a narrow, self-contained program, isolated from everything else that is happening in the schools.

All this becomes clear as day when we think rightly about basic aims. It can be just as clear to general educators as to music educators. So constant and earnest thinking about basic aims can be the heart of cooperative action, and can lead music educators to see that modern developments, far from being a menace, are a great opportunity.

2. There are a great many questions and issues, less far-reaching than that just discussed, but still urgent, with which the present-day music educator must deal. He can deal with them aright only in the light of a clear understanding of his basic aims.

Modern music education is in a very experimental state. Many different and often conflicting practices are being tried out and recommended. When should we introduce music reading? How should we teach it? How much should we emphasize it? Should we use simple instruments, such as melody flutes, tone bells, autoharps? Should children make such instruments? How should rhythmic activities be carried out? How far up the grades should they go? Should we have rhythm bands? Should children sing with or without piano accompaniment? Should we have an elementary school choir? An elementary school band? What is "music appreciation" and how should we teach it? These are typical questions on which the music educator has to take some stand, even though he cannot always decide alone on what will finally be done.

How is he to arrive at decisions?

He may, perhaps, try to follow what he considers "modern" practice. But this is not very satisfactory, for modern practice covers a great deal, and some of it is probably wrong. Or he may accept the ideas of some "authority"—perhaps an individual, perhaps an organization such as the Music Educators National Conference. But individual authorities differ, and even the Conference may not be perfectly consistent and infallible. In the last resort, the working music educator, faced with a bewildering range of choices, is likely to decide pretty much on the basis of his likes and dislikes, his preferences and prejudices, after which he invents reasons to justify himself.

There is only one adequate way of getting a good answer to all these inescapable questions, and that is by having a reason for one's choice. Why introduce music reading at a certain stage? Why handle it in a certain way? Why use or avoid simple instruments? Why introduce rhythmic activities? Why have or refuse to have a rhythm band? Why acquaint children with recordings? It all depends on what one is trying to do, on where one wants to go. It all depends, that is to say, on one's aims. Until one is clear about one's aims, one cannot think intelligently about procedures. Here is another reason why it is important to give constant, earnest thought to the problem of basic aims.

3. Constant and earnest thought about ultimate aims, and a constant endeavor to see more and more clearly what they mean and how they apply is by far the surest means of continuing professional growth for any teacher.

A very interesting research study once indicated that many teachers improve through experience in service for about seven years, and then strike a level of effectiveness which lasts for the rest of their careers. What this means is that it takes an ordinary teacher six or seven years to learn the routines of the job, such as keeping records, making reports, preparing lessons and tests, marking, managing a classroom, handling discipline, and so forth. An experienced teacher, in the ordinary sense, is one who can do such things smoothly and confidently. After such a person has mastered these professional techniques he is quite apt to stop developing and improving. He tends to lose enthusiasm, to become impatient with new ideas (not because they are wrong but because they are inconvenient), to get into a rut, stay there, and like it.

But good teaching is far more than a matter of smooth routines. It is an art whose challenges are endless and whose possibilities are unlimited. A good, a growing teacher does not swallow each new *nostrum* just because it is new; but he welcomes and assays each new suggestion, because he knows that there is always more to learn about his business. He realizes that he has in himself unrealized possibilities. Above all, he remains flexible, willing and eager to change and to grow.

If a teacher wants to retain this precious flexibility, nothing will help so much as being haunted by such questions as these: What, ultimately, am I trying to accomplish? What are my associates trying to accomplish? What is our program really for? What good does it do? How far am I really accomplishing what I should? How can I tell what I am, in fact, accomplishing? That is to say, to retain a career-long flexibility, a teacher needs to be haunted by the question of ultimate aims.

4. Constant and earnest thought about determining aims sets up a challenge needed by every teacher and every group of teachers. This is the challenge constantly to assess their own success and failure.

What about that lesson I just taught? Was it a success, or a failure, or perhaps a bit of both? What were the strong points and the weak points of my work last year? What are the strong and weak points of the program which I and my associates are carrying on? Did that program really get anywhere last year? If so, where? What about this new practice we have introduced? Perhaps there were some rough spots, some difficulties; but does it give promise of working out? If so, in what direction and in what sense? These are the sort of questions that every teacher and every group of teachers should constantly have in mind. But if they are to be answered—nay, if they are to be intelligently asked—it is necessary to have a yardstick, a criterion. And the only yardstick is a clear notion of where we are trying to go, and of what we are trying to accomplish. The only possible yardstick is a clear notion of determining aims.

II. How Should We Think About Aims?

It is an undeniable certainty that a clear understanding of the aims of the music program has immense practical value. But to think about these aims successfully and to formulate them to good effect takes some doing.

I once tried the experiment of asking a group of competent and experienced music educators to write down what they considered to be the basic aims of music in education, and to indicate the sort of program they thought was indicated by the aims they chose. Nearly all of them "fell flat on their faces." They were smitten with a feeling of helplessness, which showed all too clearly in the ideas they produced. If you, yourself, will try this same experiment before reading any further, you too may have this same frustrating experience. I am inclined to think that the difficulty, the intangibility of the problem of ultimate aims is a main reason why so many music educators tend to brush it aside, comforting themselves with the thought that it does not matter much.

Now there is a very definite reason why the group of music educators with whom I worked failed in their attempt to think through the problem of aims. *They did not know how to set about the job.* But it is a job that is not only well worth doing, but that can be done, if only one tackles it properly. The following points will not tell you everything. They will not do your thinking for you. But they will give you a helpful and promising approach to the vital business of earnest, constant, constructive thinking about the aims of the music program.

1. *When you think about aims, think first of all about people.*
What people? Those from four years old and upwards with

whom you deal from day to day. These are the people whom the music program exists to serve. Think of them as they are, here and now, all around you. Name names, remember faces, recall personalities.

What should you think about? About what music can do for these people, as people; about what it can do for them here and now, and later on. These are the questions on which you should center. Your answers will be your aims.

Notice that you should think about *people,* not about pupils, not even about children. Think about real people, whom you see, and deal with, and know. Think about them as human beings, in the setting of their own lives. Think about them in the setting of their homes, their enjoyments, their friends, their feelings, their duties, their opportunities, their limitations What can music do for them? Be as specific as you know how. Do some thinking about this or that particular person, troublesome, shy, bright, privileged, underprivileged, sick, robust. Your music program exists to serve this person, now and later on, to bring into his life lasting values that otherwise would not be there. What are these services? What are these values? When you have answered those questions, you have your aims.

That is how to start thinking about aims.

2. *Think about these people both as they now are, and as they will be in the future.*

A large order? Yes, indeed! But a necessary one, for education must deal with the future, or there is no point to it at all. Yet the future cannot be foreseen. Who can predict what Tommy or Sally will be, or what they will be doing twenty years from now? No one, surely! How then, can you possibly think to good purpose about these people, not only as they now are but also as they will be in the years to come?

You can do this seemingly difficult bit of thinking if you will cling to one great and releasing idea. This is the idea of *growth*. You cannot tell what the future holds for Tommy or Sally, but you do know for certain that both of them and all the rest are growing up. They will change and mature. They will meet responsibility, trial, success, failure, grief, joy, work, marriage, parenthood, citizenship, and last of all, old age. They are growing up right now, as you well know. But they will, or at any rate they can, keep on growing as long as they live.

Here is your cue. Is it possible for your music program, here and now, to give them anything that will help them to carry through better with the great adventure of their lives? Anything that will help to keep them from frustration and defeat, that will help to keep them from becoming warped and stunted, that will help to keep them growing as long as life lasts? If so, just what? Your answers to this question are your aims.

So we have carried our thinking one step further. The aims of your music program are ways of growing with which music can help.

3. *In your thinking, be very sure to distinguish between ends and means.*

Music itself is a means, not an end. The effects of music on living, on people, on growing—these are the ends you must formulate and clarify.

This distinction between means and ends is vital, and if you disregard it you will never clarify your aims. One often hears talk about finer taste, better discrimination, the ability to sing, the ability to read, as proper outcomes of the music program. But these are not really ends or aims at all.

Desirable outcomes, are they? Why are they desirable? Who desires them, why, and for whom? If such musical accomplishments and insights are desirable at all, they are so only because they are good influences on living and growing. Is it really true that a person will succeed better in the great adventure of living if he prefers Bach to Boogiewoogie, if he can play the violin, if he can read the musical notation? If so, just why? Just how? Until you can answer questions as specific, as

sharp-edged as these, you have not even begun to think in terms
of genuine aims. For music is a means, not an end; and everything desirable in your program is so because it is a desirable
human influence.

4. *In your thinking about aims, always search for a genuine
relationship between means and ends.*

To dream up various high-falutin' aims without a glimmer
about how music can actually help to accomplish them is very
easy. It is also quite useless, quite futile, and very bad thinking. Valid aims are not pipe-dreams. They are practical possibilities, with practical meanings.

One often sees music courses of study with an introduction
formulating fine, large, sweeping statements of what are intended as aims, such as democratic behavior, respect for in-
tegrity, power of concentration, cooperativeness, and what not.
Such statements are supposed to be formulations of aims, and
are labelled and presented as such. But they are not really aims
at all, and for an excellent reason. No one really shoots at them.
And an aim that is not a target is simply not an aim.

If you want to think with good effect about the aims of your
program, you must certainly define the actual desirable effects
that music can have on the living and growing of actual people.
This much we have already seen. But, too, you must go a step
further. You must also see, dimly at first no doubt, but more
and more clearly and definitely, just how your program must
be shaped to produce these desired effects. Unless you can see,
at least to some extent, this relationship—the relationship between means and ends—you are wasting your time and probably
deceiving yourself.

5. *Pinpoint your aims.*

From time to time, formulate your aims in brief, carefully
phrased statements. Write them down. List them. Examine
them. Revise them. There is always a risk, when one does a
job of thinking, that one may be satisfied with a headful of

ideas that are quite good but never very definite. One of the best of all ways of knowing exactly where you are is to put such ideas down on paper. Then you can look at them, consider them, study them, reflect about them. You have arrived at a specific stage, and thinking can go onward from there.

Exactly what human influences do you think your music program can and should bring to bear? Unless you can answer that question briefly and in writing, the probability is that your mind is not yet entirely clear. And clarity and definiteness about your aims is essential if they are to be of real value.

6. *Do your own thinking and deciding.*

Now we come to the most formidable and the most fundamental point of all. Perhaps I can put it best in the form of a question. How can one think out, decide upon, and formulate the proper aims of the music program at all? We have seen that music itself is a means, not an end. The aims to have in mind are the desirable effects that music can have on people. They are influences that music can and should exert, directions or tendencies that music can give to growth. How can you, or I, or anyone properly decide what these ought to be?

Only through your own reflection, insight, meditation, wisdom! That is the only possible answer.

There are plenty of research studies and surveys dealing with the problem of educational aims in general, and some of them have a bearing on music. All such work is worth considering and examining. But none of it will give you ready-made answers. For instance, one such study showed that in this country people do very little music reading. One is quite willing to believe that this is a fact. But in and of itself it tells you very little. Perhaps a great deal of music reading would go on if more people could read music well. Perhaps people who never read music would be better off as human beings if they did read it. Perhaps not. It is not the fact itself, but the issues it raises that are important for you. The question is not what actually happens, but what should happen. And this is something that the facts alone cannot decide.

There are many excellent statements of general educational aims, drawn up sometimes by individuals, sometimes by committee groups. These statements also bear upon music in many cases. Sometimes they have been very influential, and you would be unwise to ignore them. You can get a great deal out of them *if you use them properly*.

My strong advice would be not to start your thinking with any ready-made formulation of educational aims, no matter how influential, no matter how much admired. When you do this, you are starting with *words,* and then your problem is to translate these words into practical meanings that will apply to your own doings from day to day, from hour to hour. This is a treacherous task, and tends to be an unrewarding one. From time to time music educators have taken some widely heralded formulation of general basic aims, and tried to work out the implications and meanings for their own field. Usually the outcome has been disappointing and unconvincing.

Remember that in thinking about aims, your proper starting point is not with words, but with people. There, and nowhere else are your basic facts. There you will find your true leads. As you begin to see for yourself what music can and should do for the people with whom you deal, as a means of better living and fuller growth, then general formulations can be very helpful indeed. By examining them you can fill in the gaps of your own thinking, pick up ideas that otherwise you might miss, see how to make good and useful formulations. But do not feel that the thing to do is to take over somebody else's notions.

In the next chapter of this book I shall put forward a number of basic aims that seem to me feasible and valid. Since these are expressly intended as aims for the music program, they have a closer and more direct relationship to your work than formulations of aims for education in general. But still do not take

them over simply as they stand. Let me say here and now what
I shall say often again, that they are intended only as starting
points, only as suggestions. They are no more than helps for
our own thinking. Such helps can certainly be useful. But the
only aims that are likely to do you much good, and that are
likely to affect your own work and your own development,
are the aims that you think out and decide upon for yourself
as you reflect about what music can and should do for the
people with whom you deal.

II. When Should We Think About Aims?

1. Your consideration of the determining aims of your program and your work should be a preoccupation constantly in the
background of your mind, and it should come to consciousness
unpredictably and often.

Frequently music educators give thought to aims only once
in a while, and on special occasions. They are called upon to
develop a new course of study in music. The curriculum director has said that all new courses of study must begin with a
statement of aims. So they wrinkle their brows and proceed to
supply one. Or they find themselves put on a committee dealing
with the aims of the curriculum as a whole, and so they
collaborate as well as they can in some sort of verbal formulation. Such "special occasion" thinking about aims is likely to be
valuable only if everyone concerned has been reflecting about
the matter more or less consciously all the time. Otherwise, all
that usually comes of it is a set of well-sounding platitudes
which have no real meaning and no practical application.

What am I trying to do for these children of mine in the long
run? What are the actual and lasting effects of my work upon
them? What is the actual influence of our music program?
These are the questions that should haunt a teacher's mind.
They are the questions out of which a real understanding of

valid aims arises. They are the questions which should always be there in the background, and often in the foreground, as a teacher deals with people from hour to hour, from day to day, from year to year. They are the master questions, and one should never get very far from them.

They are questions to which there is no quick or easy answer. Indeed they are questions to which there is no final answer at all. When one thinks as one should about aims, one is thinking about people, about the true values of their lives, and of how music can help in the achievement of those values. Such thinking, in the very nature of things, is bound always to be unfinished business. True, a teacher does well to formulate his understanding of his aims from time to time. But any such formulation should always be in effect a progress report to himself, and nothing more. For what is required is that he must grow in wisdom, in insight, in comprehension of his own purposes, and in understanding of how to achieve them better.

2. Some of the most fruitful thinking you are ever likely to do about the aims of the music program can occur in connection with your daily work.

Here, for instance, is a boy who "just hasn't liked music." When the class sings, he sits dumb and cross-looking. Listening experiences seem to bore him, and he keeps out of rhythmic activities as much as he can. In the late third grade he has a chance to experiment with a simple instrument, and like magic all is changed. He gets permission to take the instrument home with him, makes himself almost a virtuoso on it, wins the admiration of the other children, and is transformed into a musical enthusiast.

Here is another boy who transfers into the school, also in grade three. Immediately he establishes himself as class problem number one. Sometimes he is a maddening smart-Alec; sometimes his role is that of sullen, unresponsive bump on a log. Nobody likes him, and the teacher begins to experience the first onset of despair. Then the class embarks on a unit on Indians, with the thought that some suitable music may be found, and other suitable music composed by the children, along with a text. Not waiting for any suggestions, this young trouble-spot arrives at school with a tune he has developed overnight. It suits the purpose perfectly. He presents it. It is tried out, accepted with astonishment and delight, learned, and written down by everybody to be kept and enjoyed. His attitude toward the group, and theirs toward him are dramatically altered. He has found himself in the social setting of the class and of the school, and music has been the means of this self-discovery.

A certain junior high school in one of the most underprivileged districts of a great city has made for itself a most formidable reputation for difficulty. Many of the children come from shockingly overcrowded tenement homes. During the night they run wild in the streets, for family care and discipline are almost unheard of. At school it is almost impossible to prevent them from creating bedlam. They spatter walls with ink, smash furniture, fight in the corridors, and from time to time there have been cases of physical assault upon the teachers. Then a band program is introduced. There is a wave of interest, and a desire to enroll and participate. The band director keeps a firm hand, but he is wise enough to allow a large measure of self-discipline. Responsibility for the care of instruments, for punctuality and behavior at rehearsals, is accepted, and those who do not measure up hear about it very quickly from their fellow performers. Music with a real challenge is undertaken, and no amount of pains, work, and care seems too much to bring it to a creditable proficiency. The influence of the activity is very manifest in the lives of all those taking part, and as time goes on it pervades the whole school.

All these are actual happenings. The music specialists concerned, and also the general teachers and administrators who are close to such events cannot help but realize at least something of what music can do and should do. It is hard to imagine any teacher being a witness of such events without being stimulated to think. He may or may not channel his thinking into a statement of feasible aims for music. But he has, before his eyes, an electrifying suggestion as to what such aims should properly be.

Episodes of this kind, even though not always so dramatic, happen continually in the daily work of every teacher. They furnish some of the best possible starting points for that earnest, constant reflection about aims which is recommended in our first principle. Do not let them go past you unheeded. They are precious opportunities for learning, for growth, for the deepening of insights.

3. Much good thinking about the aims of the music program can and should go on in the privacy of your own mind; but also much fruitful thinking is social thinking. Seek and cherish and use opportunities for thinking along with other people about this fundamental topic.

A personal discussion with a parent, for instance, about the musical interests and proclivities of his child, can be a learning, thought-provoking experience for you. It very often happens that a parent who is a musical layman will see certain fundamental things with a directness and simplicity which you find startling. He raises points, asks questions, makes comments which perhaps have never occurred to you because they seem so obvious—once they are said.

"May loves music," a mother once said in the course of conversation with a music specialist, "She's taking piano, and there's never the least trouble getting her to practice. I even have to call her away from the piano sometimes. And she listens to music programs on the radio and really knows quite an amazing lot of classical music. But she just hates singing songs with syllables. I wonder why you do that in school?"

A vital topic was opened up. The music specialist had to

clarify his own position and practice, and not merely to clarify it but to re-think it so as to make it convincing both to the mother and to himself. The great question "Why?" had been raised, and once that question really comes up, thinking does not naturally stop short of some conclusions about where one is heading and about the ultimate aims one is seeking.

For the teacher who has the problem of aims on his mind, conferences and discussions with parents can be illuminating and thought-provoking. So also can conversations with pupils. From time to time there have been rather elaborate questionnaire and opinionnaire studies, in which children have been asked what they think of this or that subject or instructional practice. On the whole I doubt if you will find such procedures very helpful. Something far simpler, far more direct, will probably bear far richer fruit. Do not expect children to present you with considered, studied opinions on educational matters. A casual interchange, a chance remark, a question briefly answered, in the corridor, on the street, in the room while classes are changing, can start a whole train of thought which may deeply affect your views and your practice.

Then, of course, a talk with your colleagues and friends at home, on trips to visit schools, in the lunchroom, can and should open up many a vista. Such opportunities are worth seeking and cherishing. Do not hesitate to raise the great question of aims, sometimes indirectly, sometimes directly, for there is no more interesting and intriguing educational topic in the world. Of course there will be, and should be, formalized, scheduled group discussions of aims. But very much of the value, the rewarding effectiveness of such discussions depends upon the thinking, both individual and social, that goes along on casual occasions where there are no agenda, no calling of a group to order, but just two or three people chatting, perhaps for a passing moment, perhaps for an hour, about something interesting and important to them all.

4. Following the last thought a step further, there should certainly be special occasions, "roundup" occasions, so to speak, when thinking comes to a head, and an effort is made group-wise, to formulate aims explicitly. Such occasions are very important, because thinking that is never brought to a focus tends to degenerate into dreaming, and to lose all touch with action. A new course of study has to be drawn up. A manual has to be prepared. A committee report must be licked into shape. A statement to the whole staff has to be formulated. These should never be mere routine challenges. They should be occasions for determing where thinking has gone so far, and for re-orienting thinking for further developments.

It often happens that groups of teachers find these special occasions which come along once in a while somewhat of a bore, and a chore, and an ungrateful task rather than a stimulating and intriguing experience. This is an almost certain sign that no constant stream of active thinking is going on. When a group of people who, for a long time, have done nothing but plod the daily round, are suddenly faced with a challenge to unfamiliar and difficult thinking, they are not likely to get very much, to give very much, or to accomplish very much. But a staff that has been thinking, individually and group-wise, about basic issues, will relish the chance to bring this thinking to a focus, and to use the focus for new departures.

It may be very well, from time to time, to have meetings of such a staff without any special business to be done, without any report to develop, without any special agenda at all, just for the sake of an evening of relaxed and schedule-free talk and discussion. To offer a hint to administrators, do not have such meetings merely for the sake of having meetings. Staff meetings should always be for some worthwhile purpose, or they fail even as morale-builders. Either there should be something definite to do, or it should be evident that some or all are full of thoughts and ideas on which time can fruitfully be spent, even though no definite conclusions and decisions may emerge at once.

IV. Who Should Think About Aims?

There are three points to be made in answer to this question. Such thinking is primarily the business of the *local* staff. It is primarily the business of the *music* staff. It should ramify as widely, and involve as extensive cooperation, as possible.

1. The business of thinking about, clarifying, defining, formulating, and applying the aims of the music program is, first and foremost, the business of the *local* staff. This is the first point to make in answer to our fourth question; and it is so important that the reasons for it must be carefully set forth.

A. The first reason arises out of the very nature of aims themselves. We have seen that the proper and valid aims of the music program are always and only the beneficial effects that music can have on people. It is these effects that we wish to achieve, and our program should be designed to achieve them. If this is so, then we ought to think first, not about people in general, or about human nature and human psychology in general, but about the actual human beings with whom we are dealing. Otherwise it is almost certain that we will lose touch with reality, and slip into mere verbalizing.

Let me go back to the underprivileged and very difficult junior high school I mentioned a little while back. The whole local staff of this school were anxious and troubled about the young people with whom they dealt. That was the point at which their thinking started, instead of beginning with some large, sweeping, verbal generalizations. They came to believe, among other things, that one of the great needs of the young people attending the school was a real sense of achievement, and the pride that goes with achievement. They could have gotten this thought out of books on psychology, and the books did, in fact, confirm their judgment. But it came to them, in the first instance, from watching, studying, and coming to know the young people. So that was one of their aims. How did they set about achieving it? By organizing a band program. They felt that orchestra would not do so well, and that chorus would not do so well in their particular situation. The outcome confirmed their decision. The aim was attained to an extent that any teacher might well envy and admire. But the formulation of the aim, and its practical application—the whole job of thinking and planning, that is to say—was a home-grown product. This meant that it was specifically and definitely fitted to the situation, in a way that otherwise would hardly have been possible.

B. The second reason why the pattern or platform of working aims is first of all the responsibility of the local staff is that it should be not only *home* grown, but home *grown*.

No person, no group of persons, however brilliant, can sit down and knock out a really good, worthwhile set of working aims in half an hour or half a day. The job takes time—*time*, the essential condition of all growth. One must feel one's way. One must let ideas lie fallow and come to maturity. One must accept delay, one must overcome confusions and frustrations by living them down. One must enrich wisdom by sharing it with others. What are the evident needs of these people with whom we are dealing? What must we do to try to meet these needs? Such questions are the very heart of all good thinking about aims, and they cannot be answered in a moment, nor can answers be obtained from any oracular source. Such answers must be developed and worked out little by little. The problem of aims can be dealt with as it should only by living with it, so that insight and understanding grow. And only the local staff can live with the problem, day by day, year by year. Indeed, this growing understanding of basic aims is the very essence of the professional growth of the working staff.

C. Yet another reason why thinking about, clarifying and formulating basic aims is, first of all, the business of the local staff is that a pattern of aims nominally accepted without thought and discussion is almost sure to amount to no more than wordy wind.

I remember once visiting a certain school system to see something of the work in music. On my arrival I was handed a brand-new course of study. It was a well-printed document, and I opened it with pleasure and interest. Sure enough, it began with a platform of formulated aims. One of these aims was to the general effect that music should give children a sense of social belonging. A little later I visited a class being taught by a person whose name was prominent on the title page of the course of study. The lady had the room arranged so that children regarded as "monotones," and designated as such, were in the front row. They were adjured not to interrupt proceedings by trying to sing, but to get what they could from listening. However, after a song or two, a couple of them were dragged to their feet, and given a work-out on tone-matching, with which they egregiously failed, to an accompaniment of titters. I can imagine that some kind of aim was being achieved in this classroom, but certainly not the aim of promoting a sense of social belonging.

I have a pretty good idea of what had been going on. The lady whose teaching I saw was active on a committee set up to prepare the new course of study. A list of aims was wanted, and so she searched around for statements that should sound well. She unearthed one about social belonging. It seemed to have the right ring, to seem sensible, and it looked as though it would please the curriculum director. So down it went. But the thought never seemed to strike her that she was really talking about her fourth-grade class and the people in it. The statement was just words, because it did not grow out of her own thinking.

That is just the sort of thing that is likely to take place, and in fact does take place very often, when aims are adopted like packaged goods, without any mental labor or developing insight. It should be realized that the adoption of a set of aims is a very serious matter. It involves a moral commitment—a commitment to live up to them as far as possible, to achieve them as far as possible. When we adopt a pattern of aims we are saying, in effect, that any and every procedure, no matter how familiar, how convenient, how time-honored, that runs counter to them will go right out of the window. Otherwise we are not being honest. *Aims are intense convictions, or they are worthless.*

2. Now we come to the second point in answering our question: Who should think about aims? And our thinking moves a step further. The *music* staff should be the powerhouse and center of such thinking. Let it be said, however, and said with emphasis, that this is only a matter of primary responsibility. No group of specialists should ever think or work in isolation, or behave as monopolists. Thinking about aims should be system-wide. But where music is concerned, the music staff has a key responsibility, and should accept it, taking initiative in thinking about determining aims from its own point of view, though always as a part of the entire team. This is another crucial point, and, as before, the reasons for it need to be clearly understood.

A. The music staff must be the prime mover in developing the aims of the program because its members are specialists, and must and should be specialists.

As we all know, the place of the specialist in the educational scheme is being challenged nowadays. It does not matter much whether he is called a supervisor, or a consultant, or something else. His place is being challenged, and the question is even being raised whether he has one at all.

This has not come upon us without cause. The danger of the specialist is that he will see nothing but his specialty. In the past the music specialist has often been a person who darts up to a school carrying a trunk-full of music books and records, teaches three or four lessons, and then darts off elsewhere. When a person has to work in this way, he cannot know much that is going on in the school. He may have brief conferences with the teachers, but there cannot be much fruitful meeting of minds. Above all, he cannot have a realistic, intimate, compelling sense of the needs of the children, and of how music can meet those needs. The pre-planned lesson, the pre-planned schedule are bound to be the main considerations. Under such conditions, the most conscientious and devoted of persons is almost bound to think first and foremost of the organized presentation of his specialty. And in a day when classroom teachers are being urged to live with, work with, and come to know their children, and when comprehensive units are being used more and more, such a person tends to find himself a misfit.

But there is another side to the case. The music specialist can see certain things more clearly than anyone else, just because he is a specialist. That is, he can see them if he will take the trouble to look. Enlightened general educators believe that the whole purpose of education is the enrichment and betterment of human living, and the guidance of human growth toward fruitful outcomes. These are the actuating ideas behind such developments as the self-contained classroom and the use of comprehensive units. With these ideas the music specialist can unreservedly agree. But just because he is a specialist, he can see in all this certain things that the general educator may miss. He can know beyond the peradventure of a doubt that music can yield certain precious and to some extent unique values, that it can make a precious and to some extent unique contribution to the enrichment and betterment of living and the guidance of growth. Moreover, he can come to see how his work must be organized and conducted if these values are to be achieved, and this contribution made. All this he can come to see in and through constant and earnest thought about his basic aims.

The music specialist, just because he is a specialist, can make his own unique contribution to the thinking and planning on which the general scheme depends. He can add his own color to the general spectrum, for there is no basic conflict at all. Then he, and everyone else concerned, can see what the pattern of his work should really be. He can plan and work fruitfully with classroom teachers. He can help to bring musical enrichment to comprehensive units. He will prize such opportunities, because he will know that, without them, music cannot make its full impact or have its full potential effects. But he will insist that, alone and by themselves, such experiences and activities are not enough, and that they must be integral elements in a coordinated, continuous, sequential program. This, as he will clearly see, is necessary for the achievement of the aims he has in mind—aims that are understandable to all concerned.

B. The second reason why thinking about aims must center in the music staff is that such thinking is certainly the best and probably the only way of binding the staff together, and of creating the mutual understanding that is the basis of cooperative effort.

The music staff is a group of specialists; but there are also specialties within it. This is not only necessary, but also very valuable, so long as it does not lead to disunion. There are the elementary school specialists, the band specialists, the orchestra specialists, the vocal specialists, and perhaps others. It is very important for all to work together for a common cause. How can this be managed?

It can be managed only on the basis of a common platform of basic aims. The elementary consultant may know very little about how to make a clarinet reed. The choral director may know very little about how to teach the violin. But they are all dealing with people. They can all believe that music can do many precious things for people. If, as a group, they come to see clearly what these things are—which, of course, means formulating their aims—they can also see what the contribution of each should be, and how it should be made.

All sub-specialists within the staff are liable to the same danger that besets every specialist—the danger of seeing nothing but his own specialty. That is how weakening conflicts arise. But these conflicts cannot be resolved by shrugging one's shoulders, shutting one's mouth, and letting others go their own way. They can be resolved only by hard thinking about basic issues. The band director complains that children do not learn to read music in the elementary school. The elementary consultant retorts that the band director is narrow and hide-bound, and thinks only of his band. What, then, should be done? Should they fight the issue out, or just leave it alone? No! They should come together to explore basic aims, and means of achieving those aims. Then each will surely find that he has much to learn from the other. So with all conflicts, all differences arising from sub-specialties. A common, intelligent concern for human values and welfare is the common basis, and the true foundation for staff cooperation.

3. Thinking about the basic aims of the program should center in the local music staff. But also it should ramify as widely, and involve as extensive cooperation as possible.

General administrators, curriculum and guidance workers, and general teachers should certainly be drawn into the process of basic thinking about the possibilities of music as a means of achieving human goods. Sometimes a music staff tends to take the position that it must propagandize for its own ideas, and try to persuade the general educators to accept them. Sometimes, and usually with reluctance, it feels that it must accept the ideas of general educators without much question or discussion, and conform to them as well as may be. Both attitudes are wrong, for both sides have much to learn and much to contribute. What is needed is a process of mutual education, a back-and-forth relationship, out of which clearer thinking, better ideas, more adequate formulations continually emerge. Any group of specialists comes to see its work in its own way, and has both a right and a duty to do so. But any group of specialists is apt to slip into a rut. On the other hand, any group of general educators can easily become ensnared by sweeping formulae, which can wreak havoc unless their limitations, exceptions, and subtleties are understood.

The opinions of outside authorities should certainly be sought, but those ideas and opinions should not be accepted like oracles. The value of outside thinking turns considerably on coming from the outside. No visitor, no consultant, no general writer can understand a local situation as well as those who work with it. But capable and experienced outsiders will often see things in a new light, will hit on weaknesses neglected because of familiarity, will reveal blind spots that afflict the best of us. So once again we return to our basic principle, for the function of the outside authority is not to tell the local workers what to do, but to stimulate and guide them in their own thinking.

A Self-Test

The central idea of this chapter is that a music educator should not be a mere classroom mechanic, however skillful, but essentially a *thinking teacher*, always growing in wisdom and human insight, always seeing more and more clearly just what music can do for people. This is what is really involved in the constant and earnest consideration of basic aims which is required by our first principle.

With this idea in mind I would like to propose a self-test. It is not a formal test, and you cannot get a percentage score on it, or even a letter grade. It is just something to think about and judge yourself by from time to time as you go on your way.

The test can be condensed into this single question: *Are you*

willing to consider change without being stampeded by gadgets?
This is exactly the attitude which I know, from many personal
contacts, develops from real thinking about basic aims.

No teacher can think hard and realistically about the basic
aims of his work without a divine discontent, without realizing
his present limitations, without becoming aware of unfulfilled
possibilities and new vistas. No teacher can do such thinking
without some reaching out for new and better ways of working.
Yet all of us know that change can be disconcerting and
troubling. It can, and in fact it does mean the breakup of some
comfortable habits, the abandonment of procedures that have
become easy and familiar, the shedding of seeming certainties.
No one who understands what the daily work of a teacher really
is can recommend change just for the sake of change, or just
for the sake of being what is called "modern." Yet growth means
change, and when we find ourselves clinging to routines, re-
lapsing into ruts, doing the same thing day after day and year
after year in just the same way, we should ask ourselves whether,
perhaps, we are becoming moribund. This is where earnest,
constant, realistic thinking about basic aims comes in. For no
teacher can do such thinking without being shaken out of the
complacencies that so easily beset us all, and without seeing
the new adventures that continually beckon.

Suggestions for Discussion, Thought, and Study

1. Suppose you are put on a committee to prepare a new music
   course of study, to what extent would you consider this an opportunity (a) to let the administrative staff know what the music staff
   wants to do, (b) to clarify and improve the basic thinking of the
   music staff about the human values in music?
2. Assemble from your own experience, from the experience of
   other members of the class, from conversation with experienced

teachers, or from any other sources that occur to you, typical ideas and comments of laymen about the place of music in education and in life. To what extent do you think workers in music education might find these ideas revealing and useful?

3. When a layman, perhaps your own principal or superintendent, opens a discussion by saying, "Well, of course I don't know anything about music," what is your own personal reaction?

4. Several times in this chapter it has been intimated that a teacher should be constantly evaluating himself. Go over the suggestions that have been made about this, and see if you can draw up a list of specific questions that a teacher might well ask himself for the sake of self-evaluation.

5. Would you be inclined to say that the sort of self-evaluation suggested in this chapter resembles evaluation by the teacher-rating forms that are in use in many school systems?

6. Bring together from reading, or conversation, or from your own memories, revealing comments that have been made by children about music in general and music in the schools in particular. Consider and discuss the significance, implications, and value of such comments.

7. In educational writings the word "aim" is used in more than one sense. We sometimes hear about "lesson aims." One such, for instance, might be to explain the dotted quarter note. How does the word "aim" used in this connection differ from the use of the word in this chapter?

8. The argument of this chapter has been that teachers should make themselves conscious of the aims of their work by thinking about them. Do you consider that pupils also should be conscious of these aims?

Readings

I think you will find the following two readings helpful in connection with the material in this chapter.

Hollis L. Caswell and D. S. Campbell, *Curriculum Development.* New York, The American Book Company, 1935. Chapter 6, "Aims of Education."

As you see, this book was published a good many years ago, but the chapter I mention is one of the best of all discussions of how to go about developing and formulating educational aims.

James L. Mursell, *Human Values in Music Education*. New York, Silver, Burdett, and Company, 1934. Chapter 1. "Introduction: Music, Education, and Human Values."

This chapter sets up the basic idea of the book, which is along the line of this chapter.

CHAPTER TWO

Some Aims Suggested

The Principle

The aims of the music program should take the form of specific statements of the tangible, practicable effects that music can and should have on human nature, human living, and human growth.

This is our second working principle. It is a direct outgrowth and extension of the first. In this chapter I shall present and discuss five aims which conform to the principle stated above.

As you read, please bear constantly in mind the purpose of the chapter. The five aims here presented are put forward to help your own thinking. They will show you how our second principle actually works out, and the sort of thing that happens when it is applied. You may feel that they are not sufficient, that additional aims should be listed. This may be so. You may feel that some changes or even extensive changes in wording would make the ideas clearer. You may wish to organize the list differently, and to make more divisions and some subdivisions. All this is entirely proper, for above all I do not want my list of aims to be accepted without thought, as though it were the last possible word on the subject. I am sure, however, that these five aims do, in fact, conform to and illustrate our principle, and I doubt if anyone could follow out the principle and simply reject the essential content of the five. In any case, I shall use these aims throughout this book, though I am sure that the great value of any such formulation is to give people leads for their own reflection.

Aim Number One: Enjoyment

Through our music program we will try in every possible way to bring to children full, rich, varied experiences of musical enjoyment.

Let us consider this as the first of our determining aims. Why do we choose it? What does it mean? How does it apply?

1. We choose the promotion of musical enjoyment as one of our basic aims because of the very nature of music itself. Music serves a great many purposes in human life. It has often been used as a means of arousing and stimulating religious and patriotic feelings. We know that it can do much to relieve fatigue, and to make hard work less hard. Research has even shown that it can be an aid to digestion! The list of such purposes and functions could be made much longer. But in a sense all purposes and functions of this kind are secondary. Unless people enjoy music, not one of them will be achieved.

No one will be aroused to a keener sense of the greatness of God by the *Hallelujah Chorus* unless he likes it. No one will be moved to an uprush of patriotic sentiment by the *Battle Hymn of the Republic* or by *Dixie* unless he enjoys them. No one will get a lift on a long hike from a stirring march unless he likes it. And if a person does not enjoy dinner music it will be likely to produce the very opposite of better digestion!

Really one hardly needs to argue the point. Music, first and foremost, is one of life's great natural pleasures. All time through and everywhere, people have enjoyed listening to it, participating in it, creating it. Why human beings enjoy music we do not fully understand. But very evidently they do. Indeed, one may go so far as to say that if human beings did not enjoy music, there would be no such thing as music in the world.

If all this is so—and it seems no more than undeniable common sense—then the promotion and fostering of musical enjoyment is not only the first of our aims. It is the most important, the most basic of them all. Enjoyment must be the keynote of the program. Our first business must be to bring to people a means of pleasure—something they can enjoy here and now, and will enjoy throughout their lives. If our program fails here, it fails everywhere. This is the central reason for selecting enjoyment as the first of our determining aims.

2. Here, then, is the central idea. But we must look at it a little more closely, for one can easily misinterpret it. To say that music is a means of enjoyment is perfectly true, but the thought needs to be carried further.

Enjoyment, we may very well believe, is one of the good things of life. But there are many kinds of enjoyment. Some are trivial and transient, and do very little to make a person stronger or abler. Some are of a kind that one cannot turn to in times of distress, or confusion, or pain. There is nothing wrong with such pleasures. Indeed, there is plenty that is right about them. But also there are some pleasures that are selfish, or injurious to others, or downright harmful, or that lead to deplorable consequences. So even though we agree that enjoyment itself is a good thing, the idea has to be qualified.

Now the great point about musical enjoyment is that it is— or rather that it *can* be, and certainly *should* be—one of the very best possible forms of human enjoyment. For one thing, it can be enormously varied. There are a great many kinds of music, so that one can find some suitable for almost any human occasion, ranging from the darkest grief to the highest delight. There are a great many ways of dealing with music. One can listen to it in what is almost a waking dream, or give scrupulous attention to its structure, and one gets pleasure from both. Music can be played. Music can be sung. Music can be created. And it has in it a rhythm which, in a mysterious but very real way, stirs our bodies and moves our hearts and minds. Moreover, as experience has proved again and again, these musical pleasures can be wonderfully refreshing and strengthening. One can turn to music in all kinds of circumstances, and know that one is the better for it. Furthermore, such musical pleasures have no sting, no after-effect, no bad consequences, no ill effects on others. Musical pleasure is keen and profound, yet it is essentially one of the most innocent of all pleasures. Finally, musical pleasure can last a lifetime, in contrast to some other good and desirable pleasures which are possible only while one is young, and strong, and well, and healthy.

So musical pleasure is no small or trivial thing. In some people's lives, of course, it can be and indeed is trivial. It may mean no more than putting an occasional dime in a juke box, or turning on a jazz TV program as an obbligato to conversation or a game of bridge. But people who get no more than this out of music, do not get anything like all that they might, or all that they should for their own advantage. And when we set up the promotion of enjoyment as a key aim for our music program, we have in mind something far richer.

Let us look at it like this. We should think of ourselves as coming to our children with a very great and precious gift in our hands. As they go on down the years, they will know sadness and distress; and our gift can stand them in good stead at such times. They will know joy and gladness, and the gift we have to offer can make such gladness brighter. Sometimes the days will seem empty and futile, and the gift we have to offer them can help to fill those days. Sometimes they will be lonely, or sick, or weak, and then our gift can be a consolation and a strength. Some of them will go on to warped and stunted, and perhaps evil lives. Our gift of music perhaps cannot make them good, but it certainly can be an influence for goodness. Some of them will go on to unhappy lives. Our gift of music perhaps cannot make them wholly happy, but it can always be at least a candle in the gloom.

Such thoughts, such possibilities, I suggest to you are tremendous and challenging. Yet we are saying nothing less than this when we say that through our music program we will try in every possible way to bring to children full, rich, and varied experiences of musical enjoyment. We cannot take it for granted that such things will happen. Plenty of musical experiences are not enjoyable at all. On the contrary, they can be made hateful, as all of us know very well. This central aim will not be achieved automatically, magically, without effort. It must have a high place in our thinking, and we must seek constantly to understand its full meaning, and weave it more and more effectively into our planning. So now we must try to see, in general at least, what it implies for our program.

3. We have now reached a point in our thinking where practical applications begin to show up. They will be dealt with extensively in later chapters. But some indication of them is worth while here, in order to make the vital connection between ends and means clear.

If our aim is to help children to discover the richness, the fullness, the variety of enjoyment that music offers, the *whole* of our program is involved. A special kind of activity called "music appreciation" will be entirely insufficient. All musical experiences, all musical learnings, must be experiences of musical enjoyment.

A. We must see to it that singing is enjoyable. It can be made dull, humiliating, frustrating, painful. When this happens, singing itself is inhibited; and one of our basic aims is negated. It is a wonderful and delightful thing to be able to sing—wonderful and delightful for children now, wonderful and delightful for them all their lives. To reveal this to people calls chiefly for two things, as we shall see more fully later on—first, the right choice of songs, secondly, the right kind of situations for singing them. By these basically simple means we can bring to many, many people the gift of song as a lasting, lifelong enrichment.

B. The study and use of musical instruments should always be a discovery of new possibilities of musical pleasure. This is true of the use of simple instruments like tone bells, melody flutes, autoharps. It is just as true of standard instruments, with their richer musical possibilities. When instrumental study becomes mere mechanical drudgery, it defeats its own ends, and negates our purpose at a vital point.

C. The instrumental specialist may wonder if this means that technique is to be disregarded. Certainly not! What it does mean is that technical study and practice should always be a search for, and a growing discovery of beauty. There is a world of difference between laboring at a mere manipulative problem, and laboring to realize and project a musical effect. It is the difference between good and bad technical practice, and between negating and fulfilling our aim.

D. Music reading! Surely now we are far afield from musical enjoyment! Surely the best we can say is that here is a grim necessity on the way toward more delightful things, the bread before the cake and ice-cream. Not at all! Reading study that is simply drill on the notation has little pleasure about it. But that is the wrong approach. The proper approach to reading is to help children to see, and in and through seeing to understand, more and more of what there is in the music. Music reading properly taught is not a routine drill, but an opening up of new vistas of musical meaning, beauty, and enjoyment.

E. Listening? Of course! I have left it until last because it is apt to be the first, even the only thought when we think about musical enjoyment. Listening has many varieties, many uses, and I cannot touch on them here. I will only say that listening to music which is not, in some way, in some sense, a discovered pleasure, is not worth while.

You will realize that there are many important matters on which I have not touched—rhythmic activities and creative activities, for instance. All I wanted to do here was to show that our first aim applies *program-wide*.

Furthermore, our aim begins to give us a basis for cooperative thinking, planning, and acting. All the sub-specialists within the music staff can get together, consider what it means for them, and work out its applications in detail. They need not for a moment fear that there is anything here to threaten their interests. On the contrary, even the most technical of musical specialties become amazingly vitalized when they are considered as ways and means of realizing the pleasures of realized musical beauty.

Then, too, this aim can help classroom teachers to see more clearly the significance and value of their contribution. Many classroom teachers hesitate to use music because they feel they can do so little with it. But assuredly there are many, many ways in which they can enable children to enjoy music, and to benefit by enjoying it. They can lead children to sing, to play, to feel and express rhythms, to listen. They can even do far more with music reading than most of them imagine, as we shall later see. In all such matters the specialist can help, and suggest, and guide. But above all, the classroom teacher can come to see that the promotion of sheer musical enjoyment, far from being trivial, is a contribution of great and authentic value. Moreover, the classroom teacher, because of her close and constant contact with the children, has opportunities for fulfilling this first aim which are hardly available to the music specialist.

Comprehensive units and general education sequences, too, provide many opportunities for fulfilling our first aim. Music can be introduced in new settings. Types of music that might otherwise be neglected can be discovered and used. Thus the effect of our aim is to expand the range of our program from being the sequence of a special subject to a program of education-wide experiences and learnings.

4. Nevertheless, the problem of sequence remains vital, for our program must reach forward. We think of our children as they now are? Very true! We must bring them rich, varied experiences of musical enjoyment suited to their present level. But we must also think of the future, toward which all our work tends. We must think of them as developing beings, moving toward a maturity which has no definable terminus, as beings starting on the adventure of personal growth, which is also the adventure of living. Very well! Then we must provide in our program for *growth* in musical enjoyment. Otherwise a time will surely come when they will outgrow the gift we try to offer, and put away from them the things we bring, as being childish things.

What does growth in musical enjoyment mean? A complete answer would be very lengthy. But it is possible to indicate what is essentially involved. Growth in musical enjoyment very largely means a growing ability to notice, respond to, and enjoy nuance, refinement, and significance. A little child can get a very real musical pleasure from simply singing a song. But as he matures he should become able to find pleasure in shaping its phrase-patterns and its dynamics and in delivering it with expressive and beautiful tone—that is to say, in singing it musically and well. A child, or for that matter an older person, can get a very real musical pleasure from listening to a piece of music simply as a flow of tone. He moves on to a more mature type of pleasure as he becomes able to respond to and enjoy its thematic content, its organization and form, its harmonic sequences, its orchestral color, which are, of course, the factors on which its beauty depends. Capacity for the simpler, less developed types of enjoyment need not be lost, but out of them emerges an enjoyment that is more insightful, more aware of musical and artistic values, more capable of discriminating and appreciating such values. This, briefly, is what growth in musical enjoyment means; and if we fail to provide for it in our program, our work will fail, for adults will be dissatisfied with nothing more than childish types of enjoyment.

5. Before passing on from this discussion of the first of our basic aims, a concluding point must be made. It can be convincingly argued that everyone ought to get from his education some means of keen, innocent enjoyment that can last him through the years; for, as we have seen, such enjoyment is certainly one of life's great blessings and values. How this can be done better or more surely than through the agency of music, it is hard to see. No doubt any area of the curriculum can yield enjoyment. One can certainly find pleasure in mathematics, or history, or natural science. But in such cases pleasure is surely incidental, for the main values are in general intellectual or practical, which of course is no disparagement. With music, however, enjoyment is central, and it can last a lifetime. To be sure music is not quite alone in the curriculum in this respect, for there are also art, and poetry. But there is no doubt that the main bias of school education is toward intellectual and practical values, naturally including social values. Music can bring to bear an influence for better and richer living which is obviously very valuable, and which certainly seems somewhat neglected in our over-all curriculum.

This is one of the strongest of all arguments for giving music an important place in the scheme of education. But if music is to realize its full possibilities, if it is to exert its proper potential, proper conditions must be provided, and a proper program must be organized. Musical enjoyment must be a point of emphasis, a focal point in all the aspects of that program. And the program must be shaped to bring about growth in musical enjoyment in the sense explained above, for without such growth there cannot be lasting results, and enduring values will not be achieved.

Aim Number Two: Success

We will endeavor to bring to children experiences of successful achievement in and through their dealings with music.

1. The experience of successful achievement is of the highest importance in personal living and personal adjustment. It is an influence of great importance in personal development. This is generally recognized. There is in all of us a natural drive to function. When we have to do with a disorderly, antisocial, disoriented person, our first thought is likely to be that, for one reason or another, he has been denied normal and constructive outlets for functioning. When we run across someone who has to cope with some impediment, perhaps a physical handicap, and has yet made a good life for himself, we usually see that he has been able to find ways of succeeding and achieving, and that his secret, if such it can be called, lies in this fact. To have some area where he feels that he can experience significant success can be the salvation of an otherwise frustrated person, and to find such an area can add to the well-being and strength of the strongest.

Strange though it may seem, the experience of successful achievement is a peculiarly urgent issue in connection with school work. For school work is haunted by failure beyond all reason or necessity. School failure may not mean getting low marks, repeating grades, or flunking courses. These are only its extreme manifestations, and they are minority manifestations. But immense numbers of pupils at all levels certainly have the feeling, dim and unformulated but very real, that they are not mastering their work, not rising adequately to challenges. How many pupils in an ordinary school have a glowing, confident inner sense that they are truly succeeding with arithmetic, English, social studies, natural science, and all the rest? Not very many, one fears. Yet this is exactly the sort of experience they ought to have. Obviously there is something absurd about studying any subject without mastering it. And the experience of not mastering it is bad in itself.

Personally I am convinced that this widespread sense of tepid non-success that haunts our schools is the real cause of many of their problems, the problem of discipline among others. I am also convinced that it is far from inevitable, and that it can be largely overcome by more expert teaching in all fields. But here we have to do with music. And my suggestion is that so far as our field is concerned we do all in our power to banish the evil spectre of failure, and to evoke the good angel of successful achievement. This should be one of the aims built into our music program.

Like the first of our aims, it will not be achieved by accident, or in a fit of absent-mindedness. Music study, both in school and studio, can be and often is, hag-ridden by failure. Pupils fail to learn to sing. They take up the study of an instrument, and get nowhere with it. These all-too-common happenings lead simply to musical dead-ends. They make music totally ineffective as a means for living and growing. And the people to whom they occur are quite likely to take their revenge by saying that, after all, music is quite trivial, and that it is suitable for only persons with some special gift, and peculiar persons at that.

So our music program must be deliberately planned for and pointed toward the widespread realization of successful achievement. Almost everything in this book bears on the question of how this can be done. But the general approach to the problem can be indicated fairly briefly.

2. The proper approach can be indicated by asking and answering the question: Exactly what and how much is meant by the "experience of successful achievement"?

At first, and perhaps in essence always, it is an individual, a personal experience. It is simply the sense of being able to achieve something, the discovery that one can really do something. A newly blinded person who discovers, with the guidance and encouragement of a skilled teacher, that he can really play the piano at least a little, has this experience, and it is very good for him. A child who discovers that he can draw or sing, has the same experience, and again it can be very good for him. How well can these people perform compared to others? At first the question need not arise at all, and to press it is extremely unwise for the time-being. At root the experience of achievement is probably not comparative. It is the opening of a doorway, the realization of a potential. Simple though such experiences may seem, they have great value for personal adjustment and personal development.

For the organized music program this means, first, *variety of opportunity*, second, *invitation and encouragement*.

A. As to variety of opportunity, this means first and most obviously that we must include rhythmic activities, the use of simple instruments, creative activities, listening, commenting, chances to choose and to display initiative, instead of almost nothing but singing. The point is to organize all possible chances for self-discovery through successful musical achievement.

But today still wider ranges of musical opportunity can open up. Classroom teachers can be helped to use music in many ways throughout the school day. One advantage they will find in doing this is that it will bring the tonic of success to many otherwise rather discouraged and perhaps indifferent children. Again, one reason why music specialists should do all they can to help with the use of music in comprehensive or integrated units is that it can bring out many children who would otherwise remain in the background.

B. Then it should be our policy to offer real musical invitations and encouragements, something that can be done in many ways.

(a) It can be done through classroom flexibility. For instance, rhythmic activities, or the use of simple instruments, can go along with singing, so that children have a choice of what they will do. Flexibility simply means providing alternatives, instead of a single line of activity for all. Here are many possibilities both for music specialists and general teachers.

(b) Another means at our disposal is social example and suggestion. Classroom teachers sometimes ask how to deal with hesitant singers, or "one-note singers." Part of the answer is to use enticement rather than forcing. When most of the children are singing happily, the hesitant few tend to be drawn in.

(c) New problems, new challenges should always be introduced in such a way that from the very first children have the sense that here is something they can do. Part-singing, for instance, should not come as a sudden shock. It should grow from simple, almost inconspicuous beginnings—perhaps just an added note here and there, sung by the teacher, echoed by some of the children, played on an instrument—moving on to simple descants and rounds. As to music reading, there should not be some formidable moment when the grim realities of the notation are forced upon the children. Music reading should emerge and develop from a natural, understandable, achievable connection of eye and ear, beginning even with gestures indicating the up and down of pitch.

(d) Above all, appealing, well-chosen music makes its own invitation. This is a point of supreme importance. Everyone concerned—music specialists, classroom teachers, general educators—must realize that *musical quality is essential*. When we allow ourselves to use drill music, essentially meaningless music, we abandon one of the most powerful influences at our command. The right kind of music convincingly invites children to sing, to dance, to play, to listen, to participate.

3. The experience of success is, at first, almost entirely individual, personal, non-comparative, non-competitive. Perhaps, in essence, it is always just the experience of "I can do." But as children mature, it takes on added complexities and new characteristics.

A. Social comparison and social standards become important. The child comes to judge himself with reference to others, and to be greatly affected by their judgments. Young children draw very freely and without inhibitions. But when they discover, as without proper guidance they certainly will, that their efforts are not socially acceptable, they usually cease to draw. Some ultra-progressive teachers claim that it does not matter if a child goes up to the seventh grade without being able to read English. All one can say is that it certainly matters to the child, or soon will, and that it can hurt and humiliate him deeply. It is certainly desirable for a young child to sing freely, even though he sings off pitch; but his satisfaction evaporates and his singing terminates if and when other children begin to notice the sounds he makes with questioning looks and smiles. For children, in their mutual dealings, are not imbued with the amiable philosophy of extreme progressive education.

What does this mean for our program?

(a) First, that we must work for developing and advancing achievement. A young child can be satisfied with very modest musical achievement, because he is not aware of his limitations. But if he does not advance, his pleasure will evaporate, humiliation will take its place, he will run into a musical roadblock, and our program will do him no lasting good.

(b) We can and should deal wisely and above all constructively with vaulting ambitions. Many young people have private dreams of themselves on the platform of Carnegie Hall or the opera stage, dreams that will not come true. Such dreams are usually harmless, perhaps beneficial. We should not throw cold water on them. What we should do is to show, by every means in our power, that music has much to offer in its own right, so that gradually they see that it is worth while for them even though they may never reach the topmost heights.

(c) We should be alert to help children to accept the self-evaluation which social comparison inevitably involves, and to do so without frustration. They may not be able to shine with the brightest light, they may not be as good as some others, but we should always try to see to it that there are some musical activities in which they can achieve satisfying success.

B. Young children need experience of more or less immediate or quick success. But as they mature they can be motivated more and more by belief in and desire for deferred or prospective success. If children are helped and encouraged, this kind of motivation becomes possible much sooner than is ordinarily understood. This was brought out by a very interesting research study.* First grade children were set various little tasks which were rather difficult for them. Usually the first result was frustration, but they were given very kind and intimate guidance, and assured that if only they would keep on trying the problems would "come out." Their persistence and confidence were quite amazing, and usually it was rewarded by success.

This indicates some very practical policy-lines for our music program. To try to bring to children experiences of successful achievement simply by removing all difficulties is impossible, because music presents unavoidable difficulties. Moreover, such a policy will not work, because easy and cheaply bought success soon loses all its savor. What has to happen is the transformation or evolution of the simple, childlike "I can do this," into the more mature "I will be able to do this if I try."

There is absolutely no argument for throwing difficulties in the pathway of the learner, and letting nature take its course. First, we must do everything we can to create and maintain a

* Mary Elizabeth Keister, "The Behavior of Young Children in Failure." University of Iowa Studies in Child Welfare, XIV (1937), pp. 29–82.

genuine belief that successful achievement is possible. Second, we must shape our teaching so that foretastes, gleams, intimations of success arrive at the earliest possible time. A good deal is said from time to time about the character-building effect of hard work. What this too often comes to is lazy teaching, which condemns learners to plod on interminably without a ray of hope or a word of encouragement. Such teaching is the very negation of our second aim. What we must work for is a program shot through with confidence, encouragement, expert teaching that quickly brings a real promise of achievement, and the enthusiastic example of teachers and of other pupils.

4. Granted that the experience of successful achievement is an important human value and a constructive developmental influence, which means that it is an important educational aim, music is peculiarly well adapted to fulfill it. Of course this aim can and doubtless should be attained in and through other areas of the curriculum. But musical achievement is peculiarly objective and direct. It does not have to be demonstrated by any more or less artificial contrivances, such as tests, objective or otherwise. Nor does it need to be expressed by percentages, letter marks, or statistical devices. It is readily recognized by all concerned, for it manifests itself in school just as it does anywhere else. Moreover, successful musical achievement is often possible to children and young people who are not making much of a success with anything else in their schooling. This aim, the second of the five, may not come nearly so close to being unique to music as did the first. But music is so extremely well adapted to it that a school without an adequate music program is certainly neglecting a most important means for achieving its general purpose of human betterment and healthy human development.

Once again, the music program must be of the right kind. Facile success on the simple "I can do" level can and certainly should be made widely possible. It can be made possible in any classroom, in connection with projects, in connection with com-

45598

prehensive units, in connection with many extracurricular activities. It is, indeed, extremely desirable, and should by no means be confined to the lower grades. The program must also provide for advancement to more mature levels of achievement and success, in which the individual matches himself with others, and works towards relatively remote goals. As always, we are thinking of the long future, as well as of what happens here and now. And it is very certain that the type of achievement and success that satisfies the child and the beginner will cease to be satisfying or to seem worth while as he goes on toward maturity, both in school and later on.

Aim Number Three: Discipline

We will constantly seek to bring to children disciplinary experiences of devoting their full efforts and energies to attain goals that they desire and that seem significant to them.

1. It is often said that children, and older people too, need to learn the lesson of hard work. Undoubtedly this is true. To go "all out," to do as well as one knows how, to work as hard as one can, to sacrifice other pursuits, to give up inviting pleasures, for the sake of a desired goal is certainly one of the tonic experiences of life. It is unquestionably a constructive, formative experience.

This is the true meaning, the true source of discipline. Discipline is sometimes considered, rather unthinkingly, to be equivalent to conformity, orderliness, obedience to regulations and to authoritative persons, dutiful routine performance of set tasks. But such ways of behaving are not likely to have any deep, positive effects on character and development unless there is something else. They are the external manifestations of discipline, not its essence. The essence of discipline consists of behaving in an orderly, regulated fashion *for the sake of a meaningful goal.* A group of young people under a strict teacher and a strict regime may come promptly to class, sit quietly through the period, go through all the motions of conformity, and leave without disturbance because they are afraid to do anything else. They are showing the appearance of discipline, but the reality is not there. The same group of young people coming to a band rehearsal with an important performance in immediate prospect, may behave just as well or even better. They may be just as prompt, just as orderly, even more eagerly attentive and scrupulously obedient. From the outside the two situations may look quite similar. But inwardly they are entirely different. In one of them the motivation is negative; in the other it is positive. In one of them there is no actively desired goal; in the other there is such a goal. In one of them there is probably little or no disciplinary and developmental effect; in the other there certainly is.

Returning to the lesson of hard work, it is often said that while it is an important lesson, children and young people do not learn it adequately in school. If this is true, and to some extent it probably is, the reason should be quite clear from what has been said. The reason is that so many school tasks are pointed to undesired goals, goals that seem pointless and without meaning to the learners. I once overheard a group of junior high school pupils planning a small escapade, mild and harmless enough, but very exciting to them. If the amount of scheming, planning, organizing, arranging, and sheer applied intelligence they were using had been brought to bear on their social studies, the effect would certainly have been spectacular. Or contrast for a moment the kind of learning and application one will find in the average algebra class and on the average football squad. In the algebra class, discipline is almost entirely from the outside. With the football squad it comes from within, and the members will accept regulations far more stringent than the algebra teacher could impose, and accept them willingly, because they all point to a desired goal. In these two sets of contrasts one sees immediately

the difference between the externals and the reality of discipline, and also the necessary condition for learning the valuable lesson of hard work.

No doubt the true and living discipline, which is the discipline of meaningful endeavor is possible everywhere in school work, although it is very far from being achieved everywhere. But in music it is difficult to avoid such disciplinary experiences. Only very bad, very unintelligent teaching can miss it. So we both can and should weave such experiences into our music program, all the way from the first grade to the rehearsals of the senior high school band, orchestra, and *a cappella* choir. We will do this both for musical reasons, and also for the realization of one of the most valuable effects that music can have on human living and human development.

2. How can these things be done? That is a very pertinent question. If I were not prepared to give a feasible answer to it, there would be a flavor of dishonesty about what I have been saying; for I would only have presented an empty verbal formula which perhaps could not be applied, and there are far too many such formulae in the business of education.

We say that children, in their dealings with music, must work for goals which they themselves consider significant and desirable. Otherwise one of our most important aims will not be achieved, and the value of our subject will be reduced. But how can we get children to desire goals and to find them meaningful? That is the crucial question, and it certainly seems like a hard one.

There is an answer to the question, a solution to the problem, and a very definite one. The solution will not work every time. Nothing will do that. But it will work surprisingly often; and it will work better and better as we ourselves become more skillful. The solution, in a sentence, is this: *Always help children consciously to set up for themselves genuine musical goals.*

Here, I am sure, is one of the most vital and helpful ideas in the whole field of music education. I myself discovered it many years ago, though a long time passed before I realized its full significance. Perhaps the story of how I came to discover this thought may help you too to understand it.

I came upon this idea through my work with a piano teacher to whom I shall always be grateful. For my first lesson with this teacher I took her a movement of a Beethoven sonata. I had studied it carefully, and thought I had it well in hand. When I was through playing it, there was a long and heavy silence. Then my teacher began to analyze my performance. Her analysis was positive, not negative. She did not simply point out mistakes, and tell me to work some more and try to do better. She pointed out to me some of the musical effects—melodic, rhythmic, harmonic—that Beethoven had intended. This was not simply dictation on her part, for she pointed out these effects so that I could see them for myself. There they were, no doubt about it. But I had been missing them. Indeed, I had never known that they were there. For my previous practicing had been indefinite, unfocalized, motivated as one might say by hope, instead of pointed straight at certain musical values. When my teacher had pointed out these effects that I was missing, or perhaps better, enabled me to see them for myself, she went on to suggest ways of practicing to bring them out. Technique, of course, was involved, for no one can deliver musical effects without it. But technique was always for the sake of the music. All my practicing was to be aimed at being able to state clearly in sound the musical intentions of Beethoven.

All this came to me as a tremendous eye-opener. It seemed so reasonable, so obviously right that I was amazed that I had never hit on it before. It transformed my whole approach to music study. I saw, once and for all, that to practice in a general kind of way, hoping that if one is good and works hard, one will progress, is nothing more nor less than stupid. Moreover, such practicing is boring, even though one may resolve to be noble and to stick to the grind. But practicing in which one is always driving to the utterance of a genuine musical effect, trying to grasp it with one's mind and get to the place where one can deliver it with one's fingers, is an utterly different proposition. One has an undeniable sense of getting somewhere. And such practicing is interesting, nay, even fascinating. For the musical goal has a charm about it. It seems to pull one like a magnet, and the closer one gets to it the stronger becomes the pull.

Now why cannot my experience be generalized? I am sure that it can! So, when somebody asks how to get children (and older learners too) to set up goals that they find meaningful and desirable, my answer is: *Always help them to set up genuine musical goals for themselves.* Music is naturally attractive. Musical effects are lovely and fascinating. Very well! Let us use this natural attractiveness and fascination in our work, and use it to the full.

I have said that my experience with my former teacher can be generalized. Let us follow through with at least a few suggestions.

A. We have a first grade singing a song. It is charming, yet simple. Of course there will be musical factors even in the simplest song that are beyond the ken of first grade children. However, there will certainly be some such factors that they can notice,—perhaps the rise and fall of the tune, perhaps a bird-call coming in again and again, perhaps a recurrent rhythm that can be brought out in movement or by using rhythm sticks. No doubt these are simple things, but they are genuinely musical, genuinely significant for all that. We indicate them, and the children can see them, not because we say so, but because they are really there. The children can aim at them, try to bring them out. The chances are good that the children will enjoy doing this, because the effects are musically *right,* and because the song sounds as it ought to sound when the effects are brought out. That, I think, is what a musical approach to any piece of music really means. Set up the song in this way, and the chances are that the children will be happy, and even eager to try to make it go well. You will not have to do much driving, or insisting, or negative correcting, because you have helped the children to establish goals that have a magnetism of their own, which is true of musical goals.

B. Now let us pass from our first grade to the other end of the scale, and consider a senior high school choir rehearsal. Surely the same idea applies here. You can simply drill your group, telling them what you want, and plugging away until you get it— more or less. But quite another policy is possible. You can enable them to grasp for themselves the possibilities, the beauties, the subtleties of the music they are to learn. Then you cease to be a domineering drillmaster, and become the humble servant of the music itself whose responsibility and privilege it is to aid and steer the group in the work of realizing its values. Surely this will make for a fruitful rehearsal. It will also mean that membership in your choir will be a convincing revelation of what is involved in devoting one's utmost effort to achieve a desired and meaningful end.

C. So far I have dealt only with performance, but our idea applies more widely than this. Certainly it applies also to listening—or at least it can. In most of our music programs, including even the superior ones, listening tends to be rather superficial, perhaps with not much carry-over. What we should really try to do is to teach people to listen in rewarding and fruitful ways, so that they come to recognize it as what it can be, namely, a business that is both serious and delightful and a great deal more than a pleasant and casual relaxation. But how can this be done? Again, by showing people how to set up musical goals for themselves, so that they are able more and more fully to realize and appreciate what they are hearing.

Listening, as we shall see later, is a complex and varied affair, and all I can do at this point is to indicate a few general leads.

With young children listening can and should amount essentially to the discovery and appreciation of the general spirit or artistic meaning of a piece of music which is itself a vital matter. From this point we should move steadily forward, always, however, staying within the scope of musical values, never wandering off into the aridities of merely factual information or merely intellectual analysis. Young people, as they grow up both personally and musically, should come to know better and better how to discover, recognize, dig out, contemplate, admire, and enjoy the manifold subtleties that make up the expressive substance of any fine composition. Listening that is mere basking is perfectly legitimate; but it is not the only rewarding kind of listening. Analytic listening, too, can be a delight, and will be when it is properly done. For its essence is not intellectual analysis, but the discovery of new flowers and jewels of musical beauty. Such listening is an almost unique union of concentration and pleasure.

D. In all this there can be a most fruitful contact between the music specialists and the general teachers whose understanding cooperation is so immensely important. A classroom teacher, let us say, is handling a social studies unit on Our South American Neighbors. She believes that the unit can be enriched and vitalized by the use of South American music. She and the music specialist together work out a plan by which the children can be helped to find some such music. Among other items, a Gaucho song is chosen. What should be done with this song? How should it be treated? Very likely, for one reason or another, the classroom teacher does not want to use it for what would be considered technical purposes in the narrow sense—that is, for learning about note names, time values, key signatures, etc. Probably she is quite right. Does this leave the music specialist with nothing further to do? Not at all! The music specialist, perhaps by means of records, or by personal performance, or by suggestion and explanation, can reveal the musical, the expressive intention of the song. The classroom teacher, perhaps all by herself, perhaps with the direct collaboration of the music specialist, can set this up as the essential thing to emphasize. Then the children have a challenge, a goal, something to shoot at, something to work for. The whole experience becomes valuable musically, and valuable personally.

Notice how vastly this differs from the hit-or-miss choosing and haphazard singing of one or two more or less appropriate songs. Music specialists rightly feel that activities of this latter kind do no good at all. They do not enrich the unit. They do not yield either musical or human values. Yet the wide use of music in the curriculum can accomplish all these three things if only musical significance itself is kept in central focus.

3. I have presented above a scatter of suggestions about how to go about achieving the third of our basic aims, which is to bring to children the disciplinary experience of hard work for desired and meaningful goals. These, and all other pertinent suggestions, turn on one essential point. We must help and guide children to set up musical goals. Obviously this has profound implications for our music program.

What it means is that our program must center on musical values, first, last, always, everywhere. This is clear as day, as obvious as one, two, three. The central core of our program must be a growing realization of what music really is, a growing responsiveness to it. We start off by helping children to set up goals that are very simple, and that are yet true musical goals. In and through this they begin to respond to the realities of music itself. Away up the line we help them to set up goals that are far more complex, more subtle, more discriminating, more exacting. Yet here again they must be true musical goals. In and through this, once more, they develop a more exact, a more refined, a more discriminating, a deeper realization of what music is, and a more mature response to it. Such a program-design is, by all odds, incomparably the best way of achieving musical re-

sults. It is the best of all possible guarantees that in and through
our music program young people will learn the disciplinary
lesson of labor, devotion, self-control, and if necessary self-sacri-
fice for the sake of achieving desired and meaningful goals.

Aim Number Four: Social Development

*In and through our music program we will seek to promote
the social development of children by means of constructive
social relationships and experiences.*

1. To learn how to deal with and get along with other people
is a very important part of anybody's education, because it is an
important part of his living. One might say that the capacity to
get along well and to deal well with others is a lesson that everyone needs to learn. It would be even better to use the word
"growth," for children acquire mature ways of social behavior by
growing into them. Social development, like all kinds of development, is brought about by the right kind of experiences. The
school should certainly be a place providing a wide range of
experiences leading to healthy social development.

Such experiences should certainly not be limited to the extracurricular, out-of-the-classroom life of the school. It has been
known for a long time that a favorable social setting has a favorable effect on learning. Investigation has frequently shown that
subject-matter is better learned in such a setting than it is in a
setting of solitary study. So we should want a good social atmosphere in the classroom, both for the sake of the subject-
matter learning, and because of its effect on the social development of the learners.

Just what is a "favorable" social setting? Just what is a "good"
social atmosphere? Here again experience and research combine
to give us some very helpful and quite definite answers. The best
all-round social setting is known to be democratic. Since the
word "democratic" suffers somewhat from over-use nowadays,

and perhaps seems a little tired, it may make things more definite to say that what we want is a "participant" social setting. This, in fact, is a term used by many investigators.

A "participant" or "democratic" social situation has quite definite characteristics. It contrasts with an *autocratic* situation on the one hand, and a *laissez-faire* situation on the other. In an autocratic situation, all the direction, all the initiative comes from the leader alone. One person only is in charge. All the rest are followers whose role is simply to obey instructions without question or discussion. A laissez-faire situation is one in which there is virtually no leadership at all. Some one responsible person may arrange for a meeting place and get the group together. But after that he lets everything go as it will. Perhaps he conducts himself as one of the group. Perhaps he just sits and watches. But he issues no instructions, gives no leads, offers no special help, and merely lets everyone have complete freedom.

It is important to understand that a participant situation is not a halfway house between autocracy and laissez-faire, nor a mixture of the two. It is different from both. A participant situation requires leadership; but it is a very distinctive kind of leadership. The business of the leader is not to tell everyone what to do, but to help the group to choose, to decide, to act together, and to help the individual members of the group to make their contributions.

Consider, for instance, three possible situations where music is the center of the picture. In the first situation, a teacher might tell a group of children that the song they were using called for melody flutes, have the instruments passed round, and have everybody play. This would be an autocratic situation. Another teacher might suggest that perhaps some kind of instruments would go well with the song. With this in mind he might have a great many different kinds of instruments on hand in the room. After making his suggestion he might let the children choose whatever instruments they liked and use them just as they preferred. This second situation would be almost pure laissez-faire, though not entirely so, for the teacher did make a suggestion. In the third situation, the teacher asks the children whether, perhaps, some of the instruments they had previously tried out would not go well with the song. Then he raises the question of which instruments would be best. If there are too many suggestions, he indicates that perhaps it might be best to settle on just one kind of instrument for a start. Who would like to play? Everybody? Well, maybe it would be best to have a preliminary try-out with just a few while the rest sing. This would be a democratic or participant situation. As you can see, the teacher guides the choices of the group, helps the group to organize its choices, steers matters away from pitfalls and frustrations. There is real, genuine leadership, for the teacher does not simply abandon control and leave the children to their own devices. But on the other hand, he does not impose his own wishes and ideas, but helps everyone to think, choose, and decide.

Research, both in education and in industry, has shown again and again that democratic or participant situations are best in every way. They yield the best results. They enable the group to do the best work. And they have the best personal effects on the individuals in the group. From the above illustrations you can easily see why. The participant situation is obviously far better than either the autocratic situation or the laissez-faire situation, both from the standpoint of musical outcomes, and from the standpoint of the social development of the children.

2. Music lends itself extremely well to participant or democratic social situations. Music is naturally a social art, in a sense that some other arts, for instance poetry and painting, are not. People play and sing in company. Even soloists make music to and for others, in a direct face-to-face relationship, and not always for themselves alone. There can hardly be a doubt that those whose music-making is largely solitary—who rarely play in an ensemble, who rarely play an accompaniment, who rarely

play or sing for anyone else—miss some of the very best values, both musical and human, that the art has to offer.

Everyone knows, more or less, that these things are so. Everyone who has ever taught music in a classroom, or directed an ensemble, or prepared for a public performance knows that he is dealing with social situations, and that he cannot avoid doing so. But many music specialists take such social situations all in the day's work, without realizing that they are educational opportunities of the first water. Here we are, presented every day with splendid chances to show some of the most valuable things that music can do for people. Why not take advantage of such chances?

What, then, should we do? We should see to it that all the numerous social situations which we cannot in any case avoid, are the best kind of social situations, i.e. participant or democratic situations. The music specialist who goes into an elementary school classroom with a set lesson, and proceeds to push it through on a preconceived line, is missing a chance. The band or choir director who treats his group simply as his instrument is missing a chance. We must not relapse into a feeble laissez-faire or abdicate our leadership. Far from it! We must try to exercise the kind of leadership that evokes the thinking, the planning, the choosing, the deciding, the cooperating of others— the sort of leadership that does not treat others as passive followers, but that builds up in them a sense of active, responsible cooperation in a common enterprise. Thinking, planning, choosing, deciding, cooperating—all of them are valuable as means of purely musical development. All of them, too, are valuable as means of social development.

This line of thought applies also to the work of the general teacher, who can use music to create group morale and further social development. To achieve such ends, music should be freely and informally introduced throughout the day; interesting and attractive music should be used; children should be enabled to choose, to decide, to plan, to participate in unforced, fluid patterns. The sort of things that ought to be done may strike a classroom teacher as so simple and easy that they may seem almost trivial. But the very opposite is true, for it is just such direct, simple doing that are right, both musically and educationally.

3. The root of the matter is to encourage free and confident participation, the sharing of initiative, group cooperation and planning, in all musical activities and learnings. In dealing with young children all this means something very simple. The social reactions of young children are circumscribed, limited to quite small groups that may often be smaller than the entire class. They are not much affected by generalized ideas of how to behave, such as rules, regulations, codes of conduct. Their social behavior is fluid and immediate. At the teacher's suggestion a few of them feel they would like to move over to one side and sing a verse of a song while the rest sing the refrain. Three or four very naturally and readily undertake a little rhythmic dramatization. Nothing need be highly organized. Nothing should be cut and dried. Such doings may not seem tremendously impressive, but they can be highly significant and valuable. They indicate an excellent approach to music itself, and in them is the seed of future growth, both musical and personal.

As children grow older, the externals of social behavior change, but its essence remains the same. The social setting of musical activities and learnings never loses its importance, and participant social experience still retains its great value. There can be, indeed must be, more complexity, foresightedness, regulation by generally understood ideas and codes. Still music provides a wealth of opportunities for mature forms of social experience. Instances are sharing in the organization and discipline of the orchestra or choir, caring for and storing instruments, planning musical events, planning programs, seeing to materials, planning and organizing musical services of various kinds both in the school and the community. Here as always, the wise teacher will consider himself, not an autocrat, but a leader who delegates responsibility just as far as possible. He will realize that such doings are rich with opportunities for musical learnings, and that out of them can come valuable and powerful influences making for personal development and adjustment.

Aim Number Five: Widening Cultural Horizons

In and through our music program we will try in every possible way to widen the cultural horizons of children and young people, and to lead them to a growing awareness of the vast range and variety of human experience.

1. All significant music flows from human experience, and expresses the values of human living. Some of it stems from life as it was lived in bygone days; some of it from life in faraway places. Some of it stems from experiences that are strange to us. Some of it stems from such great universal experiences as patriotism, worship, romance, love of country, love of home, love of nature, death, sadness, bereavement, joy. Music is not mere manipulation and arrangement of tone and rhythm. Always and everywhere it is an expressive art.

Laymen often ask what this or that musical composition "means," what the composer was "saying" when he created it. Musicians tend to find the question annoying, and even to condemn it as stupid. On the contrary, it is an excellent question, and it deserves a plain and careful answer. The answer in general is that music conveys a meaning, but that the meaning cannot be expressed in words. Words can often indicate or suggest what that meaning is, but only the music itself can convey it. Beethoven has told us that his Sixth Symphony conveys the spirit and feeling of country life. This gives us a clue, but only the symphony itself brings us the composer's message. It is quite true that Dixie conveys the patriotic sentiment of the Confederate States. But one must hear and perhaps participate in the music itself to catch the thrill that is its real meaning.

There is nothing in this conception that need be difficult or puzzling. Words are capable of expressing and conveying intellectual meanings. They can be used to present arguments, to explain problems, to recount happenings. But intellectual meanings are not the only possible kind of meanings. There are also emotional meanings. To some extent emotional meanings can be conveyed by words—by the tone in which they are spoken, or by arranging them in rhythmical and harmonious patterns, as happens in poetry. But music is peculiarly well able to convey these emotional meanings. Music, in fact, does convey, not the intellectual but the emotional meanings of human life and experience.

This leads at once to a practical and helpful conclusion. To catch the full import of any piece of music, we should not try, as it were, to translate it into words. We should not try to dream up some kind of exposition or program to go along with it—at this point the composer is angry, now he becomes calm, now he sees his lady-love coming towards him, now he is looking at a cloud in the sky—and suchlike without end. That is not at all the way to get at the music. But to catch anything like its full import, we should know at least something of the circumstances, the experiences, the way of life out of which it arose. With this understanding as our background we should let the music convey its own message, a message which we have prepared ourselves to accept.

2. Coming more specifically to our program and its practical management, we can see very clearly that if children sing, or play, or listen to music with no other awareness than that it is there in the book, a great deal is sure to be lost. A high school choir is rehearsing one of the works of Palestrina. If it is nothing more than a piece of octavo music passed out at the right moment, some very essential things will be hidden from the singers.

If, by one means or another, they learn who Palestrina was, the sort of life he lived, the sort of circumstances that surrounded him, and what his work as a musician meant to him, then there is a great illumination. This illumination is valuable for purely musical reasons, for by it the singers can see something of what they should try to do in dealing with the music, instead of following what must seem to them the arbitrary decisions of the director. It is also valuable because then, through the experience of dealing with this music, they are brought into contact with a phase of human life as it was lived long ago.

The same idea, the same approach, is valid everywhere. It applies to the Haydn symphony being rehearsed by the orchestra, to the Swiss folk song being sung in the sixth grade. Children should always be aware that, in every piece of music, something is being said, something is being conveyed, by some person or (in the case of folk music) by some group of people, about the life they live, its values, and the ways of feeling it arouses. To repeat, this has a double value. It helps the children to find the right approach in dealing with the music itself, and it makes the musical experience a means of widening their cultural horizons.

3. Children should not deal with music in isolation, simply as a pattern of tone and rhythm. Always they should deal with it in its setting of human life and experience, the setting from which its whole significance derives. With young children this means something quite simple—stories, discussions, suggestions, anecdotes about composers, tales of living in far places and in the long-ago, pictures, and so forth. As children grow older, the process becomes more mature, and more generalized, with reading and more and more independent research entering in. The exploration and discovery of backgrounds should not be limited to listening experience, to "appreciation" lessons, or to general music. It has an essential place in connection with all musical activities, including rehearsals and lessons in applied music.

Moreover, investigation, reading, research, and the arousal of interest should not only be from the music to the setting, but also from setting to music. Comprehensive or "integrated" units, projects, and programs of general education offer excellent opportunities for the alert music specialist. For he can pressingly raise the question as to what music arose in connection with this or that phase of living which is under consideration. Here is a unit on Indians, here is another on Our Community, here is yet another on Our Southern Neighbors. The music specialist can make a contribution to all of them, raising the question of relevant music, and indicating how to go about finding it, and also what to do with it when it has been found.

Notice that this is a very valuable contribution. We may read about Indians, or about the history of our state or region, or about the South American countries. From our reading and discussion we may gain considerable knowledge and understanding. If we actually experience Indian melodies and rhythms, tunes and songs used by our local pioneers, the music of the Pampas, we can have a sense of intimacy with these people and their lives that words and understandings can never yield.

Overview and Preview

In this chapter I have dealt with five aims for the music program. They are intended essentially as samples. My purpose has been to show how our second principle applies, to show what a set of valid aims looks like, and to show what thinking about and working with such aims involves.

Already much has become clear. Our aims are influences that we wish music to exert on the behavior and development of human beings. They refer both to the present and to the future. They indicate a program that is broad and comprehensive but at the same time sequential. They provide a basis for cooperation both within the music staff itself, and between the music staff and the whole personnel of the school. This is the line of thinking that has been established so far; and now we must go on to deal with it more specifically.

Suggestions for Discussion, Thought, and Study

1. It is often said that "appreciation" is the true aim of music education. Consider this idea. How is it related to the aims presented in this chapter? How much will it help us practically in organizing our music program?
2. The claim has sometimes been made that music is valuable because it will train the mind. What truth, if any, is in this idea? How is it related to the aims presented in this chapter?
3. One might set up the aims of the music program in social terms—to promote the use of music at home, in the community, in the church, etc. etc. You might find it interesting to see what you can do with this approach. In any case, what do you think of it? Is it better or worse than, consistent or inconsistent with, the aims here set up?
4. Why would social aims of the above kind still require a program of musical growth?
5. With reference to the aim of enjoyment, is there any danger of a person becoming so sophisticated about music that he ceases really to enjoy it?
6. To what extent can music that comes from some historical period or some social situation tell us anything about them that we could not get out of books?
7. Some people say that children should have "rich experiences" with music. What do you think this means? Would this statement be a feasible aim for our music program? What would be some of its practical consequences.
8. Some people say that children should have music as part of their education because it gives them opportunities for "self-expression." Does this seem to you a sound idea? Is it consistent with the material in this chapter? Should we take self-expression as one of our basic aims?
9. This chapter presents five important benefits that music can bring

into a person's life. Can you think of any others? Should these also be regarded as educational aims?

Readings

Ethelyn Lenore Stinson, *How to Teach Music to Children*. New York and London, Harper and Brothers, 1941. Chapter 3, "The Value of Music For Children."
This is one of the rather few explicit discussions of aims in the literature of music education.

Beatrice Landeck, *Children and Music*. New York, William Sloan Associates, Inc., 1952. "What is the Social Value of Music?" pp. 74–86.
A rather more specialized treatment of aims than the preceding.

James L. Mursell, *Music and the Classroom Teacher*. New York, Silver, Burdett Company, 1951. Chapter 1, "Why Music for your Children?"
This chapter deals with aims without expressly saying so.

Educational Policies Commission, *The Purposes of Education in American Democracy*. Washington, D.C., National Education Association, 1938.
I mention this because it is the most influential recent formulation of over-all educational aims.

CHAPTER THREE

The Orientation of the Program:
Musical Growth

The Principle

A program which is to achieve human aims and to realize human values must be oriented, planned, and organized throughout for the promotion of musical growth.

There have already been hints and intimations of this third working principle in the previous chapter. The five aims there suggested were, all of them, effects that music can and should have on people—influences that music can and should have on human living and human development. In each case it was pointed out that these effects, these influences, should never be thought of as transient or fleeting. What we should have in mind, what we should want to do, is to make music a lifelong benefit. But if this is to happen, then clearly people's responses to and dealings with music must become more and more mature as they themselves move onward from childhood to maturity in the great adventure of personal growth.

Music can yield lasting and abiding values in anybody's life only if he himself achieves a developing grasp of, feeling for, and understanding of it; only, that is to say, if he grows musically. From this it follows that the basic direction of our whole program must be towards the furtherance of musical growth.

As I say, this has already been intimated. But now we must bring the idea into focus, and look at it carefully and steadily. In so doing we will carry our thinking a stage further, and come to see many things which we must try to do, and many things which we must avoid.

In saying that our program must center on the promotion of musical growth—that it must be what may be conveniently called a *developmental program*—we are taking a very definite stand. We are saying that it must be a certain *kind* of program, that it must have certain definite characteristics. It is the business of this chapter to explain what these characteristics are.

Music educators will find it easy to understand the characteristics and requirements of a developmental music program. They can also readily see how to go about putting those requirements into practice. A developmental program provides the basis for school-wide cooperation. If our program centers on musical growth, then not only music specialists and sub-specialists, but also classroom teachers, curriculum workers, and guidance workers will see that they can make a real and significant contribution to it.

All this will become more and more evident as I proceed. But it can be made clearer at the very start by introducing a negative thought, and by pointing out what a developmental music program can *not* be.

1. A program centering on musical growth is not and cannot be a program consisting of routine, mechanical music study. Learning the fundamentals as if they were a sort of formal grammar, learning the notation as if it were merely a sort of code, studying a piece merely to get the notes right, practicing technique merely for the sake of agility—these are instances of routine, mechanical music study. They do not bring about musical growth, and they do not lead to the attainment of human values except by accident.

The exclusion of routine and mechanical learnings means a great deal for the music specialist. It also means a great deal for general teachers and general educators. One of the main reasons why so many classroom teachers feel that they can do nothing worthwhile with music is that the whole program, as they know it, is narrowly technical. One of the main reasons why many curriculum workers, guidance workers, and administrators have grave doubts about music in the school is that it is handled as a self-contained technical subject. But if the essential idea is always the promotion of musical growth, then a sensitive and perceptive classroom teacher, with aid and guidance, can make a vital contribution; and music itself becomes a school-wide sequence of experiences and activities aiming at human values.

2. Again, a program centering on musical growth cannot be made up of fragmentary, occasional, casual, superficial musical experiences and activities. Listening to an occasional piece, singing an occasional song, bringing in a little music here and there because it happens to fit in with some topic, are instances of such experiences and activities. They may be pleasant and attractive in themselves. But by themselves they are not enough. The reason, obviously, is that they can do little or nothing to promote musical growth.

Perhaps when I speak of these superficial, incidental musical experiences and activities, you may have a suspicion that I have in mind the sort of musical doings often found in self-contained classrooms, in connection with comprehensive or integrated units, and in activity programs. Well, I am afraid that, without a doubt, such musical doings can be very feeble or even negligible influences making for musical growth. The point to get hold of is that *they need not be*. For one thing, they can have genuine quality and real significance. Suppose, for instance, that a song celebrating the rice harvest is brought into a unit on the Philippines. It can be a song with a moving melody and a haunting rhythm—in other words, a fine song. Also the children can be helped to deal with it as a fine, though simple, art work deserves to be dealt with—feeling what is in it, understanding what is in it, bringing out what is in it. Such a song, so treated, can be a very powerful developmental influence; and of course it will enrich the unit far more than a hack piece of music performed in a hit-or-miss way. Then, secondly, the musical doings in self-contained classrooms, comprehensive units, and so on, can be integral parts of a larger planned pattern of musical experiences, which, of course, is the music program itself. If these two conditions—quality and coordination—are fulfilled, then these musical doings are no longer fragmentary, superficial, or casual. They all point toward a developmental effect.

Of course the cooperation of music specialists and classroom teachers is required if these two conditions are to be met. But this is just what the developmental program itself requires. Such a program can hardly get on without rich musical experiences in the classroom, in connection with units, and so on. Such experiences and activities, I might even say, are indispensible for the adequate promotion of musical growth, and for the achievement of the human values that we have in mind.

I have stressed these two negative statements at the outset, because it is important to see, once and for all, that when we talk about musical growth we are not talking about something vague, or hazy, or indefinite. On the contrary, the idea is full of very definite, very exacting, and often startling implications. I shall present these implications, and their bearing on our program, by means of a series of propositions.

Proposition One: From the Essential to the External

In a program planned to promote musical growth we will work always from the essential to the external. This is the first thing to have in mind in planning, organizing, and carrying on our program. Let us see just what it means.

When you look at a piece of music, you see various marks on paper. You see lines and spaces, clefs, sharps and flats, time signatures, notes of various lengths, rests, slurs, measure bars, and so on. All these are externals. What, then, is the essential thing? Clearly, the music itself!

Think of it in this way. The man who composed the piece you are looking at had an idea in his head. It was a musical idea. Putting it roughly and simply, you might say that he had a tune in his head. He wanted to put this tune down on paper so that he could remember it clearly, and so that he could pass it on to others. Therefore he made the marks that you are looking at. But clearly, the tune—or to speak more precisely, the music— and not the marks, is the essential thing. Furthermore, if you want to play or sing this piece, either by reading it at sight or after much practice, it is certainly the music itself that you are after. You must get at what the composer had in mind, and whether you do so at the first glance or only by a great deal of digging does not matter for our present purpose. The marks are there only to tell you what the music is, what the composer meant. So they are externals. The music itself, the composer's meaning itself, is the essential thing. There is nothing difficult or strange about this. It is only common sense.

Now let us take another illustration. You start work on a new song or piece, and you find many difficulties in it. There are technical problems that, at first, you cannot manage—octave passages on the piano, fourth position on the violin, awkward intervals and sustained phrases in the song. To execute the piece you must deal with these problems. Still they are not essentials. After all, your real aim is not to do gymnastics with your fingers, and wrists, and bowing arm, or with your breathing apparatus, and larynx, and tongue, and lips. Your true aim is to make the music sound as it should—to realize it—to realize the composer's intention, if you will. So, once again, the music itself is the essential. You cannot realize or project it without technique, to be sure. But the technique is only a means to an end. It is not the root of the matter. It belongs among the externals.

Or consider music theory. Music theory is a body of rules, suggestions, and doctrines about the management of harmony and counterpoint. It is often called the grammar of music. This is not a bad description, for it has in music very much the same place that grammar has in language. Now I am sure you would never say that when a man is creating a poem the essential thing is for him to use correct grammar. You might think that without grammar he could hardly create a poem, and you could be right. But all the grammar in the world, all by itself, would never enable him to do so. To create a poem, he must have a poetic thought, which is obviously essential. With music the case is exactly the same. The musical thought, the musical content itself is the essential. The rules of harmony and counterpoint, important though they are, are simply the means of shaping it up and projecting it. And so they are the externals.

All this should make the distinction between the essential and the externals quite easy to understand. What we have said is that in a program centered on musical growth we will always work from the essential to the externals. Let us consider this for a little.

We will always do everything we can to enable children to get hold of, be aware of, respond to the expressive pattern of tone and rhythm which actually *is* the thing called music. We will begin with this emphasis. We will continue with it. We will never let go of it. In the first grade we will make very sure above all that children are conscious of the spirit, the content, the musical beauty of the songs they sing, the pieces they play, the music they hear. In the senior high school orchestra rehearsal we will do exactly the same thing, only, of course, in a far more thorough and complicated way. When we introduce note reading we will always, above all, be sure that children are learning to see how the music itself should sound; and we will develop them into better and better readers by helping them to see this more completely, more surely, more quickly. When, in teaching an instrument, we run into a technical difficulty, we will approach it with this question: How should the rhythm, the melody, the harmony of this passage sound? Then we proceed to the mechanical means of making it sound as it should. Always, everywhere, at all levels, we begin with the musical thought itself, and go on to the means of realizing it and symbolizing it.

How can such a thing be done? There are many ways, and the second part of this book deals with them extensively. So here I will only give a hint or two, and not a full answer. We can do it by helping children to listen as they should before they perform and while they are performing; by helping them to become more and more able to think and image music in their minds; by suggestion, precept, and example. Once we have the idea, many ways of applying it can certainly be found.

Of course we will not ignore the externals, or allow ourselves to think for a moment that they do not matter. Please notice this point particularly. Of course we want a growing mastery of the notation. Of course we want a growing technical competence. Of course we want an advancing theoretical understanding of the structure of music. It is in and through such advances, such developments that people come to respond more and more adequately to music itself—*so long as these advances are always related to, and always grow out of musical responsiveness.* The argument is not for ignoring or depreciating externals, but for putting first things first. If we do this, all other things will be added unto us.

A contrast with routine, mechanical music study will help to clinch and clarify this argument. There are elementary school courses of study in music whose staple content consists of lessons on note lengths, keys, key signatures, time signatures, measure bars, ways of counting the beat, and the like, with very obvious made-to-order musical applications. There are books for instrumental beginners made up almost entirely of information about the notation and problems in manipulative technique. In all such cases it is the lesson—the dotted quarter note, the melodic minor scale, the trill, or what not—that is the center of emphasis. No one can doubt, no one can deny, that these plans begin, not with the essential, but with the externals. In fact one nearly always finds that no attempt at all is made to emphasize the essential—the musical content itself. Children are invited to learn the symbols with, at the very best, a verbal understanding of what they mean, to learn technical gymnastics without any idea of how to use those gymnastics to produce the musical effects for the sake of which they were invented. The assumption usually is that if a learner will stick long enough at the mechanics, the routines, the externals of music-making, the real meaning of music will one day dawn on him. But this is wildly contrary to common experience. What usually happens is that the learner held to routine and mechanical study becomes bored and discouraged and abandons the whole business, so that music does him very little good. By far our best assurance that music will be a continuing and constructive influence in the learner's life is to bring him face to face with its beauty and reality from the very start, and to make sure that he never loses touch with this reality and beauty which is the great essential.

The idea of going always from the essential to the external affects music teaching in all its aspects. Also it is a releasing idea for the classroom teacher and the general educator. A classroom teacher considers using music with her children. But what shall she do with it? For her that is quite a question. Shall she teach note lengths, key signatures, time signatures? Shall she go in for tone-matching to cure monotones? She questions whether such doings are desirable, and doubts her own ability. The solution is as clear as day. She should above all bring out the beauty, the charm, the appeal of the music. There are simple ways of doing this, as conferences with the music specialist can show, and it is supremely worth doing. When she does these simple things she is right, musically and educationally. As for the externals, she can go as far with them as her own equipment and her knowledge of her children may indicate.

Another teacher is conducting an integrated unit, and wants to introduce some music. Again the question of what to do with it arises. She certainly does not want to make it a drill on music reading. But if this is not done, will not the experience be trivial and superficial? Not if she brings out the spirit, the meaning, the beauty of the music! That, of course, is how to make the music really contribute to the unit. A Chinese work-song, a Polish folk-song has an emotional meaning, and when that meaning is caught, the topical unit itself is enriched. Also when that meaning, that spirit is caught and felt, we have an authentic musical experience of great value. For the essential thing has been emphasized, and out of that everything else can grow.

Proposition Two: Unfolding Rather than Accumulating

In a program planned to promote musical growth, we will think and work always in terms of unfolding or evolving, rather than of adding or accumulating.

Here is an idea whose applications are many and far-reaching To see quickly what it means, let us take one of these applications, and, in dealing with it, draw a contrast.

In programs and courses of study in music we often find a list of specific items set up to be learned, and also a time schedule, telling when each of them is to be learned. First, perhaps, quarter notes are presented, explained, and illustrated from music specially chosen or even written for this purpose. Following this there may be half notes, eighth notes, whole notes, treble clef, bass clef, various key signatures, the 4/4, 3/4, and 6/8 time signatures, syllables for the major, syllables for the minor, and so forth. Each of these items is brought in at a certain point in the sequence, and often a good deal of thought is given to deciding just when it should come. The controlling idea throughout is very evident. That idea is that each item should be mastered once and for all when it is presented, and thereafter retained. Obviously the whole plan, the whole purpose, is to bring about an accumulation of bits of learning. One thing is added to another until everything necessary has been acquired, or supposed to have been.

This plan of operation looks very sensible and practical. It has been tried out in many subjects—arithmetic, spelling, and English grammar, for instance. But it never works very well. It does not live up to what seems to be its promise because of a very simple fact. This is the fact that children—and older people too—forget. In November a child may seem to have learned how to spell "marsupial," or how to "carry" in doing a subtraction sum. By March his seeming knowledge may have gone from him, and in fact it very often does just that. Exactly the same thing is certain to happen to his learning about dotted quarter notes or the melodic minor scale.

The reason is that the human mind is not a very good storage receptacle. We cannot just put things into it, and expect them to stay there, ready to be produced on call. The real business of the mind is thinking and understanding; and if we make plans to treat it as a filing cabinet, our work will not go well. Moreover, when you or I or anyone else undertakes to think about, understand, and finally grasp anything, comprehension rarely comes all at once, complete in a moment. It dawns upon us gradually. We come to see more and more in what we are considering. We grasp its meaning better and better. There is a process of unfolding, or evolution, of growing insight and certainty. A little reflection about some problem you have mastered, some learning you have done, will easily convince you that this is how the mind really works.

This gives us the proper clue for organizing our music program. Instead of introducing, let us say, our note lengths one by one, bringing in each at a stated time and then passing on to the next, we will introduce them just as they occur in music that has worth and interest. An attractive song that is musically suitable for first or second-grade children may have quarter notes, half notes, eighth notes, and even sixteenth notes in it. But this does not mean that we expect young children to learn all these different note lengths all at one fell swoop. That would be quite absurd! What it does mean is that we will pick out one kind of note length (or perhaps two) that happens to be particularly important and interesting in this particular song, and help the children to get the effect intended. In dealing with first graders or second graders we will certainly not make elaborate explanations. For instance, if there is a fast little passage in sixteenth notes, we may say "Let's make our tune scamper here!" Of course this is not a complete, logical, adequate account of sixteenth notes. But it is perfectly right as far as it goes. That is the proper way to deal with children, in music and everywhere else. Help them to understand and realize as far as they can. Be sure that they understand and realize *rightly* as far as they go. Then they have a basis for understanding and realizing better and better as they become older and get more experience.

For, to return to our illustration of note lengths in general and sixteenth notes in particular, our program will provide for many, many experiences with note lengths of all kinds as children move onward. These note lengths will not be brought in according to some schedule which we have cooked up in advance.

They will come in when and as the music requires. We will help children to understand them, to grasp them, to respond to their musical meaning better and better as they become more mature and as their background builds up. The full meaning of note lengths will dawn upon them, beginning with a glimmer, and gradually turning into full day. This is entirely different from learning each separate note length at a stated time, and storing the bit of knowledge for future use. It is precisely the process of evolving or unfolding about which we are talking.

It is this sequence of unfolding or evolving that we should organize everywhere. A young child can sense the difference between major and minor. This is far from the whole story, but it is the beginning of it. It is the glimmer; and he can be brought into the full daylight of complete understanding by many musical experiences under our help and guidance. A young child can very early begin to feel key relationships, for instance the tendency of *so* or *ti* to go to *do*. This again is the glimmer; and it too can grow into full daylight.

The idea of working always for unfolding or evolving gives us all kinds of practical and useful clues for our work. Here are a few of them. A child's first experience with the piano might consist simply of experimenting with it, to get his earliest glimmer of what playing it might be. A child's first glimmer of musical form might consist simply of enjoying the singing of appealing and beautiful phrases. A child's first glimmer of part-singing might consist simply of hearing someone play or sing a few notes a third away from the tune he is carrying. A child's first glimmer of harmony might be the finding of the I chord and the V7 chord on the autoharp to go with a song. Notice these are promises, forecastings, rather than lessons. They are the beginnings of the dawn which, through many and varied guided musical experiences, can be brought to brighten into full day.

Then again, this idea of starting with a glimmer that broadens toward full day is a releasing thought for the classroom teacher. Many a classroom teacher will hesitate about trying to teach the dotted quarter note, or the 6/8 time signature. Perhaps she does not understand these things very well herself. But to give the children a glimmer here and a glimmer there of musical insight is a very different affair. This, probably, is well within her capacity. Is it worth doing? Does the glimmer sometimes seem dim? Well, so is the dawn of the brightest day.

Notice, finally, that what has been said in this section is entirely in keeping with our first proposition. That proposition was that we must always center upon the essential thing, which is the musical content itself, and work from that to the externals. As children move toward a better and surer grasp of note values, time values, key relationships, and suchlike, they do so always in musical settings, always in and through rich, vital, guided musical experiences. The meaning of the minor mode dawns upon them through minor music, and guided experiences with minor music help the dawn to brighten into day. The meaning of syncopation dawns upon them through authentic syncopated rhythms, and once more, guided experiences with syncopated music help the dawn to brighten into day. As children's grasp of specifics, fundamentals, techniques, concepts becomes firmer and surer, and evolves toward completeness, their grasp of music itself and their response to it evolves toward greater adequacy. This is, precisely, the process of musical growth, and it is the guiding clue for our whole program.

Proposition Three: Fuller and Clearer Understanding

In a program planned to promote musical growth, we will work constantly toward a more and more adequate and clear understanding of music.

To explain this third proposition, let us consider the following musical example, which, as you will see, is the first line of *America*.

A person who knows nothing whatever about key, or time values, or even the very names of the notes, can still recognize this tune when he hears it; and he can sing or hum it, doing so by imitation, or, to use the familiar but rather unfortunate expression, by "rote." (Why I think this expression unfortunate, I shall explain later.) Would it be proper to say that such a person has absolutely no musical understanding at all? No, it would not; or at least, not quite. For, after all, he does grasp the tune as an organized pattern, and he does respond to its appeal and expressiveness; and here is at least the beginning of understanding.

As a matter of fact a great many human beings do and always have dealt with music on just this level. With many primitive peoples, music consists simply of tunes, passed on from generation to generation by imitation. They may not even think of these tunes as made up of notes, still less as having a relationship to what we would call a scale. They recognize and sing the tune as a whole, and that is all. Young children, too, recognize music, feel it, and sing it long before they become note-conscious. It is hard for trained musicians to realize that anyone can deal with music at all without at least thinking of it as made up of notes. Yet such is certainly the case. As a matter of fact, a composer may often get a tune in his head as a whole, before beginning to consider the notes it contains. So this tune-wise, whole-wise approach is the most basic of all responses to music.

There is not much understanding about it. But there is at least a glimmer of it. And unquestionably, a young child, or an adult with no musical background at all, can sense, feel, and respond to the first line of *America,* simply and solely as a tune.

This, of course, is a very inadequate, a very limited response. It moves forward a little when a person is helped to see that the tune rises and falls, that at certain places it goes up, at certain places down, and at other places stays on the level. When a person sees this, he understands a little bit more than he did before.

Here is at least something, but still not very much. Our learner may go on to notice not merely directions, but specific notes. We may, perhaps tell him that the notes have names— G, A, and so forth—because names, as always, will bring the things named sharply before his mind. Then we help him to discover that one of these notes seems to have a special importance. One seems always to want to come back to it, to return to it; and when the tune ends on this note, as it does in our example, it seems to reach a terminal point. In this case, of course, the note is G. Our learner can readily sense its importance; and when he has done so, he finds that the note in question has a special name or designation, being called the "home tone," or, more technically, the "tonic," or "key-note." Now his musical understanding has gone forward quite a step, but there is still much more. Perhaps we may help him to see that the second-last note of our tune "wants" in a special way to go on to the last note, which is the "home tone" or "key-note." This also is an effect that he can sense and feel; and we may find it advisable to bring this effect into sharp focus by giving it a label and a name, and calling it the *"ti-do,"* or leading-tone-tonic effect. Our learner is now beginning to recognize that the tune is made up of notes separated from each other by exact distances, and that it also has something called a key center. He has sensed all these factors from the very first, but they have not been brought to his attention. Little by little he comes to see that the effect of the tune, of which he was always aware, depends on these and similar factors.

From this point one can go on indefinitely. One can call attention to other key-relationships in the tune. They are right there in the music, and our learner has always responded to them, though without being conscious of them. We call his attention to them, and help him to notice them by attaching names, or labels, or symbols to them, perhaps using numbers, or movable *do* syllables, and finally arriving at the key signature itself.

Naturally we will not ignore rhythm, for that also is an important component of our tune. Our learner feels it from the first, and he can be led to feel it more definitely by moving to it. As his feeling for the rhythm becomes sharper and clearer, he can be helped and carried still further along by discovering that there are ways of talking about it, naming its components, and writing it down. Hence note-lengths, time signatures, and measure bars come in.

Perhaps, too, we may wish to introduce harmony. We do this by helping our learner to experiment with some harmonic instrument, such as the autoharp. Soon he can feel that certain chords sound right and that others do not. Moreover, he finds that chords have designations or names. And if we have in mind to push on to still higher levels, we can help him to discover the difference between triads and discords.

All this should give you a pretty good idea of what is meant by musical understanding, and of how it develops. The idea is that our learner comes to understand better and better what makes the tune sound the way it does—to understand better and better what he is feeling, hearing, singing. In a word, he comes to a better and better understanding of the music.

Which of these factors—notes, note lengths, key relationships, rhythm—should be taken up first, or in what order they should be taken up, nobody knows. Probably there is no "best" order, applicable in all cases. They need to be taken up, not for their own sake, but for the sake of building more and more understanding into musical experiences. That, certainly, is the important point.

One often finds what are usually called the "fundamentals," i.e. note names, note lengths, key signatures, time signatures, measure bars, and so on, set up as lessons to be learned in their own right, as it were. This is a very great mistake, because all these so-called "fundamentals" are simply designations for musical effects that can be felt by a person who does not know a half-note from the key signature of F#. They are labels, or signs, or symbols that call attention to the crucial points that make a piece of music what it is. They ought always to be learned with this in mind; and the learning of them should bring about better and more adequate musical understanding.

It is this apparatus of technical terms and symbols—notation, syllables, and all the rest of it—that daunts many a classroom teacher. She has been led to believe that to teach music is to teach these things; and she herself contributes the belief that she can't teach them. What she needs to be shown is that although the symbols are useful, they need not be taught lesson-wise at all. She can pick one out here and there, understand for herself what it tells her about this or that particular piece of music, and pass the understanding on to her children. No doubt the specialist can carry the process further, but it is still the same kind of process, for symbols should always be taught to further understanding, and not in their own right. So the classroom teacher can be confident that she is proceeding along the right line, and that the development of musical understanding is by no manner of means beyond her capacity.

Our third proposition tells us, in effect, that the development

of musical understanding is a necessary part of any program aiming at musical growth. Why is this so? Perhaps the answer is
obvious; but to consider it briefly will not be a waste of time.

1. When a person reaches a better understanding of *some*
music, it enables him to deal better with *all* music. In the case
we are considering, our learner has discovered that *America*
has a key center, and that this key center is very important in
producing the proper musical effect. Now he is in a position to
realize that most music has a key center; and since he has found
that the key center of *America* is designated by certain symbols,
he is ready to find out how to discover the key center of any
music. So on for all the musical factors that he has come to
recognize and comprehend.

2. As a person arrives at a better and better understanding of
music, he becomes able to enjoy it in a more and more mature
way. To understand music means something far more than
having in one's mind a body of theory which one can express
in words. This, I hope, will be quite clear from our example
above. To understand music means to be able to notice, to
respond to, the factors that make music beautiful and expressive—the factors that make music what it really is.

3. To understand music is to have the real and proper basis
for every kind of musical competence. Suppose that after our
learner has moved forward quite a distance, he comes back and
looks at the score of *America*. He has come to understand what
all the symbols on the page mean in a musical sense—what they
tell him about how the music should sound. So he is able to read
the song; and since the same factors are present and the same
symbols are used in all music, he has the proper basis for music
reading. Or suppose that he wants to learn to sing a new song
or to play a new piece. Since he understands the musical meaning of the symbols on the score, he can study it, examine it,
and get the music in his mind before he begins to try to make
it sound. At least he does not have to spell it out laboriously

note by note, without any real notion of how it ought to go. He has, in other words, the proper basis for technique, which is always musical understanding.

Clearly then, the development of musical understanding belongs in a program centering on musical growth, which is the only sort of program that will realize lasting human values. Indeed we will never have fruitful musical growth unless we do in fact emphasize and work for musical understanding.

Proposition Four: Technique

In a program planned to promote musical growth, we will work for technique as a means of creating desired musical effects and achieving musical satisfactions.

An executant technique, vocal or instrumental, may be defined as a pattern of movement by means of which a person can create or project intended musical effects. Technical study has a very important place in music education, and rightly so. Any notion that it can be slighted, or even disregarded or bypassed, in a program aimed at musical growth, is entirely wrong. The only question is, how to go about developing it. This question is answered in our fourth proposition. Technique should always be developed in the closest possible relationship to the purposes for which it exists, which are musical purposes.

A very simple illustration will help to make this clear. Every vocalist knows that proper breath-control is essential for good singing—an essential factor in the pattern of action that we call the vocal technique. How, then, should we set about developing it in our work with children? Should we call attention to it in the early grades? Should we introduce breath-control drills or exercises such as some vocal teachers use, modified to be suitable for young children? This would almost certainly be a great mistake. From the very start we should give many opportunities for the singing of appealing songs. At first there may be no

conscious attention paid to any of the problems of voice production, including breath-control. However, from the very first we
should call attention to this and that in the music which the
children can notice and understand, and which can make the
singing go better and more enjoyably. As time goes on, their
feeling for phrase, for tone-quality, and for pitch contour becomes more exact. Then it becomes very natural to show them
that these desired musical effects require more or less conscious
breath-control. Here is the way one factor of technique can
emerge out of music.

Now let us see how our proposition applies at a considerably
higher level of maturity, namely, the beginning study of a
woodwind instrument. Here the technique is more external, and
in a sense more artificial than in the case of voice. For instance,
a proper embouchure must be achieved to make the instrument
sound, and attention must be given to this and other related
problems if the learner is to get anywhere at all. Does this mean
that we have on our hands a job of teaching manipulation pure
and simple, without any reference to anything else? By no
means! For one thing, a child should not even start the study
of clarinet until he has heard considerable good clarinet music,
both on records, radio, and television, and in live performance.
Moreover, he should have had opportunities to see the clarinet
played, to watch at close quarters, with some explanation of
what the performer is doing and how the instrument produces
sound. Also he should have had opportunities to handle the
instrument informally, to examine it, to experiment with it. A
beginner who starts definite study with this kind of background
will already have an intelligent musical goal. He will know the
sort of music he wants to be able to make, and will have some
notion, at least, of what he must do to make it. The goal will be
somewhat remote. It will not be a concentration on this or that
immediate effect. But it will be a genuine musical goal; and a
child is probably not old enough to get what he should from

studying clarinet until he is old enough to set up and work for fairly remote goals.

But this does not mean that quite immediate musical goals should be ruled out. When our beginner starts his specific clarinet study, he should not be engaged in manipulative problems pure and simple, with nothing more than the hope that he will be able to make satisfying music when he has solved them. Even from the first he should be attentive to the kind of tone he wants to make and the kind of tone he is making, to the problems of attack and release, and so forth. Study should go on always in a setting of conscious musical goals. It should not be concentrated simply and solely on a kind of acrobatics with tongue, lips, breathing muscles, hands, fingers.

The two illustrative applications given so far have dealt with the beginnings of technique. Now let us see how our fourth proposition bears on the refinements of technique—that is, to agility, speed, shadings of accentuation which are essential components of what we call an excellent technique. How should one go about acquiring these?

To make our discussion specific, let us consider the technical problem of the *Rondo alla Turca* third movement of the Mozart piano sonata in A major. This problem—or better, these problems—are exacting, and many intermediate piano pupils do not cope with them adequately. There are a number of rapid passages; the music must be very crisp and clear; it must be finely phrased and shaded. Unquestionably the best approach to the technical problems involved is the musical approach. The question which should be first and constantly in the learner's mind is: How should this sound? How should the melodic line flow? How should the accompaniment figuration be subordinated? And above all, what should be the rhythmic accentuation that carries the music along? Then comes the question of means—fingering, adjustments of hand position, perhaps certain special dexterities which call for independent consideration. These questions certainly cannot be shirked. They should be dealt with, not by mere repetitive practice, but by intelligent analysis designed to shape up the best possible pattern of movement. It is amazing how what seem like pure manipulative difficulties will tend to melt away when the learner has a sharply focused awareness of the desired musical effects, and above all, of the desired rhythmic effects.

These, then, are sample applications of our fourth proposition, and they serve to make its meaning clear. A number of comments remain to be made, and some questions still need to be answered.

1. Setting up technique as an end in itself is a thoroughly self-defeating business. One can say with confidence that abstract exercises, abstract formal manipulative drills are amazingly sterile and un-rewarding. Technical problems should be dealt with as they arise in music, and studied with musical goals in mind. Material in books of studies and exercises is valuable when items from it are picked out that bear directly on the technical problems that actually arise in musical settings. To grind through such books in the vague hope that something favorable will happen is almost always a delusion and a waste of time.

2. The idea that a person must first acquire a technique and then use it musically is a disastrous fallacy. It is a good way to make sure that most learners will get nowhere and go nowhere musically, and that the musical development of even the most talented and ambitious will be delayed and warped. Technical study should be always an integral part of music study, not something separate from it, and technical development and musical development should go hand in hand.

3. In connection with technical study and the musical approach to it, an interesting pair of alternative questions is often raised. Should a learner form a clear and definite notion of how a passage should sound *before* he begins to deal intensively with

the executant problem? Or should he develop this notion *along with* his intensive executant study? There is no decisive answer. It all depends on the learner, and particularly on his maturity. In fact, the same person may work in these two different ways on different occasions. The vital point is always that the learner should never for an instant lose grip on his musical intention even in the midst of the most careful and analytic technical study.

4. From all that has been said it is evident that technical development is an integral component of musical growth. There is a technical problem whenever we wish to create and project musical beauty. There is a technical problem in the simplest of first grade songs—only we do not pull it out of context for separate consideration, but treat it simply as the problem of making the song go as enjoyably, as expressively, as charmingly as possible. As children mature, technique is just as readily learned, but with less conscious effort. Even at the most advanced level, technical study should always be an endeavor to capture, to realize, to project the expressive content and beauty of music. Technical study so conducted is neither more nor less than music study itself; and it is the kind of music study that, at the same time and in the same motion, yields both technical proficiency and musical growth.

Proposition Five: Continuity and Coordination

Our music program must be planned and conducted to promote a sequence of development that is continuous throughout its entire course, and coordinated in all its aspects.

This fifth proposition presents two ideas, the idea of continuity, and the idea of coordination. They do, of course, have different meanings, but they are so closely inter-related that they need to be considered together.

1. We must think, plan, and work always in terms of a

continuity of development. This statement has both a positive and a negative meaning.

On the positive side it means that our whole program, from its earliest beginnings and throughout its course, must be the development of a single central theme. That theme is response to the beauty and expressiveness of music itself. A little child's response to music differs enormously in degree from that of a mature musician, but it is the same in kind. A little child responds to music very simply. He responds, one might say, in a very general way to its charm, to its appeal, to the moods and ways of feeling it conveys. There will be many subtleties which he will not notice, many refinements which he will not grasp, many insights which he will lack, many skills which he will not possess. One can easily call the child's musical response inadequate, and so it is, in a sense, but if his response is vital and real, its inadequacy is only that of the bud as compared to the blossom. For the whole of musical growth is simply the making of this early vital response more discriminating, more subtle, more understanding, more skillful. It remains always the same in kind, but goes on to become fuller, richer, deeper, more finely structured. This is the process we are trying to promote; and it is the positive meaning of the statement that the process is essentially continuous.

But that statement also has a negative meaning. It amounts to saying that the process with which we are dealing does not pass through self-contained stages, and that it must not be treated as if it did. This needs particular emphasis, because it is so often ignored or misunderstood. Many makers of music programs talk about musical growth, and then violate one of its most essential conditions by organizing discontinuity instead of continuity.

A. The proposition that we must plan in terms of a continuous sequence means that it is wrong to begin with routine learnings and move from them to a realization of meanings. We must not begin by teaching the symbols, the notation, the elementary grammar in the abstract, and then go on to the music. We must not teach manipulative technique, and then go on to the music. Such practices are far from rare, but their whole tendency is to kill musical growth, because they violate one of its most essential conditions. They are violations of continuity. On the contrary, we develop an understanding of the symbols out of the music, and in so doing bring about a more comprehending response to the music. Similarly, we develop technical skills out of the music, and in so doing achieve, not merely technical competence but also a more discriminating, precise, and certain musical response.

B. Once again, the proposition that we must plan in terms of a continuous sequence of development means that we must give up the time-honored formula of going "from rote to note." The singing of a little child should not be a "rote" response at all. It should be something entirely different from slavish copying which the word "rote" strongly suggests. It should be an authentic musical act, an expressive act, coming from within himself, helped as much as need be by imitation and example and encouragement. And the visualization, the eye-representation of music should be introduced when and as needed, to help him sing more and more discriminatingly, and with more and more conscious satisfaction and control. This, very clearly, is what is involved, for an abrupt transition from no-notes to notes is a glaring breach of continuity.

C. Once again, the proposition that we must plan in terms of a continuous sequence means that the idea of a "pre-reading-stage," or a "music-reading-readiness-stage" must be abandoned. In practice this means that for several years children make and respond to music largely or entirely "by ear," and that in the late second grade, or the third grade, or even the fourth grade— for there is no universal agreement about the proper moment— they are introduced to the notation. Here is a clear breach of continuity, for children are supposed to pass through a non-reading stage, and then, at a certain time, to enter a reading stage of their musical development.

The basic trouble with this familiar plan is that it involves an altogether unduly limited notion of what music reading really is. Music reading starts whenever the eye first helps the ear, and this can happen very early indeed. It begins with gestures, diagrams, pictures, the space layout of simple instruments —with any *seen* object or arrangement or movement that can be related to sound. Experiences of this kind are not preparatory to music reading. They are actual experiences of music reading itself, rudimentary of course, but still valid. They involve the use of visual symbols for musical responses. From the use of these crude but still genuine symbols, the child moves forward to the use of symbols that are more and more complex, precise, and abstract, namely, the symbols of the standard notation. These notational symbols are introduced little by little, to point up and refine musical responses in a way that is not possible with the simpler, cruder gesture-symbols and picture-symbols. So music-reading ability is gained by a continuous evolution toward more and more precision and refinement, rather than being introduced at some set moment, previous to which nothing at all has been done with it.

2. We come now to the second part of our fifth proposition, to wit, that a program planned to promote musical growth must be *coordinated* in all its aspects. In other words, it must be a *unified* program. Let us explore some of the meanings and applications of this statement.

A. We will not have a separate music-reading program within our general program. On the contrary, we will constantly use eye-symbols of many kinds to help the ear and to develop understanding. We will use eye-symbols and eye-experiences in connection with singing, playing, listening, rhythmic activities, dramatizations, the creating of music—in connection with the entire gamut of musical activities and experiences. This tie-up between eye, ear, and understanding is the very essence of music reading, and it is also a prime agency for musical growth. It should, so far as possible, be established with all children, and it should be emphasized at all points throughout our program, from the beginning on.

B. We will secure a free, constant, flexible interplay between singing, playing, listening, rhythmic response, and creation. Instead of regarding these as separate activities, each within its own channel, we will move from one to another with the greatest freedom. For we are not essentially teaching children to sing, to play, to listen, to respond rhythmically, to compose music. Basically we are teaching them to respond more and more adequately to music itself; and these activities are the means we use.

C. Our developmental program will provide a common platform, and a basis for understanding cooperation between the sub-specialists of the music staff. General music teachers at all levels, band directors, orchestra directors, choir directors, are all working each in their own way for a common goal, the goal of musical growth. Each specialist has his own special contribution to make, and his own work will gain in effectiveness as he comes to see its true place and value in the larger whole.

D. Our developmental program will provide a basis for understanding cooperation between music specialists and general teachers. Our program will have a sequence, but it will be a sequence of living growth, not of rigid, predetermined topical arrangement. At all levels it will always emphasize different aspects of the same thing, i.e. of musical responsiveness. So the classroom teacher can readily find a place in it and make a contribution to it. Comprehensive or integrated units, too, will be found rich in opportunities for significant musical experience; and these can vitalize the units, strengthen the music program, and make for the attainment of those human goals and human values which are the determining aims of all our efforts.

Proposition Six: The Arousal and Defining of Purpose

In a program planned to promote musical growth, we will work always for the arousal, unfolding, and defining of purpose.

A person takes up a new hobby—woodworking or gardening, let us say. He takes it up because it seems a pleasant thing to do, and perhaps because he has a skillful friend who encourages him and offers to help him out. He starts, that is to say, with a general interest that may be quite mild. Little by little he acquires skill and "know how." He also acquires understanding, so that he not only knows what the right techniques are, but also sees why they are right. Along with his increasing skill and understanding, interest and purpose develop too. He thinks about his hobby, plans for it. His over-all interest still remains and indeed becomes stronger, but also it becomes much more definite, much more grooved. He considers buying this or that new appliance, trying out this or that new process. As time goes on, the general mild interest with which he started tends to turn into fascination. He is well on his way to becoming a "fan."

It would be quite right to say that our man has grown as a woodworker or a gardener. He has become better, more skillful, more discriminating, more intelligent. The standards that pleased him at first no longer satisfy. Along with this gain in skill, there has been an evolution, a development of interest and purpose. This evolution, this development is an essential factor in his growth. Without the developing purpose there would have been no growth at all.

The case is exactly the same with music. Musical growth depends essentially upon purpose, upon will. It depends essentially upon an aroused, deepening, and continuing interest.

It is the learner interested in musical experiences, activities, and achievements who grows musically. It is the bored, uninterested learner who does not grow. So, if we want to promote musical growth, we must always work for the arousal, unfolding, and defining of purpose and interest.

But how can we go about doing such a thing? The answer is implied in everything in this chapter. Let us look at the problem in the light of what has been said.

We can begin with the confident belief that musical activities and experiences are naturally attractive and appealing. Children will like these activities and experiences; they will like to sing, to play, to listen, to respond rhythmically, to make up little tunes, if only we will give them a reasonable chance to do so. Giving them a reasonable chance simply means choosing suitable music, i.e. music with real worth and appeal, and featuring its worth and appeal above everything else. Music itself will do most of the enticing, if only we will avoid standing in the way. Here, then, is the beginning of interest.

Quite soon, however, we must begin to move forward. At the very start children can just enjoy singing, playing, listening, responding rhythmically, without much or perhaps any thought or analysis. Before very long we must begin to help them to do these things better, to show them how to do these things better. Far from destroying the basic musical interest and impulse, such help tends to reinforce them. For the children come to see more and more in the music, to recognize and respond to its finer points, to grasp its effects more and more completely, to find that they have an increasing competence in dealing with it. Just as the interest of our woodworking hobbyist develops from a general, over-all liking to a fascination with some special process, so the child's interest in music develops from a general over-all liking to an interest in noticing, bringing out, understanding this or that specific effect or artistic value. This is what the development or maturing of interest and purpose means.

But the essential condition for this development is a constant, central emphasis upon the expressive content of music itself. A child may have found real pleasure in singing, in playing simple instruments, in responding rhythmically. Then he is suddenly put up against routine piano lessons, set to work on dull and worthless pieces, and made to concentrate on nothing but the right notes. His interest dries up and blows away. An eighteen-year-old learner has enjoyed making music for perhaps ten years. Then he enters a music school and is enrolled in a required course in theory. He is set to work on strange rules, difficult concepts, and exercises of the driest and most formal kind. The result is frustration and boredom. In both these cases, and in all others like them, musical growth is brought to a dead stop. It is brought to a dead stop because purpose and interest are obliterated. And purpose and interest are obliterated for just one reason. The learner has been allowed to get out of touch with the essential thing, which is the living, appealing, beautiful musical content, and has been required to make a diet of the husks of externals. Musical purpose and musical interest starts simply with the natural appeal of music itself. They are brought to greater and greater maturity and vigor by working always for the better grasp of, understanding of, realization of the expressive and aesthetic effects of music.

A distinction is often made, in educational writings, between intrinsic and extrinsic interest. To return for a moment to our woodworker, he may become fascinated with some process or technique, and exceedingly anxious to do the best possible job with it. So far he is moved by intrinsic motivation. But he may also look forward to having his friends admire the piece he is making, or perhaps to selling it for a nice price. These would be extrinsic motives. Interest in the job itself is intrinsic. Interest engendered by praise, by rewards, by marks, by the admiration of others, is extrinsic.

Which kind of motivation should we have in mind in our music program? The answer is—both! By all means let us recognize children's efforts; let us be generous with praise when praise is due; let us create a warm, appreciative social atmosphere. Such things are very important. But unless, at the same time, we arouse, foster, and direct the musical purpose itself—and this is the purpose to realize music more completely, to respond to it more adequately, to project it more perfectly— our extrinsic motivation alone will not have much effect.

A program made up of routine and mechanical learning must rely almost altogether upon extrinsic motivation. The music itself is likely to be dull. The problems set up to be learned and mastered have little meaning. There is, for instance, very little pulling power in the dotted quarter note, or in a formal exercise for passing the thumb under the hand. The learner has to be held to the task by rewards and penalties, by promises and threats, by low and high marks. What else is there to hold him to it? Johnny practices, not because he likes the music, or is interested in what he is doing, but because he will otherwise be punished. Musically speaking, he gets strictly nowhere, and the moment the pressure is released, he quits. That is why a program of routine learnings cannot possibly yield musical growth.

Now Johnny is not naturally hostile to music. Of that we may be quite confident. Indeed, he would never have become hostile to it if his teacher had not stupidly blocked the daylight. Right now he is laboring unwillingly on his piece because his teacher tells him to, and because his parents back the teacher up. But suppose that, from the very first, his teacher had given him music that had some real life to it, and had shown him ways of bringing out that life! Then, surely, the situation might be very different. The chances are that Johnny would now have something to work for that he himself felt worthwhile. Praise, encouragement, helpfulness, the chance to shine at some little musicale, would no doubt all have helped. But the essential factor would be Johnny's direct, intrinsic interest in the music itself.

When this subject of motivation or interest comes up, teachers often ask this question: Should we try to make our material interesting? The question is based on a great misunderstanding, and music teachers should be the very last to ask it. *Music already is interesting.* It has in it more pulling power than you, or I, or the most skillful teacher that ever lived can create. What we have to do is to reveal to children, by direct experience, what music is, and to lead them into a never-ending discovery of its nature, its appeal, its inexhaustible treasures. This is how we work for the arousal, unfolding, and defining of purpose; and it is also how we promote and foster musical growth.

Proposition Seven: The Future

In planning and carrying on our program we must have in mind the influence that music can have, not only on the lives of children here and now, but also on their future living.

It is often said that education prepares for the future. Of course the statement is true in substance, but it raises an awkward question. We do not know what the future will bring. How, then, can we prepare for it? To give a specific instance, fifty years ago (or indeed considerably less) no one could have foreseen the tremendous vogue of the phonograph, radio, and television, or the tremendous role they now play in people's lives. How could educators possibly have prepared for such a situation? The answer, obviously, is that they could have done no such thing. Today, as always, the future is full of unforeseeable possibilities and events, for which no specific preparation can be made.

Yet education must look ahead. It must be concerned with the future. It cannot concentrate simply on the present. Otherwise it becomes a sort of highly organized baby-sitting.

What, then, is the solution? It is this. Education cannot prepare for an unknown future, except in the most general way. But it can do a great deal to shape and influence that future. As you look at Johnny and Suzy in the first grade, you would be extremely rash even to hazard a guess at what sort of lives they will be living when they are fifty. If you try to prepare them for living forty or fifty years hence, a time will probably come when they will remember you with pitying smiles. Nevertheless, there is a great deal that you can do. You can bring certain influences to bear, you can establish focal points of interest and purpose, you can inaugurate certain directions of growth. If you do this, the chances are that your work will last; for once growth is well started along any line it seems to gain a momentum of its own, and to continue, even though you cannot foresee its specific outcomes. This is exactly what you ought to try to do in and through your music program.

Here let us return to the five aims dealt with in the previous chapter, which I will assume that you are willing to accept, or at least to consider, for the time-being. You want music to bring opportunities for enjoyment, opportunities for achievement, disciplinary experiences, opportunities for social togetherness, incentives for cultural enlargement and enrichment. These are all developmental influences, growth-producing influences, life-shaping influences, and music can bring them all to bear. Certainly you want music to exert these influences on children here and now. But also you want it to go on exerting them on these children in years to come. This too is possible, but it will only happen if you promote a process of musical growth.

The musical responsiveness of a little child can be vital. It can have a real appeal, a real importance in his life. But it is sure to be indefinite and ill-defined. To say that he grows musically is to say that his response takes on shape, becomes more definite, more discriminating, more comprehending, more competent, more assured. It does not lose vitality. On the contrary, it gains. At first it is like a sapling that must be coddled and nurtured, and that will be killed by a light frost. But growth transforms it into a sturdy tree, able to withstand the winter storms. Growth might be thought of as an affair of putting down roots and putting out branches. So, as a child grows musically, music takes a stronger hold upon his life and exercises a more significant influence.

That is why musical growth is an absolute necessity, if music is to exert the life-influences of which it is capable, both now and later. A program of routine and mechanical learnings, a program committed to the accumulation of bits and pieces, will not do at all. The reason is that such a program has no life within it. It generates no increasing purpose, pointing forward to the future years. So, again, sporadic, superficial, incidental musical doings and experiences can never accomplish what we have in mind. If we have nothing but such experiences, musical responsiveness remains at an immature, a childish level, so that it can mean very little as the years pass and children grow up. Nothing but a planned, continuous, coordinated program centering on musical growth will serve to achieve the human values that we seek.

Questions for Discussion, Thought, and Study

1. You may find it helpful in understanding the propositions put forward in this chapter if you apply them to some of your own experiences as a music student, and consider to what extent these experiences have promoted musical growth.

2. Do you think the kind of singing called "community singing" can do much to promote musical growth?

3. Can you see any possible relationship between musical growth and the business of learning to read music?

4. What answer would you give to those who insist that in bringing music to children we should have nothing to do with its technical aspects? Do these people seem to you to have a wrong conception of techniques?

5. It is very often said that in planning a sequence of learning we should always go from the simple to the complex, and from the known to the unknown. These are very tricky statements. Analyze them carefully with illustrations, and relate them to the discussion in this chapter.

6. Bring together and examine the fallacies of the idea that we ought to set up a sequence of learnings by the calendar and stick to it. Why is this very thing so often done?

7. If a teacher is to do anything very effective in promoting musical growth, is it essential for him to be a thoroughly trained musician? If not, what are some of the things that a teacher with only a little musical training can do effectively?

8. Carefully re-read the section of this chapter dealing with The Future. Do you see any relationship between what is said there with what is said in the section dealing with Purpose?

9. Clarify in your mind, and illustrate, the distinction between co-ordination and continuity.

10. Considering the characteristics of musical growth, would a program planned to promote it have any place for technical exercises, technical drills, or drills on the notation?

Readings

James L. Mursell, *Education for Musical Growth*. Boston, Ginn and Company, 1948; Chapter 1, "The Developmental Approach in Music Education"; Chapter 3, "Characteristics of Musical Growth"; Chapter 4, "The Rhythm of Musical Growth."

These chapters deal somewhat more at length with the topics here presented.

Beatrice Landeck, *Children and Music*. New York, William Sloan Associates, Inc., 1952. "How Do Children Grow with Music?" pp. 229–241.

Arthur Jersild, *Child Psychology*. New York, Prentice Hall, Inc., 1947. Chapter 2.

This whole book has greatly influenced the thinking of educational workers. It is all worth reading, but I refer you particularly to Chapter 2.

CHAPTER FOUR

A Program of Learning Experiences

The Principle

A program planned to promote musical growth will consist of a wide and varied range of learning experiences.

This principle tells us what *kind* of content our program must have, without as yet going into any details about singing, playing instruments, listening, and so on. It must consist of learning experiences. Probably two questions occur to you immediately. What is a "learning experience"? Why is it important to say that our program must consist of them? I shall now try to indicate the answers.

1. Here is an instance of a learning experience. A famous woodwind quartet visited a small mid-western city to give a short series of concerts. The music program in the city schools was a good one, and there was an excellent high school band. The band director called the attention of all the boys in the woodwind section to the concerts, and they attended every one of them. Not only did they attend, but also it was evident that they were keenly interested. They studied the programs in advance, and went over some of the numbers afterwards. Through arrangements made by the band director, they were able to get front-row seats; and they watched everything that went on with eager attention. They were fascinated by the beautiful instru-

ments used by the artists, and eagerly noted all that was done on the platform. When the series of concerts was over, the band director arranged for them to meet the artists personally, and the boys were much impressed.

This shows you pretty well what is meant by a learning experience. One could not, perhaps, point to this or that specific thing that was learned; but it was evident that a great deal of learning went on. The experience had a great effect on the boys' work in the band, and on their personal music study. There was a new enthusiasm, a new reaching for exacting standards. One could not doubt that they had gotten something they might remember for years to come, and that might even affect the course of their lives to some extent.

The great advantage of the term "learning experience" is its inclusiveness. It means simply an experience in which something is learned. That something may be very definite and identifiable; or it may be something that cannot be specifically labelled. The experience itself may be carefully organized in every detail; or it may be very informal and even unexpected. These differences are not unimportant, but they do not go to the root of the matter. A learning experience is any experience through which one learns; and our principle tells us that our developmental program must be built out of such experiences.

2. Why is this an important idea? Why is it worth stating? Because musical growth, like every other kind of personal growth, can be caused by an immense variety of experiences, formal and informal, planned and unplanned. These differences do not matter, so long as the experiences bring about learning.

Consider your own development. You have grown professionally from working on a committee, from an evening of discussion with some friends, from contact with a fine administrator, and also from formal study in courses. You have grown musically from listening to a great artist, as well as from taking music lessons. If you were asked exactly what you had learned from many of these experiences, you might be at a loss to answer. But you have no doubt that you learned a great deal. It may even be that you are in your present line of work largely because of some learning experience that came almost by chance, and the exact result of which you could not define. But it is also true that you have been helped by other experiences which were carefully planned, and which did have definite outcomes. All these were learning experiences.

The point is that growth of every kind, including musical growth, is brought about by any experience through which a person learns. For this reason such an experience is often called a *developmental* experience—a *growth-producing* experience, that is to say. This is a familiar and often-used term, and I shall feel free to use it interchangeably with the term "learning experience."

You can now begin to see how our fourth principle leads us to think about our program. An experience may be scheduled in advance, or it may come along by chance; it may be elaborately organized, or it may be very simple and direct; it may lead to definable results, or to outcomes which can only be sensed and felt. No matter! If it is an experience through which children learn, it is the right kind of stuff for our program. That is what our principle says.

But it also goes on to say expressly that our program must consist of a *wide and varied* range of such experiences. This may seem to you so obviously implied in the very conception of a learning experience that it is hardly worth saying. I think not. I think it is very important indeed to say, in so many words, that we must have a wide and varied range of learning experiences in our program.

One reason is that an experience that produces learning in one person may not produce it in another; and we need to be reminded of this. The boys in the woodwind section were greatly influenced by the concerts they attended. Would members of the choir have been influenced as deeply? Quite probably not. Perhaps, indeed, they would hardly have been influenced at all. Such things often happen. What reaches one person may not so much as touch another. This is a strong and convincing reason for building our program out of many kinds of learning experiences—out of a wide and varied range of them, as our principle puts it.

Then there is another reason. Every person needs many kinds of developmental experiences if his growth is to go ahead as it should. You may have grown professionally from serving on a committee, but the careful reading of certain books, which is a learning experience of quite another kind, is also necessary if your growth is to be well rounded. The privilege of listening to some great artist may have affected your whole life, but hard, intensive music study is also necessary if you are to grow into a good musician. Those boys got a great deal from attending the series of concerts; but one hopes that they also got a great deal from their lessons on their instruments, which were also developmental experiences, or should have been. In each of these cases, as you will see, a range, a variety of experiences is necessary if there is to be well-balanced, well-rounded growth. And so our principle does not stop short by saying that our developmental program must consist of learning experiences. It goes on also to say that there must be a wide and varied range of such experiences.

So much for a general explanation of our fourth principle. Now I go on to consider its more specific meanings and implications.

Learning Experiences or Lessons?

Our fourth principle seems to go dead against a very common assumption. It is an assumption not often put into words, but very influential none the less. This is the assumption that any music program must be made up of *lessons;* that it must, in effect, be a planned scheme of lessons. What should we say about this assumption in the face of the assertion that our program should consist of *learning experiences?*

The first thing to say is that we had better be as clear as we can about just what we mean by the word "lesson." I believe it would be fair to claim that the distinguished mark of a lesson is that it is intended and planned to bring about some specific, identifiable bit of learning. We might have a lesson on the dotted quarter note, or on the key signature and scale of E major, or on the 6/8 time signature, or on the singing of a certain song or the playing of a certain piece, or on the characteristics of Schubert's music. The word "lesson," of course, is often loosely used to cover a great deal, and to refer to many procedures. But as one watches teaching, reads courses of study, and examines lesson plans, one comes to think that its distinguishing mark is the intention to get some specific, definable job of learning done.

Now, of course, there will be innumerable occasions when it will be important to get this or that specific bit of learning done. We may want children to sing a certain phrase with good expression and intonation, or to understand and feel how to execute a syncopated passage, or to know how to find *do* from a key signature. These are all specific learnings, and if we want them to happen we may set up learning experiences to bring them about. But planning and carrying out an assembly program, or making drums and becoming able to play them, or attending a children's concert are certainly learning experiences too. Yet most of us would be puzzled to say in advance what the children ought to learn, and equally puzzled to tell afterwards what they had learned, even though we might be quite sure that they had learned a great deal.

So our principle already tells us something of very great importance. It tells us that if we are trying to promote musical growth, we must not limit ourselves to specific, identifiable learnings. On the contrary, we must study to include a whole range of various learning experiences; and if, in many cases, there seem to be no specific outcomes, such learning experiences can still be very important and very valuable. Obviously there is much food for thought here for the music specialist, and perhaps even more for the classroom teacher. The classroom teacher who does not feel able to set up music lessons in the conventional sense, need not feel inferior, or self-distrustful, or discouraged. She can contribute something of the utmost importance. Indeed, her contribution is even essential; for without the classroom teacher it is impossible to have the range of learning experiences required for the effective promotion of musical growth.

If a distinction must be drawn between lessons and learning experiences, would it not be best to say that our program must contain both? Should not our fourth principle be re-formulated? Should it not point out that, while lessons are indeed necessary, general learning experiences are necessary as well? There is a very decisive reason why this would be a bad solution. What must be done, and what can be done, is to see that lessons have the qualities and characteristics of good learning experiences. Very often they do not. Very often there is such a businesslike concentration on the specific outcome that everything else is neglected. Then the lesson actually tends to defeat its own purpose, and its contrast with a good learning experience is glaring and extreme. But this need not be so. Whether the desired outcome is specific and definable, or whether it is general and more or less unpredictable (though none the less real), any superior learning experience has the same basic characteristics. What these characteristics are, and what they require in the way of planning and organization, we shall now proceed to see.

I. Quality, Vitality, Significance

A good learning experience must have quality, vitality, significance. This is its first, and by far its most important characteristic.

A third-grade group is preparing an assembly program. For them it can be a growth-producing experience of great value. On the other hand, it can be nothing of the sort. What, then, must be done? The opportunity of presenting some music in the assembly must be met thoughtfully and carefully. It must not be approached haphazardly, or with the assumption that anything but the best the children can do will be good enough. Much of the value that the occasion will have for the children will depend on the preparation that is made for it; and so they should have as much to do with the planning as possible. Suitable music must be chosen; and they must be led to see the importance of selecting music that has real worth and interest, and also as much variety as can be managed. Then the music must be prepared. How can its beauty, its worth, its interest be best brought out? That must be the dominating question. Neither the third-grade teacher nor the music specialist should impose the answers. On the other hand, they should not leave everything to the unguided decisions of the children. The business of the teachers is to help the children themselves to realize how best to deal with the music. Possibly this may mean the sacrifice of a little extra polish here and there. But some sacrifice of fine points may be well worth accepting if children can be led to feel that this is *their* musical occasion, *their* musical opportunity. Certainly the teachers will see to it that a downright bad performance is avoided; for the effects of such a failure, both musical and personal, can be highly unfortunate. What the children must be led to work for—and this is something entirely possible—is a sincerely felt sharing of musical pleasure. This, of course, is quite a different thing from a series of over-rehearsed stunts, with every note meticulously in place and every phrase mechanically correct—and perhaps with not a note or a phrase worth delivering or hearing.

Again, a first-grade teacher would like to have in hand a few songs which she can use from time to time, introducing them as occasion offers. Where shall she find them? How shall she choose them? Song books and school music series contain a great many songs intended for first-grade children. Some of these songs are dull and hackneyed, without any musical or poetic interest or appeal. Our first-grade teacher should avoid all such; and if she distrusts her own judgment, she will probably welcome help in making up her mind. So before long she has a good handful of suitable songs, suitable chiefly because they have genuine musical interest. Then comes the question of what to do with them. Should she use them to develop the beginnings of reading readiness? Should she make a great point of getting the children's voices up, of developing so-called "head tones"? The best advice to give her is not to worry at all about such matters. First and foremost she must feel and transmit the charm, the musical interest, the expressiveness of these songs. She must begin by feeling it herself. She can get recordings of the songs and try them over. She can think about them, and come to understand them. She can experiment with and discuss them with the music specialist. She herself must learn to enjoy them fully; and then she is ready to transmit this enjoyment to the children. All this may seem very simple, very natural, very obvious, and perhaps on the whole rather trivial. But a teacher who manages to transmit musical pleasure in this way has done what can easily be a momentous piece of work, even though one cannot point to specific learnings, or say that this or that specific thing has been achieved.

Now let us consider a much more lesson-like situation, perhaps the teaching of the structure of the minor mode to a fifth-grade group. For our teaching material we choose a beautiful and appealing minor song. The children listen to it, try it over perhaps without the notation, for the first aim is to enable them to feel and sense it as a piece of music. They are already well aware of the difference between the major and the minor as an effect, and understand something of how the effect is caused; for they have sung many minor songs with chorded accompaniments, and have observed the lowered third in the tonic triad. Now we want to go further. The rise and fall, the lapse of the phrases depend very largely on key relationships; and if these relationships are grasped, the song can be more adequately appreciated and more musically sung. Very likely we make use of the valuable device of the movable *do* syllables (or numbers, if we prefer them). For the central purpose of the syllables is to focus attention on these effects, subtle and delicate, yet immensely important in interpretation. So the better appreciation and the more satisfying execution of the song go hand in hand with an advance in understanding its structure as a piece of minor music.

So here are three learning experiences. One of them is pointed towards a specific, predetermined outcome, while the other two are not. But none of them is a routine or relatively meaningless experience. All of them have quality. All of them have vitality. All of them have significance. This is what makes all of them good learning experiences—growth-producing experiences, developmental experiences.

These three instances, and the proposition they are intended to illustrate, serve to warn us of two errors which must be recognized and avoided.

1. In setting up a lesson, the danger always is to concentrate so entirely on the specific outcome desired, that everything else is forgotten. We might teach the minor mode out of a book on the fundamentals of music, or we might use some carpentered song put together as easy teaching material. Then we would ignore quality, vitality, significance. We would have a very

inferior learning experience. Probably our specific outcome would fail, and we would be doing nothing to promote musical growth.

2. In organizing a learning experience for non-specific outcomes, the danger always is to do something haphazard, or slovenly, or negligible. The assembly program might consist of trashy stunts, clumsily done. The first-grade teacher might pick out worthless songs without an artistic glimmer in them, and present them with a "don't care" demeanor. In each case, again, we would have a poor, and probably a worthless learning experience, fruitless both in immediate effect and long-time influence.

II. Growth the Essential Purpose

The esssential purpose of the learning experiences we organize as the substance of our program is, first and foremost, to promote growth, rather than to bring about the immediate and complete mastery of any specific item. This proposition follows, almost as a matter of course, from all that has been said so far in this chapter. But repetition at this point is needed, because this is the second criterion to have in mind in answering our question: What is a good learning experience?

One immediate practical implication is that we should have a great wealth and variety of free, informal musical activities and experiences, with no ulterior motive except the pure pleasure and interest of singing, dancing, listening, and playing. Activities of this kind should not be confined to the lower grades. They should continue right along up the line. We should not tell ourselves that we are fostering music-reading readiness, or preparing for the great transition from rote to note. Such excuses are quite needless, and are likely to be damaging. What is wanted is free participation and enjoyment.

Will anything of value be accomplished? Emphatically yes!

Music education, both in school and studio, tends to be astonishingly hidebound and inhibited. Always there must be painful labor, anxious analysis, searching self-criticism. It never seems to occur to many teachers that music naturally lends itself to pure enjoyment, and that young learners may be cramped and limited by having their noses held perpetually to the grindstone.

Undoubtedly a certain danger must be recognized and guarded against. Free, uninhibited musical participation, exemplified, for instance, in community singing, too often emphasizes nothing but social jollity and disregards musical quality. Then, indeed, its great potential values are on the way to being destroyed. But such a mistake is avoidable. Much fine and inspiring music, well adapted to these uses, is available. And when such music is chosen, its intrinsic appeal combines with the freedom and pleasure of the social occasion to provide a rich, memorable, growth-producing experience.

There is, of course, no doubt whatever that specific understanding of musical concepts and symbols must be developed. Without such specific understanding, musical growth itself is bound to be impaired. But such understandings and insights should not be taught as if they were isolated nuggets of knowledge, to be imparted once and for all at some pre-determined moment. On the contrary, they should emerge as integral elements in the process of growth itself.

The teaching of the minor mode, to which reference has already been made, is a case in point. Many music specialists would feel that it belongs in the fifth grade, and often they may be right. But the point is not the grade-placement of the item, but the body of experience which is its setting. Previous experiences with minor music should not be thought of as a process of getting ready to learn the technical pattern of the minor scale. That technical pattern should be introduced and explained at a moment when it will enrich and give new significance to musical experience. One cannot say in advance just when this moment will arrive, for much will depend on the children, the teacher, and the whole scheme of the program. Moreover, when the explanation has been made, we must not assume that the minor mode has been learned once and for all. The process of growth must still continue, which means that the children must be led to grasp more and more of the true inwardness of the minor mode by experiencing it in a whole range of new expressive settings. Similarly, when children have learned to do the polka, they have already learned a great deal about music with subdivided beats. At some point in the sequence this learning can be pinned down and also generalized by introducing the relevant arithmetical notational symbols. But the polka is not a readiness stage for a lesson on the notation. The notation is used to bring significance and precision to the physical rhythmic experience.

In all this we see once more the great advantage of thinking always in terms of learning experiences or developmental experiences. The teaching of the minor mode, or of the symbols for a subdivided beat, would certainly be lessons, in the sense that a specific, definite outcome is contemplated. Yet they would not be lessons in the sense that everything but the specific outcome is ignored, that all procedures center on the outcome and nothing else, and that we assume the outcome to have been achieved once the lesson is over.

Lessons of this latter kind are, unfortunately, all too common. They are what I have elsewhere ventured to call "closed circuit" learning situations. A task or problem is set up. Teaching procedures are concentrated on it. A test is run to find out if the task has been accomplished. If and when it has (or sometimes even if it has not), we pass on to the next task, and proceed as before. The idea behind the plan is obviously that we should work for the addition or accumulation of specific masteries. But it is beyond question a fallacy. People very rarely learn even a specific item completely, once and for all, at a given moment. They need time to take it in, to clear it up, to look at it from different angles, to see its bearings and implications. If it is to do them any good at all, it must grow in their minds, rather than being stored as an inert possession like a letter in a file. And also the learning of it, however specific the item may be, must be an integral part of a continuous process of growth.

The closed circuit lesson usually seems very businesslike and practical. But it is certain to be wasteful and likely to be futile. It is, however, needless and avoidable. A learning experience may be lesson-wise in the sense of being pointed to some specific item. But it can still be a good learning experience if it arises out of the continuous process of growth, and has the effect of carrying that process further.

All this makes the problem of grade-placement very difficult. To teach any specific item prematurely is to make sure that it will not be learned. To postpone it indefinitely is to impede musical growth. What, then, is the right moment? How can we tell when it will arrive? The plain truth is that there is no universal answer to these questions. Those who put forward universal answers, as a good many people actually do, are simply deceiving themselves. No one knows in advance at what point or at what age-level any specific musical item ought to be taught and learned. The idea of going from simple to complex will not help us, because what seems simple is often complex, and what is simple to one child will not be simple to another. The idea of readiness will not help us; for while it is obvious that no one will learn anything until he is ready to do so, the whole problem is to find out when he is ready. The idea that specifics should always be developed out of music begins to get us somewhere. But even this is only a general guide. Third grade children who are singing a minor song may get something worth while from discovering that the effect of the minor triad depends on the lowered third; but they may get absolutely nothing out of a complete logical exposition of the minor scale. The only advice that can be given is to say that we must feel our way, sense our human situation, maintain an experimental attitude, and never forget that no set stereotype can by any possibility be universally right.

Here is a point for fruitful collaboration between the music specialist and the classroom teacher. The classroom teacher should know and understand her children better and more completely than the music specialist can. She should have a keener and more just sense of what will help them and what will not. The music specialist, on the other hand, knows better than the classroom teacher what can, should, and must be developed if the process of musical growth is to go on. By pooling their viewpoints and sharing their insights the two of them working together, can come as near as is humanly possible to deciding wisely when such and such a specific item should be introduced, how it should be approached, how it should be followed up.

III. Decision, Choice, Motivation

Learning experiences must arise out of the decisions and choices of the learners. This is the third characteristic of a good learning situation.

To organize a learning experience that arises out of and expresses the decisions and choices of the learners, a certain kind of leadership by the teacher is necessary. This takes us back to our previous analysis of three types of social situations. In an *autocratic* situation all decisions, all choices are made by the leader, and all other members of the group are cast in the role of followers. In a *laissez-faire* social situation there is no leadership at all, and everyone is free to do just as he pleases. In a *democratic* or *participant* situation the function of the leader is to enable the group to arrive at effective decisions, and to carry them through in a satisfactory way.

The effect of these three types of situation on growth is very evident when we remember that growth is brought about by choosing, by deciding, by acting—by positive and active experience, that is to say. In an autocratic situation, the members of the group have no choice at all. In a *laissez-faire* situation, they have so many possible choices that they might as well have none. Children, and older people too, need help, guidance, organization if they are to make effective decisions; and it is through effective decisions that they learn and grow. To supply such help and guidance is the function of the teacher as leader.

Consider how this function might work out in handling a song with young children. The song, let us say, has to do with birds. The teacher has the thought that dramatization might be valuable. She will, perhaps, begin by saying a little something about the song; and then she will let the children hear it. Moreover, she will be careful to let them listen to it enough so that they can catch its meaning, its tune, and its rhythm. In so doing she has already begun to organize choices. Sometimes teachers who propose to set up rhythmic activity or dramatization make the mistake of not letting children hear the music enough to catch its drift. When this mistake is made, the children either have to be told what to do, or they are left to flounder along and get nowhere. But our teacher has already set up a focal point—or, to use a scientific term, she has already "polarized" her group. The suggestion to act the song out will then come very naturally, and the children have something to go on. Several of them decide they would like to be flying birds. Again, the teacher does not tell them how, for it is not unlikely that some of them will do better than she could. In any case, she relies on the music to do a good deal of the "telling." Of course the teacher can make suggestions, and bring up ideas that might not otherwise appear.

This is just another way of helping the children to make good decisions for themselves. Perhaps some might like to perch while others fly, or to sit on a nest, or to sing bird calls if the music permits. What we have is a pattern of activity that is free and varied. Yet it has a focus and a meaning, for it centers in the music itself. It is brought about by the constructive leadership of the teacher, which enables the children to make their own choices and to carry them out.

There is nothing in the least mysterious or unrealistic in this process of organizing choices and decisions. It happens whenever and wherever we have democratic leadership, and such leadership lends itself perfectly to the music program. For instance, many teachers have been very successful in arranging free and informal musical opportunities during the lunch hour. Some instruments, probably including an autoharp, are made available in the classroom, and children are encouraged to use them and try them out just as they wish. Again, the employment of simple instruments of both tonal and rhythm type in the classroom creates many opportunities for personal choice. The teacher who simply imposes the use of such and such an instrument, or who imposes the instrumentation of a song, loses much of the value of instrumental activity. On the other hand, it would be a mistake to swamp the children by providing so many different instruments that they would not know how to choose. At first they should be helped to explore the instruments using one kind at a time, so as to learn their possibilities. Then they should be encouraged to decide which would go best with any given song—a flute, perhaps, with a shepherd's song, or bells with a song about a desert caravan. Of course the question as to how to use the chosen instrument, and at what point in the song to play it, will also come up. Here again the teacher should not impose the decision. What she should do is to give the children a basis for deciding, by helping them to see that the instrument must be used to enhance and add interest to the music.

Such a simple matter as keeping instruments available on a table or in a music corner can have a great effect in the organization of genuine choosing and deciding.

Unfortunately, one often finds simple instruments, and particularly rhythm instruments, very differently used. For one thing, instrumental activity very easily takes on the guise of an orchestra for small children, with everyone carrying an assigned part and following the lead of the teacher-director. For another thing, such activity is often extremely unmusical, and is very apt to amount to little more than a showy, noisy stunt, lacking in the quality and significance so absolutely essential for a good developmental experience in the field of music. However, we do not question the value of rhythm instruments, correctly and tastefully used, as an adjunct to and vital part of the total music program.

But what of the teaching of musical specifics, the so-called fundamentals? Does not this require an entirely different treatment? It may be both desirable and possible to develop a suitable dramatization or to select instruments for use with a song on the basis of the children's own choice and decision. Can such a thing be done when it comes to teaching sixteenth notes, or the singing of a passage with syllables or numbers? Is it not necessary in such cases for the teacher to do the choosing and deciding, to tell the children what they are expected to learn, and to see that they learn it?

The difference is more apparent than real. Let us remember once again that the learning of all specifics should arise directly out of musical situations. We have a fast-moving passage in a song. This much the children have already grasped. The concept of *sixteenth note* can give this passage a more exact and satisfactory shape. So we introduce the concept to enable the children to do better what they can already do to some extent, to bring about an improvement which they will find significant and enjoyable. So also with the use of syllables. We introduce them

in a passage much of whose expressiveness and interest depend
on key relationships or tonality trends. The syllables serve to
feature these relationships or trends, to define them, to bring
them sharply to attention. So once more the learning of the
syllables enhances a musical experience, and becomes an influence for musical growth. Here as previously it is evident that
what is a lesson in the sense of being directed toward a specific
outcome both can and should conform to the requirements of a
good learning experience. Sixteenth notes, syllables, and all
other musical specifics become desirable when they are presented
in such a way that their true musical significance is revealed.

Note once again that the organization of learning experiences
based on the choices and desires of the learners is entirely practical, and in fact remarkably simple. It is the proper way of
dealing with the problem of motivation. The conventional, narrow, closed-circuit lesson sets up a learning task which has no
evident significance, uses material lacking in quality and appeal,
and is entirely unrelated to the choices and desires of the learners. Obviously the only kind of motivation we can use is entirely
artificial. It may consist of absurdities, such as giving notes the
names of birds or animals, of blandishments of various kinds,
and of implied threats and penalties. Such motivation cannot
yield good learning or effective growth. For good learning and
effective growth we must have a direct positive motivation spring-
ing from the appeal of the music itself, and the wish to appreciate and enjoy it more fully.

Again, the conventional closed-circuit lesson tends to draw a
sharp line between those who succeed and those who fail. We
propose to set up a drill on tone-matching, or on finding *do* from
various key signatures. In doing so we have created either-or
situations. In each case some children will manage the job, and
some will not. But the point of a good learning situation is that
while some will do better than others, all can get something from

it. Some children may make what we consider a poor choice of instruments, or be clumsy when they undertake a dramatization. But this is quite different from a flat, definite failure. Or again, some children will grasp the concept of sixteenth notes or the significance of the syllables quite well, while others will not. But there will still be something constructive and helpful in the experience even for these others. For they can still grasp the shape and expressiveness of the music itself, and know that there are ways of defining this shape and expressiveness which, later on, they may come clearly to understand.

IV. Flexibility

Learning experiences must be flexibly adapted to the maturity, interests, and needs of the learners. This is the fourth characteristic of a good, an effective learning experience. The reason for it is not hard to see. If we organize an experience that is too abstract, or too complicated for our learners, or that is entirely remote from their interests and concerns, they get nothing from it. It ceases, therefore, to be a learning experience at all.

One of the great advantages of thinking, planning, and working in terms of learning experiences is that it gives our music program great flexibility. On the other hand, a program that is entirely a sequence of specific lessons, or that has such a sequence as its solid core, is almost bound to be rigid. In making such a program one begins by getting together all the specifics that seem important. Next one decides as well as one can at what stage each of these specifics should be presented. Then one provides suitable teaching materials, i.e. songs and pieces, with the various specifics in mind. Then one indicates, at any rate in a general way, a plan or "method" for using the specifics. The program goes into operation as the teachers present the specific items, one by one, in the designated order, using the materials

that are furnished, and applying the indicated teaching procedure. A little variation may be introduced here and there. A
few "trimmings" in the way of free learning experiences may be
tolerated. But the main business is the pre-planned sequence of
lessons, dealing with the specifics as they have been laid out in
the basic plan.

A program organized in this way (and such programs are
found in many subjects besides music) is often said to be
logically rather than psychologically organized. Psychologically
organized it is certainly not; for every psychological assumption
that underlies it is about as wrong as it well could be. But it is
not logically organized either. I have seen a good many courses
of study, in many subjects, developed by this kind of planning.
Not one of them really exemplifies what a competent scholar
would consider the basic logic of the field. All such courses of
study, all such programs, are really *arbitrary* arrangements. The
sequence of topics, the choice of materials, the indicated teaching procedures are decided upon for some sort of reasons. But
the reasons are always debatable, not founded on any basic
principles, and wide open to disagreement on the part of anyone
who feels like disagreeing. *The real defense of such curricular
schemes is not that they are logical, but that they are convenient.*

So long as practically all the music teaching in a school system
is done by the music specialist, there will be a very strong tendency to set up just such a scheme as I have described. Let us
consider a situation that is probably rather more favorable than
most. There are three music specialists working in the elementary schools. Between them, each can manage to visit each elementary classroom for twenty minutes once a week. That is the
extent of instruction in music, but it taxes each of the workers to
the limit. Preparations, the making of reports, the transportation
of materials, absorb both time and strength. Without a very
definite plan, stretching ahead week after week, they will cer-

tainly be lost. To make such a plan, and to stick to it, is almost a necessity for them.

Now suppose that there is a radical change of policy. Our three elementary music specialists are no longer expected to carry an impossible load of hurried teaching. Some teaching they will always continue to do, one reason being that it is bad for any educational workers to get out of touch with the children. But much of their thought, time, and energy is now devoted to developing the music program throughout the schools, and above all with the classroom teachers. This will keep them as busy as ever they were; but their work will pay greater dividends, and the dividends will tend to increase. They do not sit in their offices awaiting calls for help. They take the initiative, with personal contacts, demonstrations, conferences, conversations, discussions, workshops. Then a very different kind of program becomes possible. There will be more music in the schools, and also more kinds of music. There will still be continuity, but it will not be the continuity of a rigid sequence. A set, pre-determined series of specific lessons will no longer be the heart of the program. For now, with effective specialist leadership, many people will become more and more able and willing to plan and organize varied learning experiences, flexibly adapted to the maturity, interests, and needs of the learners with whom they deal and whom they intimately know.

A music program consisting of learning experiences can and should be flexible in three respects. There should be flexibility in planning, flexibility in scheduling, and flexibility in the total sequence.

1. There should be flexibility in planning. A good learning experience often requires a great deal of careful preparation and pre-planning. Instances are the stage-managing of a listening experience, the choice of the most suitable song out of several alternates, the way of introducing a novel instrument, the de-

cision to use syllables to highlight the musical values of a selected passage.* But some of the best learning experiences are
extemporized.

In a kindergarten, the teacher may have planned certain musical experiences, perhaps intending to use certain songs. One of
the children brings a kitty to school, and everyone is fascinated.
Obviously, the pre-conceived plans should be abandoned, or at
any rate altered enough so that music activities may center about
the kitty, including singing, making up rhythms, making up
poetry, etc. Or a teacher may have in mind to teach a song about
the sunshine. On the day, the rain is pouring down, and a whole
unforeseen set of activities is indicated.

By way of a negative instance, I once visited a classroom
where an elaborate unit on Indians was being developed. There
were decorations, pictures, models, tools, utensils, maps, and
even a wigwam. At the appointed time the music specialist arrived, and proceeded for twenty minutes to teach the use of the
head voice and something about triplets. I fully sympathize. I
am sure he was under such pressures that he could hardly have
done anything else. But still, I deplore!

2. There should be flexibility in scheduling. Music can and
should be used freely and frequently throughout the day. When
so used it is a very valuable influence. Songs, rhythms, listening
can be used for rest, for relaxation, for a refreshing change of
occupation. Music, in any of its manifestations, can do much to
create a good social morale in the classroom. It can be brought
into touch with experiences of other kinds. The children are
reading a story about a puppy. Why not have some appropriate
musical activity there and then? An extended comprehensive
unit is being developed, and music can do much to enrich and
vitalize it.

Such free and frequent uses of music, however, should not

_____

* Notice, however, that such planning is always with reference to the particular
group of children, not the planning of steps to put a specific across.

preclude the setting off of a special music-time each day. Indeed, if we wish music to exert its proper and potential influence, a special assigned music period is essential. A wide, varied range of musical experience, some of them perhaps quite casual, is an excellent thing—*if there is some center, some focus, some point of coordination somewhere.* This is what the assigned music period is for.

The assigned music period is not an opportunity for us to abruptly introduce a fixed sequence of specific lessons. But it is a chance for us to show children many things about music that they would otherwise miss. When we have a run of time, say twenty minutes, at our disposal, much can be done in a classroom where music is being freely and frequently used throughout the day. Types of music, and types of musical activity that would otherwise be missed can be introduced. Or one can go a little more deeply into music that has already been used and enjoyed in some other connection. One cannot effectively promote musical growth with no more than twenty minutes daily (still less twenty minutes weekly) to do it in. Nor can one promote it effectively with nothing but a spread of experiences, even though they may have authentic musical quality and appeal. But when there is both the spread and the focus, then indeed conditions for development are favorable.

3. There should be a flexible sequence. So much has already been said about this matter in the present chapter that it calls for little more than mention here. We should certainly work for growing understanding, growing discrimination, growing skill. But just when some new type of learning experience should be introduced cannot be told in advance. The introduction of the study of the minor mode, which was previously discussed, is a case in point. So is the introduction of the standard instruments. Some experienced workers like to begin instruction in the instruments in the fifth grade; but in a good many cases it can certainly come earlier. Here are two illustrations of a general truth. With-

out internal significance, sequence, and continuity, our music program will certainly fail. It will not achieve the human values that we have in mind. But a rigid, imposed sequence is a sequence only in name. What we must have is a sequence geared to the learners themselves, and determined, not in accordance with some pre-determined plan, but on the basis of our understanding of those learners.

Questions for Discussion, Thought, and Study

1. To get a good understanding of what the term "learning experience" means, get together examples of as many different kinds of such experiences as you can think of, consider them carefully, and try to see what makes them real learning experiences.

2. It is sometimes said that children should have "rich" experiences with music. Is a "rich" experience the same thing as a learning experience?

3. In the light of what is said in this chapter, can you see any reason why ordinary private music lessons (i.e. piano or violin lessons, etc.) should not be very valuable as means of producing musical growth?

4. Would it be possible to arrange a program made up of learning experiences so as to go from simple to complex?

5. As you probably know, courses of study in music often follow what is called a "logical" order. This sort of arrangement might not suit a program made up of learning experiences. In that case, would such a program be organized illogically?

6. Conscientious teachers often feel that they are wasting time if they put aside some lesson they had planned to teach at a given time, and give attention to some point of immediate interest that may have come up unexpectedly. Is this a good attitude? What reasons do you think account for it?

7. Teachers often feel that a certain amount of ground must be covered in a certain length of time. Must we give up the whole

idea of ground covering if we have a program consisting of learning experiences?

8. Various comments are made in this book about the type of musical experience offered by the rhythm band. Bring them together by looking up the topic Rhythm Band in the index, and relating what is said to the discussions in this chapter.

9. If we have a program consisting of learning experiences, is it possible for a child to fail?

10. Which would you say is more important, the number and variety of learning experiences, or their quality?

Readings

Marion Nesbitt, *A Public School for Tomorrow*. New York, Harper and Brothers, 1953. Chapter V, "We Need Music Everyday."

Gives you some good instances of learning experiences.

Emma Sheehy, *There's Music in Children*. New York, Henry Holt and Company, revised edition, 1952.

Later I shall give some specific references to this excellent little book.

Here I suggest that you glance through it for instances of learning experiences.

Beatrice Landeck, *Children and Music*. William Sloan Associates, Inc., New York, 1952. "What is Good Music?" pp. 218–228.

Another good source for learning experiences.

James L. Mursell, *Education for Musical Growth*. Boston, Ginn and Company, 1948. Chapter 5, "Developmental Experiences in Music."

The topic of this chapter with a somewhat different treatment.

PART ONE

Retrospect and Preview

We have now blocked out the general outlines of our music program, and it is well to pause for a moment and glance over the road we have travelled before turning our eyes to the prospect ahead.

1. Our program must be based on thinking and must arise out of thinking. It must arise out of thinking about human nature, human needs, human values, and about what music can do in relation to them. Our thinking will never be complete. It will never be final. And so our program itself will never reach finality.

2. Our program must center on musical growth, because music can have lasting, life-long values only for people who are growing musically.

3. It must be a program of experiences rather than of narrow and specific lessons. Specifics, indeed, must be acquired; understandings must be clarified; skills must be developed. But all this must happen in a setting of experience, and as an integral part of the process of growth.

4. Our program must be cooperative. Music specialists alone cannot do all that needs to be done. Their function becomes that of leadership, and their task is to draw other workers into the adventure of cooperative thinking, cooperative planning, and cooperative action that is the developmental music program.

PART TWO

THE SPECIAL AREAS OF THE PROGRAM

CHAPTER FIVE

Music Reading and Musical Growth:
I: Basic Concepts

The Principle

*In a program planned to promote musical growth, the develop-
ment of music-reading ability will proceed as the development
of a progressively clearer, fuller, and better understanding of
music.*

This principle, together with the next one, which is closely
related to it, shows the bearing of our developmental point of
view on the teaching of music reading. *The effect is revolutionary.*

Even the best and most enlightened music educators often
seem to have ideas about music reading that are entirely at vari-
ance with these two principles. Here I will take my courage in
both hands, and try to summarize what I believe their ideas are.

Music reading is a tool skill. It is valuable. It is important. But
its importance lies in its usefulness. A person who can read can
do more with music than a person who cannot. Learning to read
music means learning to understand certain symbols, namely,
the notation and perhaps the syllables. These symbols are ingenious artificial devices. They are an ingenious code. Their
function is to tell a person what to do when he sees them. To
learn them is to understand them intellectually. In and of themselves they have little to do with musical beauty. The business

of coming to understand them has little to do with making musical response and feeling deeper, keener, and more satisfying. Music reading, to repeat, is a tool skill. But it is such an important one that it ought to be taught and learned. This, I hope, is a fair summary of much enlightened opinion.

Now, what does our principle tell us? *Something very different!* It tells us that learning to read music is learning to understand, *not symbols, but music.* Understanding music is far from a merely intellectual process. You do not come to understand a piece of music by being able to say that it is in three-four time and in the key of G major, and by being able to identify and name its notes and tell their lengths. You come to understand it by becoming aware of its expressive content, by responding to and feeling more and more completely what there is in it, by recognizing more and more fully and surely, not the notes it contains, but the beauties it contains. What of the notation? What of the syllables? They are not code-symbols to be understood just with your mind. They are means of highlighting, of calling your attention to, of making you aware of the beauties contained in music. That is how they should be taught. That is how they should be learned. That is how they should be understood. When the symbols that we use in music reading are properly grasped, they are means of revealing to us the beauty and expressiveness of music.

I have already said many times that the very essence of the developmental approach is that we must never, never get away from the beauty, the charm, the appeal of music itself. This applies, most emphatically, to the teaching of music reading. To learn music reading is not to learn an intellectual technique. It is to learn *music.* Music reading is far more than a tool skill.

That is what our fifth principle tells us. The same idea is carried further by the sixth principle. I believe it well deserves to be called a revolutionary idea. But I am sure it is a sound one, and I shall try to do justice to it in this chapter and the next.

Music Reading Is Essential

Right at the start, we run into a very striking implication. *The teaching of music reading has an essential place in a developmental program of music education.* This faces up to a highly controversial issue about as squarely as anything could.

The reason? To learn to read music is to learn to understand music. The whole value of the symbols is to help us to understand music better. Without an understanding of the symbols, musical understanding is bound to lag, just as without the symbols called numbers, arithmetical understanding is bound to lag. But if musical understanding lags, musical growth lags. So the teaching of music reading is a "must" in a program planned to promote musical growth.

At this point I think a glance back over the history of music education will be repaying, because it puts the statement I have just made in its proper setting, and shows its extreme importance. For many years, in many but not all school systems, music reading was the staple content of the elementary music program. Musical materials were chosen for the sake of teaching children to read; and a good deal of music was composed—or, perhaps better, constructed—for this purpose. Very specific teaching procedures were devised, and teachers were expected to follow them carefully and in detail. In effect it was prevailingly true that music in the elementary school meant the teaching of reading.

For some considerable time this type of work has been subjected to growing criticism, both from general educators and music educators. Many objections have been raised; but the most important of them are as follows:

(a) A program that centers almost entirely on reading is monopolistic. It entirely neglects many other very significant aspects of music. (b) The quality of the music used is, in general, very poor, because all that is wanted is a collection of suitable exercises on the notation. (c) Teaching procedures are extremely mechanical, much being made of routine drills, note-pointing, note-spelling, and the like. Such procedures have long been abandoned by experts in the teaching of language-reading. (d) Results in general are very poor. Few children finish the sixth grade as good readers. Enthusiasts for the old-fashioned music-reading program deny this, but they have no convincing data to support their claim. Moreover, it is obvious that our schools have not produced a generation of competent music-readers. (e) A great many children, and indeed a majority, will certainly fail to read music. They are likely to develop an antipathy to music, which is a poor outcome for the elementary music program. (f) This type of work is contrary to enlightened elementary-school procedure in other fields. So the music program becomes an anomaly, a sort of enclave or beleagured fortress. This is certainly the opinion of many general teachers and administrators, and it is recognized more or less clearly by music educators, often with pain and bewilderment.

These and other similar criticisms have had a great effect. They have caused much stir, confusion, trouble, and angry debate. What ought to be done? That has become a very pressing question. Three answers have emerged, none of which is very satisfactory.

First, there are those who would greatly reduce the emphasis on music reading. Here, the most extreme position is that which was taken by a widely-known and distinguished music educator who claimed that music reading should be entirely given up and that children should not even see the notation until after the sixth grade. Very few would go that far, but a good many seem willing to go at least a good part of the way. In answer it is said that the abandonment of music reading, or even a serious reduction of emphasis on it, would tend to take away the solid content of music education, and would tend to make elementary school music nothing but mere play. People who press this objection have not always thought their way down to basic principles, but they sense something that is very important, and that cannot be ignored. Music educators cannot emasculate their subject without undermining their own position.

Second, there are those who still cling to the old-line type of program, with its almost exclusive emphasis on music reading, its musically worthless materials, and its routine methods. They insist that many children, in fact, do learn to read, although they certainly have never proved it, and almost certainly could not prove it. They insist that the program does not produce any widespread antipathy to music; but again without an atom of convincing proof. One has to say with regret that these are the claims of interested parties who are committed in advance to a position and propose to defend it no matter what. Still, these people are right in their strong feeling, in general, that the music program must have real substance, and, in particular, that music reading is extremely important.

Third, there are those—and there are many such—who are actively seeking for new and better procedures for the teaching of music reading. They wish to use music with genuine artistic value, to set up less mechanical and more attractive classroom methods, and to give ample recognition to a wide range of musical experiences and activities. Obviously the future lies here. Yet the solution will not come from experimentation merely on the level of procedure. This is likely to yield nothing better than an uneasy compromise between the old and the new—between reading-and-nothing-else, and no-reading-at-all. The reading problem can be satisfactorily met only in terms of basic principle.

Such a solution is proposed in our fifth principle. It says that the development of music-reading ability should proceed as the development of a fuller, clearer, better understanding of music. When a child is being properly taught to read music, he is being taught to understand music. When a child is being properly taught to understand music, he is being taught to read music. I will go so far as to say that no one can be taught really to understand music without being taught to understand the symbols and concepts on which reading depends. For music reading is not a separate, segregated stunt, or skill, or knack. *It is applied musical understanding.* To read music and to understand music are two aspects of the same process. This is why music reading necessarily belongs in a program planned for the promotion of musical growth, and pointed toward the realization of human values through musical growth.

Three further comments are in order here. To some extent they anticipate later discussions; but they will help to clarify the bearings of this position from the start.

1. The primary, compelling reason why our program must include music reading is not that it is a useful or practical ability, although it may be useful and practical. Possibly, in future years, some children may be better off if they can read music fluently. That is, at least, conceivable. But for us it is not the main point. The main point is that through gaining a grasp of musical concepts and of the symbols that stand for them, children will develop an understanding appreciation of music itself. And if they have such an understanding appreciation, they will certainly have secured a life-long resource.

2. If the development of music-reading ability is linked with the development of musical understanding, then all the learning experiences, all the musical activities of the program can and should contribute to it. The teaching of music reading means something far wider, far more inclusive, than concentrating from time to time on the notes and syllables of a "study song." It means leading children toward a steadily better and clearer grasp of musical content in and through all their musical activities and experiences—in and through listening, playing instruments, rhythmics, dramatizations, creative work. Once we link music reading with musical understanding, its development ceases to be a specialty, and becomes program-wide.

3. It follows from what has just been said that the teaching

of music reading is not the exclusive business of the music specialist. The average classroom teacher is likely to think of the
teaching of music reading as the elaborate presentation of what
is, to her, a rather unintelligible code called the notation. This
is part of the business, but only part of it. There is much more
than this to the teaching of music reading—much that is just as
important, much that is far more accessible to the timid—and
often quite unduly timid—layman. When a classroom teacher
uses some simple, self-invented device for helping children to
realize, through seeing, that music rises and falls, goes fast and
slow, hesitates and proceeds, she is helping them to understand
music; and by that very act she is helping them to develop the
ability to read it.

Ear, Eye, and Understanding

*The development of music reading depends altogether on the
establishment of working connections between ear, eye, and
understanding.* This proposition is the key to the whole teaching
of music reading. In explaining it I wish to revert to our previous discussion of musical understanding (pp.84–87), with
the addition of one very important factor, namely, the effect of
the eye in helping people to understand music better and better.
To make things as specific as possible, I will use once more the
previous example of the first line of *America*.

Nearly everybody can at least recognize this tune when he
hears it. This means that he can tell it from *Dixie,* or the *Londonderry Air,* or *Pop Goes the Weasel.* To say this, is to say
that nearly everyone can understand the tune *America* as having
an individual pattern, or shape, or structure, of tone and rhythm
that sets it off from other tunes. Some unfortunates, so we are
told, cannot even do this. They know when *The Star-Spangled
Banner* is being played only because everyone stands up and the
men take off their hats. For such persons music must be just a

meaningless jumble of sound. Their musical understanding is at zero, or very close to it. But to recognize a tune, to grasp it as an individual, organized pattern or structure, is proof of at least a little musical understanding.

Nearly everyone who can recognize *America* can also sing or hum it, at least after a fashion. A person may hum it so badly that he wants nobody to overhear. He may do his best humming in solitude. But at least he gets the tune as an organized shape, however roughly and crudely. That means that he has some mental grasp of it, some understanding of it, as a tune.

So far we have nothing that even seems like music reading, but only the possibility of developing it later on. The eye has not come into use at all. But now we point out to our learner that the tune he can recognize and even hum, sometimes goes up, and sometimes goes down. If we are wise, we will not just use the words "up" and "down." We will make gestures in the air at the right places, and perhaps draw curves on the blackboard. Our learner recognizes that what we are saying is quite true. It is something he never thought of before, but there it is! He can now concentrate on some fine points. When he hums, he can consciously make his voice go *up,* and then make it go *down* again. How pleasing! How interesting! How much better the humming gets to be! The eye has helped the mind. Musical understanding has advanced quite a long step.

After a good many experiences of these simple ups and downs, we think our learner may be able to take in something more. Just how far should these ups and downs go? Should they go all in one bound, or in a series of steps? If in a series of steps, how many steps? If we had to try to explain all this in words, our learner might be in difficulties. But we can show it to him in graphic form, and that makes everything far clearer. We bring in the staff, and put notes on it. We do not notate the whole tune, because this might overwhelm the learner. So we pick out bits of it that, for one reason or another, we consider salient. We tell him to have a good, careful look. *This* is that bit that he has always recognized in a general kind of way, and has rather liked; and that he has been able to hum fairly well. This, here, is *exactly* what it is, so far as its up and down are concerned. Another pleasing discovery! Another fine point in the music recognized and understood! Again the eye has helped the mind.

Of course we will not forget the rhythm. In his earliest stages our learner has certainly never thought of the rhythm as something separate from the tune itself, as indeed it is not. But we can begin pulling it out for special attention, and we can enable him to look at it. Perhaps if our learner is a child, we encourage him to walk, or dance, or otherwise move to the rhythm (although, of course *America* might not be the best choice for this). He feels his movements, and he also sees them; and this feeling and seeing brings out something else in the pattern of the music, so that his mind can get hold of it. Another thing we might do is to invite our learner to tap out the rhythm on a drum, which gives an interesting combination of eye experience, ear experience, and muscle experience, and so plays up the rhythm even more clearly than before. Then, at a certain point, we can graph the beat by marks on the board, or by conducting gestures, without necessarily explaining that it goes *one*-two-three, *one*-two-three. All this can lead to clearer recognition, and to improved humming; for the eye has helped the mind to a better understanding of the shape, or pattern, or structure which is the tune *America*.

I could go on and on with this account, bringing in key relationship, time signature, key signature, measure bars, harmonic background—indeed everything in the musical pattern that makes the tune *America* what it is. But I have probably said quite enough to explain my meaning. The eye helps the mind to disentangle, and to make good sense and good order out of what comes in through the ear. It must, I think, be pretty clear that our learner is at least on the way to being able to look at certain marks on paper, and tell from them how the music that they indicate is supposed to sound. This, of course, is what we mean by music reading at its higher level. It is all brought about by using eye experiences to help the mind to clarify, to disentangle, to make sense out of ear experiences.

There are a number of explanatory comments that need to be made about this account.

1. First, a word should be said about the term "musical understanding," which is open to a great deal of misinterpretation. Musical understanding is not, in essence, verbal. I know a very fine pianist who can present a wonderfully delicate and discriminating performance. He seems to bring out and reveal everything that there is in the music—all the rhythmic subtleties, all the inner voices, all the changing harmonies, all the delicate phrasing. But if he tries to use words to tell you what he does and why he does it, he gets into a muddle. Yet he has musical understanding of a very high order. A piece of music makes the most perfect sense to him. Every little bit fits in. Every detail belongs. Nothing is brought out too prominently. Nothing is lost in the fog. It is all clear, beautiful, expressive. He grasps the music as a pattern, a structure. That is what musical understanding means.

If we remember this, we can see at once why it is a mistake to begin with verbal explanations. To go back to our learner, we might feel that in order to teach him to read *America* we must first explain the 3/4 time signature to him. We might set the explanation up in words, giving a few examples, have him learn them, and test him on them; and he might pass with a perfect mark. But it could easily be that, in a musical sense, he would not understand the 3/4 time signature in the least. When he saw it at the start of *America* it might tell him absolutely nothing about how the music was supposed to sound. The visual symbol would have no musical meaning for him. Yet this is the sort of mistake that is quite often made. People try to teach children to read by having them learn the musical symbols in terms of word meanings only. Then the eye does not help the mind. Any understanding that may be generated—and it is usually not much—is not musical understanding. It is, at best, verbal understanding only. And children do not learn to read, because they have not been made aware, from the start and all the time, of the vital connection between the symbol and the musical experience in which lies the whole meaning of the symbol.

2. Music reading, properly understood, is quite different from what might be called note-spelling. If our learner had been taught by a procedure that was very common some years ago, and that is still in use, he would have been required to point at each of the separate notes of the tune *America,* one by one, and to try to sing each note as he pointed at it. One might say that he would have been expected to develop his reading ability by spelling out the separate notes. Our procedure is fundamentally different. We introduce our visual symbols, which may consist of diagrams or gestures as well as the standard notation, in order to clarify and define the learner's musical responses. We may not, and indeed we often will not, attach symbols to the whole of the song. Often we will pick out one or two places in it that have a special interest, and concentrate on those alone. For instance, much of the effect of *The First Noel* depends on its rising and falling scale passages; and if these are represented in such a form that the learner can see them, he is helped to grasp them clearly with his mind, notice them with his ear, and so execute them better with his voice. Sometimes, indeed, we may concentrate on one single note. But then the reason will be, not that it is a note, but that it is an effect. For instance, the opening note of the refrain of *Home on the Range* comes on the dominant. This gives a very strong effect of being, as it were, on the verge of something, just ready to take off even though the tonic chord is used. Singers of the song who have no musical training at all are likely to feel this effect, and perhaps to

bring it out to an extent that we may be inclined to call "corny." But if we have some simple, clear-cut symbol that identifies this effect, that calls attention to it, then our learner will be able to notice it consciously, to bring it out properly, and to recognize it when he finds it elsewhere in music. We have, in fact, just such a symbol, for the note in question can be labeled *so*. Thus it is that we use (and teach) musical symbols to bring to the learner's mind effects that are actually present in the music, so that the music becomes a more and more sense-making, organized pattern to him. And as time goes on, he will come to know, when he sees certain musical symbols, that they indicate certain musical effects, which is entirely different from note-spelling.

3. Independent music reading is the ability to sing or play a new piece of music immediately and at sight. It is an ability that develops gradually. As our learner studies and uses the various musical symbols, he becomes more and more aware of key, time, rhythm, duration, melodic shape, phrase, and harmony in any piece of music with which he deals. His musical understanding, which is his grasp of music as an expressive organized pattern, improves. Little by little he finds himself more and more able to tell how a piece of music will sound just by looking at it. Eye, ear, and understanding have been brought closely enough into relationship so that he can "hear with his eyes," as is often said. Or he can sing or play it right away, if it is within his technical capacity, for his fingers or his voice are steered by the musical effects that his mind tells him have to be produced. It is doubtful whether much independent sight reading can be developed by children before the end of the sixth grade, although there will certainly be wide differences. But this should not give us any great concern. If children have built up a good connection between ear, eye, and understanding, they have developed the best possible basis for independent sight reading. And they have developed something still more impor-

tant, namely, a real grasp of music as an organized expressive pattern or structure—a real measure of musical understanding.

4. Much that has been said about independent music reading applies also to highly skilled sight reading. This is the sort of reading that enables a person to play a full orchestral score on the piano at the first glance, or to play a difficult accompaniment in a transposed key the first time he sees it. Such an expert reader certainly does not spell out the separate notes. He looks at the score, instantly grasps the intended effect, and produces it on his instrument. One might say that he understands very quickly, very promptly, very clearly. He becomes able to do this by long and varied practice in understanding. He does the same kind of thing that our learner did when he first realized that the tune of *America* rises and falls. But he does it far faster, better, and more completely. For music reading, from its humblest beginnings to its most spectacular manifestations is always a projection of musical understanding.

5. The last remark that needs to be made here is to point out what a tremendous advantage it is that we have, in music, a really adequate system of visual symbols. The art of the dance makes an interesting comparison, for it has almost nothing of the kind. One consequence has been that we have no very good idea of how the ballets of the reign of Louis XIV were performed, whereas we have a very good idea indeed of the music of the period. But, more important for us, the absence of symbolism makes the dance harder to understand than it would otherwise be. A person can sit and watch a ballet, and have very little realization of what is going on. This is much more than an intellectual lack, much more than not being able to put a name to the figures and the steps. Such a person gets only a vague impression of something that has been carefully organized as a pattern to convey a specific effect. He operates, so to speak, on a low level of "dance-understanding"; which amounts to saying that he does not know what to look for and notice. To raise his level

of "dance understanding" (or appreciation), he must learn what to look for. The fact that the things he ought to notice have no clear, standard labels or symbols, makes this learning difficult.

Musical symbols, on the other hand, are labels or indications of the things that a person must notice if he is to get the full effect of a piece of music, whether he wants to sing it, play it, dance to it, or listen to it. To teach these symbols mechanically, or by rote, or to explain them only in language or by means of arithmetic, is absurd. But it is just as absurd to think that we can afford to ignore them in a program pointed toward musical growth. For they show us what to notice in music. They are the means by which the mind can take hold of music, and by which we can grasp the expressive pattern of tone and rhythm which is the stuff and substance of music. They are indispensible means for developing musical understanding.

Musical Symbols

A good deal has already been said in this chapter about musical symbols. Now the time has come to consider them in a more systematic way. There are two important things to realize. First, there are more kinds of musical symbols than most people suppose. Second, each kind has its own particular utility and value.

1. First, there are *picture-gesture* symbols. Both language and music have symbols that are simpler and more primitive than those which we have become accustomed to accept as standard. People all over the world have employed sign-language or gesture-language, and it is still employed to some extent, even among ourselves. The interpretation of sign-language is true reading. When one Indian out on the Western prairie saw another Indian make the peace sign, the first man read what the other man was saying, for reading is always the interpretation of visual symbols. Music, too, has its sign-language, or gesture-language. Gestures can indicate up, down, emphasis, loud, quiet, fast, slow.

The advantage of these gesture-symbols is that they are easy to make, and easy to understand. Their limitation is that they are not very exact. However, they really do convey musical meanings, and it is very proper to use them with young children. When they are so used, and children understand them, this constitutes the beginning of music reading.

Much the same is true of the use of pictures, including diagrams. We have all heard of the picture-writings found on the walls of caves which were the habitations of primitive tribes. And if there was picture-writing, there must have been picture-reading. Even today we have not entirely broken away from the use of pictures to convey ideas, as witness any good political cartoon. All this, once again, is true of music. One can draw pictures, diagrams, curves on the blackboard or elsewhere to indicate the movement of the melody; and one can make the line heavy where the music should be loud and light where it should be soft. Many instruments, too, offer very useful visualizations of music. The piano keyboard is one example. Or we may have a set of tone bells hanging from the wall, with the small bell highest and the large bell lowest. Or we may have a set of tuned water-glasses or bottles arranged in order of descending pitch. These are all true musical symbols, for they indicate musical effects and meanings. And when anyone looks at them and understands what they mean, he is doing what can be called true music reading.

We should certainly make free use of these simple types of symbols in dealing with children. Like all musical symbols, they call attention to the things that need to be noticed in a piece of music. They are means of developing musical understanding, and of developing music-reading ability at the same time. As a matter of fact, even the most sophisticated musicians never really get away from these simple forms of symbolism. This is particularly true of gestures. An operatic coach may indicate the shape, the structure of a phrase to a soloist by moving his hand through the air. And the movements made by a conductor are nothing more nor less than a musical sign-language, by means of which he wants to get the members of the orchestra to understand his conception of the music, and which they can read.

You will notice at once how enormously the recognition of gesture-symbols and picture-symbols extends the range of music reading. Music reading ceases to be the exclusive business of the specialist, with his trained understanding of the standard notation. Its beginnings, at any rate, come well within the scope of any classroom teacher. And its beginnings are neither negligible nor unimportant. By gestures, by pictures, by diagrams, the classroom teacher can help the children to recognize something of what there is in the music, something of how the music ought to sound. Such symbols cannot, of course, convey as much as the standard notation, but they have the great advantage of being both simple, direct, and meaningful. They can certainly be used to develop the coordination of ear, eye, and understanding which is the heart of music reading.

2. Next we consider the movable *do* system of syllables. There is probably no musical device about which has been raised a fuss so enormous and so absurd. Those who oppose the teaching of music reading naturally claim that the syllables should be given up entirely. Some others try to introduce them incidentally, and, as it were, apologetically. Others insist that numbers are superior to syllables and should be used in their place. Others, again, insist that the letter names of the notes are enough, and that nothing more is needed. The whole issue is in a fog; and the reason is that the true meaning and intention of these symbols are so little understood.

The movable *do* syllables have one great and decisive value. They are our best and clearest indications of tonality-relationships, or key-relationships. They bring into focus the position of a note in the key-system, that is to say, in the scale. Let us say that some given note is designated as D. This tells us something important about it, namely, its absolute pitch-location. If we wished to do so, we could define it as the note produced by a certain vibration-frequency. The absolute pitch-location of the note is, of course, musically important. But something else about it is musically important too, and of this the letter name tells us nothing. The note may be the tonic of D major, in which case it is what is, not too precisely, called a "rest tone," and also the "home tone" or key center of music in D major. All this is brought immediately to attention by calling it *do*. Or it may be the dominant of G major, in which case it has a directional tendency, namely toward G. Again, the letter name tells us nothing of all this. But it becomes instantly conspicuous if the note is designated as *so*. Or, once again, it may be the leading tone of the key of E♭, in which case it has a strong upward tendency toward E♭. This, too, is brought to attention by designating it *ti*.

There are those who argue that it would be better to use ordinary number words in place of syllables. If numbers are to be used, then the note D would be designated 1, 5, and 7 in the three instances cited above. An absurd amount of heat has been generated over this contention, as if it went right down to ultimate fundamentals. As a matter of fact, the argument is almost completely pointless. *The syllables of the movable do system are simply substitute number names.* Do, re, mi, fa, so, la, ti, do mean 1, 2, 3, 4, 5, 6, 7, 8—neither more nor less. Numbers do not cease to be numbers if they are not called one, two, three, and so forth. These entities may be called *uno, duo, tre,* or *un, deux, trois,* or indeed anything we please, without the very slightest change in their characteristics or nature. Old shepherds in northern England still count their sheep with a set of number names beginning yahn, tiahn, tethera, methera, dick; but these words, which seem so curious to us, stand for precisely the same entities as our own familiar one, two, three, four, five. So, too, the movable *do* syllables are still numbers in another guise, and nothing but numbers. And so the heated argument as to whether to use syllables or numbers turns on almost nothing but one's taste in words.

Almost, but not quite nothing more; for there is one further consideration. Ordinary number names, i.e. one, two, three, etc. have the definite advantage of familarity. The syllable number names have the definite advantage of being more singable. This advantage is particularly conspicuous when we compare "seven" to *ti;* but it applies to all the syllables, which have a superior euphony, and for the simple and obvious reason that they were chosen for euphony, whereas the ordinary number names were not. But the syllables have all the characteristics of positive integral numbers. One could do arithmetic with them just as well as with the ordinary number names, so long as one did not need to go above eight. They are, to repeat an obvious but preposterously misunderstood point, substitute number names, and nothing more.

It has been suggested that the movable *do* syllables might be called "singing names." But this at least implies, and indeed suggests, quite a serious confusion of thought. The adjective— "singing"—is quite all right; because the outstanding advantage of the syllables is singability or euphony. But names in the general sense they are certainly not. In particular, the movable *do* syllables are *not substitutes for letter names.* If we want to speak precisely, we may call the syllables *singing numbers.* In using the precise and only correct expression in this connection we may, perhaps, manage to free our minds from one of the silliest muddles in music education.

To clear our minds on this point is of genuine importance. A very distinguished music educator once complained to me that we have too many names for the same thing. What he had in mind was that we use both syllables (or ordinary numbers) and letter names to designate notes. But syllables (or ordinary numbers) and letter names are not different names for the same thing. They are different names for two quite different things—and two different things each with its own significance. The letter name indicates absolute pitch position, which is the characteristic by which we agree to identify what we call a "note," and which obviously has musical importance. But the syllable does not indicate pitch position at all. It indicates *relationship* or *tendency*. And this also has great musical importance.

Key relationship or tonal tendency is an extremely important factor in the expressiveness of almost all music. It is an important factor even in the most extreme of "modernistic" music. In such music tonal tendencies are not eliminated. They are only used in strange and unfamiliar ways.* And in almost all the music used in school, they play an extremely important role. Instances are so numerous that one hesitates to choose. Consider, for example, the very striking and impressive ending effect of the "Taps" bugle-call. Obviously it is produced entirely by the dominant-tonic sequence. If we attach letter names to the notes, we pass over the effect entirely, and yet it is the most important thing about the call. But if we designate these final tones *so do,* we feature their characteristic musical and expressive meaning; and presumably a bugler who knows how the effect is produced will be more keenly and discriminatingly aware of it, and able to produce it better on the instrument. Or, to revert to a former instance, I have already mentioned the very distinctive "pause-and-lead-on" effect of the first note of the refrain of *Home on the Range*. If we designate this note E, nothing in the symbol, nothing in the eye-experience, fixes the mind on what the crudest of singers recognizes as a fine expressive opportunity. But if it is designated as *so*, attention is instantly called to a crucial

* So-called atonal or polytonal music does not really eliminate tonal tendencies. It uses these tendencies in highly idiosyncratic ways, to which we are not accustomed, to produce the effects the composer has in mind. Modal music and pentatonic music, too, do not simply eliminate tonal tendencies. Such music employs them otherwise than our ordinary diatonic music, and thus produces its distinctive effects.

interpretive element in the song. So I could go on, giving endless instances, but surely it would be a waste of time and space. Carefully examine any school song whatever, and you will certainly find that a great deal of its charm, its character, its expressiveness depends on the tonal relationships of its notes. I would be inclined to say that tonal relationship has just as much to do with musical expressiveness and beauty as the much-boosted factor of rhythm. And the movable *do* syllables are the best direct device we have for featuring these relationships, making them apparent to the eye, and thereby making them noticeable and understandable to the mind.

As to ways of using the syllables, I have already given some broad hints earlier in this chapter, and the subject will come up for more complete discussion in dealing with teaching procedures. Here I will only say that I would not teach the syllables as a systematic code prior to use. I would introduce them when and as they would bring to attention something of the musical character of interesting and striking passages. A yodel call, a bird call, a bugle call, a passage climbing towards a point of finality and falling back just short of it would be a few among many possible examples. The syllables have no more difficulty in themselves than the numbers from one to eight; and if they were used freely and extensively in this way—which is by all means the proper way—children would soon assimilate them as a system.

In concluding this discussion of the movable *do* syllables, a number of points should be briefly noted.

A. John Curwen himself, who was the originator and propagator of the movable *do,* always insisted that the true function of the syllables was to bring out and feature tonal relationships. He said that their purpose was to bring out what he called the "mental effect"; but as one studies his writings, one sees clearly that by this he meant what we would call tonal relationship.

B. Curwen invented seven hand-signs or gestures for the syllables *do, re, mi, fa, so, la, ti*. These old hand-signs have long gone out of general use. Present-day teachers consider them old-fashioned, or mechanistic, or queer, or what not. As a matter of fact, they are ingenious, and indeed quite excellent gesture-symbols for important musical effects. There is no logical reason why they could not be used to good purpose today.

C. Admitting that the function of the syllables is to play up tonality effects, and that they are, on the whole, the best direct device we have for doing this, leads to an interesting corollary. There is no logical reason for confining their use to singing. Players of wind instruments can think them. Players of other instruments can sing or say them. Listeners can think, or sing, or say them. Remember, of course, that the recommendation is not to use them throughout a whole composition, even though it be a short one—at least not as a regular or necessary practice. The recommendation is to attach them to this or that passage where tonality relationships are peculiarly conspicuous and important. If this is done, the effect will undoubtedly be to sharpen up an understanding of the key-setting and key-relationships of the passage—factors on which much of its character and expressive value depend.

D. Another implication of this discussion is the entire wrongness of the approach to the minor by the devious and unrealistic route of the relative major, something on which a comment has already been made. The syllables, we say, are designations for tonal tendencies. *Ti* tends to go to *do*, *so* tends to go to *do*, and so forth. Very well, but what happens when we call the tonic *la* instead of *do*? All our syllable-meanings are altered; all our mental effects are confused. Here my good friend's complaint about having different names for the same thing is all too amply justified.

E. The movable *do* system, like any other code or set of symbols, has its limitations. Modulations and accidentals create serious, and in all but the simplest cases, insuperable difficulties. Be it remembered, however, that the system was never intended for highly modulated music, and that it was intended to bring out certain effects and values in music that are quite shockingly over-looked. A system ought to be used for what it is worth, for the purpose for which it was planned. If that purpose is important—and in this case it most certainly is—then the system or device should not be criticized, still less rejected, for not doing what it was never meant to do.

F. The syllables, as I have already remarked, have a long time been a sort of storm-center. They have been called various hard names, and stigmatized as mechanistic atrocities and brain-shattering puzzles. Some music educators apologize for them; many classroom teachers reject them; very many children hate them. *But the trouble is not with the syllables themselves. It is entirely with the way they are used.* Very often—perhaps, even, usually—they are treated as arbitrary, meaningless designations, without charm, rhyme, or reason. In effect, the tendency is to use them without a glimmer of understanding, virtually as nonsense-syllables. Why should anyone get any benefit from a nonsense-syllable? Why should anyone love it? Why should not any reasonable person, child or adult, hate having such a thing crammed down his throat?

But the movable *do* syllables are *not* nonsense-syllables. On the contrary, they are signs or designations for some of the most interesting, appealing, vital, and essential elements in the art of music. When properly presented and properly taught, they can reveal certain values and effects in music that are indefensibly neglected and extremely important. They can call attention to certain constitutive factors in musical beauty, and they can lead to that better and better apprehension of the musical shape and structure which, as we have found, is the development of musical understanding.

3. Coming now to the standard musical notation, the treat-

ment of many of its detailed components will be considered at some length in the following chapter; so here I shall confine myself to some general comments.

The standard notation of music is a very ingenious and effective system of symbolism. It is important to realize that the standard notation has gone through a lengthy evolution, and that it is still evolving. In the days of Bach and Händel much music was notated simply as a figured bass. Compared with what is done today, the composer indicated comparatively little of his intention, and left far more to the musical judgment of the performer. In general, the symbolism has become more and more elaborate and complete. Measure bars, slurs, indications for phrasing, for *staccato,* for fine dynamic changes, and for metronome tempi, are all relatively recent. The use of shaped notes, and (with modern advances in printing) of colored notes to indicate tone quality has been suggested; so the evolution still goes on. The constant tendency is to indicate more and more of the composer's intention, more and more of how the music is meant to sound.

But one must always remember that the notation cannot tell everything. It can only feature the high points of the musical structure. To read a musical score is always an act of interpretation. This is true whether the reading is done immediately and at sight, or whether it is a process of intensive and lengthy study and practice. The notation can only give the performer certain cues. To make a proper use of these cues, he must rely on his musical understanding. For instance, one may find in the score a passage printed in such a way as to make evident that it is a passage in eighth-note triplets. This tells a performer something important; but it does not tell him nearly everything. He must also recognize, again from the score indications, that the passage is in ¾ time, that the triplets coincide with a series of chords in quarter notes, and that the whole passage moves to a final resolution on the tonic. All these factors determine the effect of the musical pattern, which, of course, was the intention of the composer. All of them must be understood, both individually, and in relationship to one another. This integration of the various indicated factors leads to a decision about how much accentuation to give to the first note of each triplet, whether to use a *crescendo* or a *diminuendo,* how much the supporting chords should be subordinated or emphasized, and so on. In other words, the execution of the passage depends upon understanding the musical sense of the indications in the score, and upon understanding the various indicated factors in relationship to each other.

The evolution and increasing elaboration of the musical notation has two values. First, the notation becomes a better means of communication. There is, for instance, considerable doubt of just how Bach intended that the *Chromatic Fantasy* should be played because he indicated his wishes only by the rough sketch of a figured bass. There is far less doubt about how Chopin wanted the *F Minor Fantasy,* because he used a far more detailed and elaborate set of indications.

Also, the increasing elaboration of the notation makes it a better and more precise instrument for musical thought and understanding. A well-edited score calls attention to a great many factors that are vitally important, both for appreciation and for performance—to tempo, rhythmic patterning, key and key relationships and changes, harmonic sequence, melodic figuration, and so forth—and it contains many hints for proper treatment, such as accents, staccato markings, slurs, and the like. One might say that it turns a spot-light on the constitutive factors that make the music what it is—the factors that must be noticed if the musical pattern itself is to be understood. Thus the notation, properly taught and used, becomes a first-rate means of developing musical understanding; which amounts to saying that it is a first-rate means of promoting musical growth.

No good reader spells the score out note by note. He understands the musical significance of what the score indicates. Thus the note-by-note, or note-pointing approach to the score with children is fundamentally wrong. What must be done is to introduce the score and its symbols to sharpen up, clarify, and define actual musical experiences; to make such experiences more adequate, more insightful. This, by all means, is the sound and proper way to develop music-reading ability. And it is also the sound and proper way to develop something far more important than any specific skill, namely, musical understanding itself.

Music Reading in the Program

The account of music reading as based upon musical understanding, and indeed as being musical understanding in action, in effect determines the place it must hold in the program.

1. Music reading and basic aims

The basic controlling aims of the music program are the beneficial effects that music should have on human conduct and development. Five such aims, which were presented as samples, are enjoyment, the experience of success, discipline, social integration, and cultural enlargement. What relationship has music reading to these aims, or to others that resemble them in principle?

Some people would certainly say that there is no relationship at all. They might even claim that such a relationship, if any, must be negative—that learning to read music is the reverse of enjoyable, that it leads to innumerable experiences of failure, that it must be imposed as a harsh and meaningless task, that it involves the social fragmentation rather than the social integration of a class, and that it calls for the narrowest and most self-contained type of music study. All this is true when music reading is conceived and taught as a narrow, mechanical stunt or special skill, to which every other musical possibility is sacrificed.

Programs so planned and organized are depleted of musical, cultural, and human values, and offer nothing to offset the loss. But they arise out of a misconception; for the development of music reading, properly interpreted, is the development of musical understanding. As soon as this is clearly seen, the relation between music reading and basic aims appears in a completely changed light.

Instead of asking you to remain satisfied with general statements, I propose to follow through with each of the five sample aims, and to show how the development of music-reading ability, rightly interpreted, helps to achieve it.

A. First, the aim of enjoyment. How does the teaching of music reading help to extend and deepen one's enjoyment of music? Remember that, in the teaching of music reading, all symbols are presented for the sake of making specific musical effects more precise and intelligible, and specific musical experiences more clearcut and significant. This is true of the simple gesture-symbols and picture-symbols with which the development of reading begins, and extends to the most subtle, complex, abstract symbols used in connection with the art of music. Thus, instead of learning the symbols, *the learner is coming to understand the music*—to understand what the symbols signify. Understanding the music, as I have previously pointed out at some length and with some emphasis, does not chiefly mean being able to expound it intellectually. It means being able to grasp its substance, its content—i.e., to grasp the organized pattern which is the root of its expressiveness. Hence learning to read music means coming to understand, respond to, appreciate, and enjoy it better and better—to realize more and more of what it contains, and thus to find an ever-deepening pleasure in it. Increased and increasing enjoyment in listening, in singing, in playing, all should and can come from the development of music-reading ability.

Then, of course, as independent reading ability begins to

appear, it serves as a tool skill. With it one can make music better, both alone and with others; one can explore new ranges of music. Obviously, the independent reader has in his possession a key which can open up many new vistas of musical pleasure. Such a key is worth having for purposes like these. But also the very process of obtaining it involves a developing capacity to find pleasure in music.

B. The development of music-reading ability leads the learner on to more and more significant and mature levels of successful achievement. Merely to sing a pleasing song may be enough to satisfy a seven-year-old, but it probably will not be nearly enough when he is ten or eleven. By this time he needs to feel that he can make music with some real competence. This evolution cannot be brought about by nothing but undirected singing. It can be brought about by making singing more and more musically insightful, which is exactly what the teaching of music reading should cause to happen. Moreover, the understanding of music, which is the grasp of its expressive pattern, is the proper basis for all musical performance, instrumental as well as vocal. So the teaching of music reading provides the foundation for convincing success in learning to play an instrument. Here again, too, it is obvious that the emergence of independent reading ability is related to our second basic aim. For the ability to read music competently at sight has a well-deserved prestige-value. Finally, and by way of contrast, I may remark that when the teaching of music reading is made a meaningless and routine process, it contravenes the basic aim we are considering, because such a process condemns many to fail and has no positive values in itself.

C. Our third basic aim is to provide, through music, for experiences of the discipline of self-adopted purpose. Here again the teaching of music reading makes a positive contribution. The development of the ability to read, as it has been analyzed and expounded here, means a developing realization of more and more in music—more finesse, more subtlety, more challenges, new depths and refinements of beauty. The more we understand music, the more challenging it becomes, and the more engrossing the challenge becomes. The evolution of musical understanding means the evolution of more and more exacting standards. When young people in the upper grades or on the secondary level play or sing, they very often do only what their teacher or director tells them to do, and only because he tells them to do it. Obviously this amounts to external motivation, external standards. But if they had been systematically taught to understand, *to see into,* music, they would be able to set their own standards, and to grasp not only the fact of the director's requirements, but also the why of those requirements. Here we have the true disciplinary situation, the discipline of self-adopted purpose. It becomes possible only through the development of musical understanding, only through seeing into music well enough to set one's own musical goals. And this, to repeat once more, is an outcome of music reading properly taught and learned.

D. When it comes to promoting social integration and social togetherness, it is obvious that even quite a modest degree of music-reading skill can go a surprisingly long way. One thinks immediately of accompanying, playing and singing at social occasions, helping with the music at church, membership in musical groups, choir membership, manifold uses of music at home, and so on. There must be few American communities where a person who has some measure of ability to read music will not find rewarding opportunities to use it. So much for music reading as a skill. But it is also true that a person who has achieved a growing understanding of music will find many opportunities to share his insights. Many such opportunities may be quite informal, but no less valuable for that. Music-lovers are numerous, and all of them welcome music-understanders into their company. Music can be enjoyed in solitude; but it can also be enjoyed, and in some respects better enjoyed, in company. There is no doubt whatever that music can open the way into a wide range of rich social contacts and relationships. No consideration more decisively brings out the extreme importance of musical growth; for if a person remains musically childish, music will not serve him well as an adult. Music reading, properly taught, is a crucial instrumentality for development toward musical maturity, because its whole tendency is to transform an originally general and superficial response into one that is profound, discriminating, and insightful.

E. The vital relationship between music and the social and personal setting out of which it arose can only be sensed when we realize the music completely, and feel it as it should be felt. To some, the music of Wagner is meaningless and perhaps annoying sound. To others the music of Bach is dull and dry, the music of Palestrina almost entirely unintelligible, and the music of Bartok mere chaos. Tastes, of course, differ, and we are certainly not obliged to like everything we hear. But when a work of art conveys precisely nothing, when it seems to make no sense and to produce no impression, then something is certainly being missed. Indeed, many things are being missed; and among them is any intimation of the nexus between the artwork and the culture in which it emerged. Just what the relationship is between a piece of music and the life experiences of its composer, or the general life and spirit of his times, no one has been able to explain convincingly. But one can, without making oneself ridiculous, maintain that there is such a relationship, and that one can often seem to sense it very impressively. However, to feel this relationship, to sense a piece of music as the expression of an individual's experience or of the spirit of an age, one must certainly understand the music. To drag a composition of Palestrina into a unit on the Middle Ages, and to present it to unhearing and uncomprehending ears, is a waste of time. But the experience can be very vital if it is part of a total music program, all of which is pointed toward musical growth, all of which is pointed toward musical understanding. Then the modal music ceases to be a mere museum specimen, and can deliver its real message, at least partially, and can touch the intellectual structure of the unit with the magic wand of authentic feeling.

So to sum up with three brief statements. *First,* music reading as a tool skill, can contribute appreciably to the achievement of all our basic aims. *Second,* and far more importantly, the development of music-reading ability can contribute to all of them because it is the development of musical understanding; and here its contribution is indispensible. *Third,* the routine, mechanical teaching of music reading can contribute to none of them, and in fact tends to make their attainment impossible.

2. *The sequential development of music reading*

It is quite impossible to construct a chart showing the proper chronological or sequential development of the ability to read music, or the proper order of topics or concepts. The reason for this difficulty is not that adequate research is lacking, although almost no significant research has ever been done on the problem. The reason is that the question itself cannot be answered at all. Too much depends on individual differences and capacities, which vary a great deal; and also too much depends on methods of presentation, where again there are great differences. However, some quite definite statements can be made, which are of genuine and practical help to teachers and makers of curricula.

A. The development of reading ability is a continuous process. It is not a process in which certain specifics, such as quarter note, eighth note, key of C major, and so forth, are presented in some pre-determined order and mastered one by one. Each specific item is introduced when it can illuminate a musical experience, and introduced again and again in connection with other musical experiences, so that its full and accurate musical meaning emerges gradually in the learner's mind. There is no formula by which the proper order of introduction can be determined in advance. All one can say is that each specific item or symbol should always be closely and directly connected with its musical meaning.

B. The teaching of music reading properly starts much earlier than is ordinarily supposed. We do not introduce it for the first time in the second grade, the third grade, or the fourth grade. Music reading begins whenever the eye begins to help the ear and the understanding. This will probably be when the child is first helped to get the shape of a melody or the organization of a rhythm pattern by gesture, by diagram, by movement—in fact by any visual means whatsoever. Symbols help the child to grasp the music. The music gives meaning to the symbols. This is always the process of learning to read music. Again it exemplifies our rule of proceeding always from the essential to the externals.

C. There is no sharp transition from a non-reading stage to a reading stage, or "from rote to note," to cite the familiar jingle. In the first place there is no truly "rote" music-making, if by this we mean purely imitative or routine music-making. There is, from the very begining, *expressive* music-making. Nor is there any sudden or wholesale introduction of the standard notation, even in simplified form. We begin with expressive music-making, and we introduce gestures, diagrams, pictures, simplified notation, standard notation, syllables for the sake of rendering music-making more and more intelligently expressive.

D. There is no specific moment of "music-reading readiness," i.e., no specific moment at which the notation should be introduced. The symbols of the notation, along with other symbols, are introduced bit by bit, at any time that they can clarify something in the music. Notational symbols for a two-note bird-call, for instance, might very well be introduced in the first grade, and the attention of the children might quite properly be called to them. Some of the children will not understand at all, and none will understand completely. But a process has been started. Similar symbolizations for turns of phrase and points of musical interest will occur again and again, and will gradually become meaningful. For we are working, not in terms of immediate forced mastery, but of long-term, continuous growth. And, of course, later on, far more extended musical patterns will be symbolized.

E. What has just been said indicates the true meaning of that much misunderstood term, "readiness." To say that a person will never learn until he is "ready" to do so, is so obvious that it is almost a truism. To say that he will only learn in response to a need is equally true, and almost equally obvious. But the practical question is how to create this condition of readiness, how to know when it has arrived, and how to produce a need, "felt" or otherwise. Certainly not by waiting. Many a person has lived his whole life without feeling the least need to learn the key signature of G major, or giving any sign of being ready to do so, in any rational sense of the word. We produce a state of readiness, or create a need, by setting up a situation. Get the children singing a song in which a hunting-horn call occurs (E B G# E). Get them to sing it with life and spirit. Get them to realize that the call must be made to ring out. Then they will probably be about as "ready" as they ever will be to see the point of calling the notes *do so mi do*; and when this is revealed to them, it will come as a satisfaction of a more or less explicitly felt need.

F. Independent, rapid reading emerges from understanding, just as any other complex skill emerges from understanding. If you are learning to fly an airplane, you must establish sequences of movements that you understand. You must work slowly and carefully, and above all, thoughtfully. But the essential point is not the slowness of the practice, but the thoughtfulness of it. Then, with much experience, these movement-sequences flow quickly and certainly, guided, not by routine habit, but by an over-riding understanding of what you are about. That is the way with music reading also. At first we should not concern ourselves in the least with independent reading, i.e., with reading as a tool skill. That will develop in its own good time, and not before. Above all, and prevailingly, we should concern ourselves with helping children to grasp more and more clearly and certainly the musical significance of the symbols, so that they establish the vital inter-connection of ear, eye, and understanding.

3. *How much emphasis on music reading?*

So long as music educators try to teach music reading as a tool skill, set off from "rote'" singing, rhythmics, "appreciation," creative activity, and the playing of instruments, the question of how much emphasis to put upon it will continue to trouble them. And they will never get a good answer to it, because their thinking is wrongly directed from the start.

Every activity in the music program can contribute to the development of reading ability, because every activity can contribute to the development of musical understanding. Every kind of visual symbol, from the simplest to the most complicated and abstract, can be brought to bear on every kind and level of musical performance, on listening, and on creative work. How much we actually decide to do along this line will depend entirely on circumstances and on people. To repeat what has been so often said, we think of music reading, not as a segregated tool skill, but as a manifestation or exteriorization of musical understanding. The moment we take this position it becomes clear that there should be no such thing as a segregated "reading program," to be taken as a whole, to be taken in part, or entirely let alone. An emphasis on musical understanding, and therefore on music reading will pervade the entire music program; and the intensity of that emphasis will be determined always by our own judgment of the circumstances and the people concerned. However, a music program which entirely ignores music reading and musical understanding will certainly not result in musical growth.

If we do not regard reading as, first and foremost, a segregated tool skill, and therefore have no segregated reading program, the teaching of reading at once ceases to be the exclusive domain of the music specialist. No doubt the average classroom teacher will not be able to go as far, or to introduce the more intricate symbolisms so effectively, as the well-trained specialist. But if she is brought clearly to see that the essential point is always and only the connecting of ear, eye, and understanding, and to realize how very simple and available are the means by which this can be done, she can make an extremely valuable contribution. This does not in the least imply that she will be called upon to attempt technical music lessons. All that is required is to make musical experiences and activities more significant and enjoyable by using visual means to indicate, from time to time, what may be done with the music to bring out its possibilities more completely.

Questions for Discussion, Thought, and Study

1. Do you consider that the outline of "enlightened opinion" about music reading is fair and reasonably accurate? If not, how would you alter it?
2. Does it seem to you to amount to a reasonably intelligent point of view?
3. Can you think of any instances of adults using "gesture symbols" to indicate musical effects, even when they are not dealing with children?
4. Coming down to details, what are some of the things that the notation can indicate that cannot be indicated by gestures? Does this mean that gesture symbols should be avoided?
5. The notation can indicate a great many things about music. But there are some things it cannot indicate. What are some of

them? Do they seem to you to be important? Can you draw any inferences for the teaching of music reading?

6. A good reader does not spell out the notes one by one. If you are a good reader yourself, check this statement against your own experience. If you are not, find a good reader, explain the statement to him, and see if he agrees.

7. Can you find any reasonable explanation of why so many music educators, fifty years ago, placed so much emphasis on music reading?

8. Do most children become able to read music well by the end of the sixth grade? What evidence have we for getting an answer to this question? If the answer is in the negative, what inferences for music education does it suggest?

9. As you go through this chapter, does it seem to you to present an argument in favor of trying to teach all children to read music independently and well?

10. In this chapter, and elsewhere throughout the book, a great deal of emphasis has been placed on "musical understanding." Try to explain just what this means, using illustrative examples. Is musical understanding entirely a matter of the intellect? Has it nothing to do with the intellect?

Readings

Beatrice Landeck, *Children and Music*. New York, William Sloan Associates, Inc., 1952. Appendix 1, "Short Cuts to Reading Music." Interesting and helpful suggestions.

James L. Mursell and Mabelle Glenn, *The Psychology of School Music Teaching*. New York, Silver Burdett Company, 2nd edition, 1938. Chapter 8, "Mastery of the Score."

A comprehensive analysis of the reading problem, differing somewhat from that here presented.

CHAPTER SIX

Music Reading and Musical Growth:
II: Teaching Procedures

The Principle

In a program planned to promote musical growth, every procedure for the teaching of reading must meet one essential requirement, which is that it must be designed to enhance and improve the learner's understanding of music.

Our sixth principle follows logically from, and might almost be considered an extension of the fifth. The sixth principle carries our thinking an important step forward, and also relates it to much that has gone before.

The principle instantly eliminates worrying, fussing, and arguing about the best "method" of teaching music reading. Shall we teach with syllables, with numbers, with note names only? Shall we teach by position? Many music educators seem to have the strongest of opinions on such questions, to be ready to fight for those opinions at the drop of a hat, and to feel that anyone who disagrees is entirely wrong. Our principle cuts right down through all this hurly-burly. Any procedure is good in so far as it helps children to gain a real and growing understanding of music. Two procedures which, on the surface, seem quite different, may be equally good. There is no standard "best" procedure. The best procedure for you is the one that best produces the desired mental effect.

This is an important thought for all teachers. It is important for music specialists, and also for classroom teachers. It means that one is quite free to invent one's own procedures, without feeling self-distrustful because one is not following the plan laid down in some book or by some "authority." Keep the essential thing in mind, and then find out the way (or ways) of working for it that suit you and your children best.

Furthermore, our principle indicates that there will be many good procedures for the teaching of reading. So you can pick up valuable suggestions from many sources. One teacher can learn from another. The classroom teacher can learn from the specialist, and the specialist can learn from the classroom teacher. A teacher who feels that there is only one "best" or "right" way to teach music reading is limited to just that. But a teacher who realizes that the one thing needful is to help children to understand music better, will build up a whole stock-pile of devices, resources, and methods of treatment, and will often be able to extemporize an excellent one on the spur of the moment.

Moreover, our principle brings the teaching of music reading into line with what was said earlier about learning experiences. We must never get it into our heads that the only proper way to teach music reading is by specific lessons, each laid out as a nicely planned series of predetermined steps. That is a very restricting way to work, and it is neither right nor necessary. Careful planning will certainly be in order, although extemporization may often be in order too. But the whole point of the planning will be to organize an experience that will reveal something, that will make something clear or at least clearer, that will help toward getting something understood. This is very different from planning to get some specific bit of learning achieved, completed, stored away, and then overpassed forever after.

This, then, is what our sixth principle means. The rest of this chapter will be devoted to showing how it applies. Since the principle opens the gates wide to inventiveness, initiative, and creativeness on the part of teachers, no one can ever enumerate all the possible applications. All that I can do is to present samples. The seven general procedures to be described are very far indeed from being the only possible ones. The various ways of dealing with what I like to call "specifics" are very far from being the only good ways. Please bear this constantly in mind; for it would be a pity if you thought I was laying down canonically correct teaching procedures, after formulating a principle whose whole effect is to tell teachers that they have the fullest freedom, so long as they never lose sight of the one essential thing.

General Procedures: I: Seeing What One Hears

To see, in symbolic form, what one hears, is one of the most natural and direct ways of coming to understand symbols through music, and coming to understand music through symbols. As a procedure, it can be extremely flexible, and can be used in many situations. The possibilities of the procedure are so numerous and so varied that one cannot hope to mention nearly all of them. But some suggestions may be helpful.

1. In organized listening experiences, even including quite early ones, it may be excellent to have the children follow the score. This should always be done to enhance the pleasure of, and give point to, the listening, and by no means as a set task. In listening to orchestral music it will usually be wise to use a piano reduction, although sometimes, with older children, a chance to look at and follow a small-sized full score may be very interesting. It is by no means necessary for the children to have learned about all the specific symbols that the score contains, although a few words of explanation here and there will often

help them to get more out of the experience. Often, too, a problem-wise approach of one kind or another may work well. For instance, children may listen to the second movement of the Beethoven *Eighth Symphony* without the notes in front of them. Then they may listen to it again with the notes; and the teacher may ask whether, on the first presentation, they really heard what the score shows them is in the music, developing a discussion on the question.

2. Another possibility is to have before the children only some part of a composition to which they are listening—perhaps its principal theme or themes, perhaps some particularly beautiful or striking effect. Then they may be asked to notice when the item before them comes in as the music moves along, when it comes in again, how it is altered, and so forth. Such problemizing is likely to pay off better than a complete formal analysis, because the aim is not to develop an understanding of standard musical forms, but to make connections between ear, eye, and mind.

3. The wide availability today of so-called "singalong" records suggests many interesting extensions of this procedure. The usual idea is that singalong records are for the sake of the classroom teacher who does not sing well, and who wants to teach songs in the lower grades by imitation, without using the notation at all. But the use of such records at any level, and also by the music specialist, is perfectly proper, and may be excellent. The children can listen to the song without looking at the notes. Then they can listen again, following the notes. Then they can discuss the change in the impression when the eye helps the ear and the understanding.

4. Children who hesitate to sing can get a good deal by following along the music while others participate. Nor need this be a passive, pointless experience for them. Perhaps in some cases they may be asked to notice how well the singing goes, where weaknesses or mistakes appear, what might be done to make it

better. Or they may be encouraged to follow along, and to come in when and as they like.

5. The introduction of instrumental effects can often be a good opportunity to connect seeing and hearing. The children listen to a song, sing it, look at it—which last tends to pull it into definite shape. Then they have a basis for making up their minds just where to introduce a bell effect, a flute effect, a drum effect, etc.

6. The experience of seeing what one hears need not be limited to the symbols of the standard notation. As young children listen to a short and simple selection, the teacher may indicate its melodic curve on the blackboard, or by an interpretive gesture. Or one or other of the children may be asked to show how the music goes, using such simple symbolic means.

7. It is very important and very valuable for children, quite early, to see some visual representation of the rhythm patterns which they hear in music, and feel in their bodily responses. The teaching of rhythm often gets off to a very good start in kindergarten and first grade, and then the development fades out like a stream sinking into desert sands. Much of the trouble is that rhythm experiences, which are often very vital, are allowed to remain at an immature level. They need to be defined, sharpened up, mentally grasped as well as physically felt. So children should not only sense the rhythm, but also see it, as represented in gestures, pictures, diagrams, simplified notation, and at last in standard notation. This is rarely done systematically and it is a real and serious lack.

8. In giving children experiences of seeing what they hear, it may from time to time, be very advisable to use the movable *do* syllables. This may cause some astonishment; but if so, it is only because we have so many fetishistic and preposterous notions about the syllables. A set of syllables on the board may very well point up one's impression of the descending scale in *Joy to the World*. To offer a much more sophisticated example,

I can think of no musical experience that would more impressively reveal the true significance of the syllables as indicators of musical beauty, than to attach them to the series of descending scales which terminates the first movement of the Tchaikowsky *Sixth Symphony*.

So much for this scatter of suggestions, which is far indeed from being complete. But before passing on, let us recall the purpose of this procedure. To see what one hears in music can enable one to hear it better, to realize it better, to enjoy it better, to understand it better. It attaches the symbols themselves directly to their musical meanings, and thus produces a growing understanding of them.

General Procedures: II: Noticing Musical Highlights

Everything in every piece of music is, of course, important. But not everything is equally important. Every piece of music will have certain very distinctive effects or "highlights." These are points of special interest in the music, crucial points, which must be grasped and brought out if the music is to be rendered to the best advantage. These points are natural opportunities to understand music better through symbols, and to understand symbols better through music—to connect ear, eye, and understanding.

In using this procedure the children may have the score of the whole song before them. But we do not call attention to it all. We call attention only to the highlight. It is defined and clarified by the symbols. Noticing and understanding it leads to more satisfaction both in listening and in performing.

A few simple examples will make the idea clear. A conspicuous feature of the song *Joy to the World* is the descending scale-passage with which the tune opens. If the children are brought to realize just what this passage is—namely a descending scale —they will be able to understand it better, to sing it better because of this clearer understanding, and also to respond better to its expressive effect, for the same reason. The passage can be symbolized by syllables, by note names, and by the notation itself. The use of some or all of these symbols, either on the blackboard, or in diagram form, or on the page of a book, can be the means of establishing this bit of musical understanding. Similarly, the notes of the horn, introduced in various ways, are a conspicuous musical feature of many hunting songs, and the yodel call is a conspicuous musical feature of many skiing and mountaineering songs. These motives can be picked out, displayed in their symbolic designations, and thus understood. I have purposely mentioned some very clear-cut and indeed obvious examples here. But any song, indeed any piece of music, will have crucial features, musical highlights, that lend themselves to this kind of treatment. The chosen highlight may be a sustained dominant; it may be the swing and lilt of the 6/8 rhythm; it may be the key center, when the music revolves very prominently about it. In all cases, however, the highlight should be chosen, not to illustrate some pre-determined grammatical point, but because of its musical and expressive significance and importance. For you should always remember that the idea is to move from the music to the symbols, and not from the symbols to the music.

As you will readily see, this "highlight" procedure is one way —and a very good way—of linking up eye, ear, and understanding. The symbols are not taught as a code. Their meanings are not taught in verbal form. Their musical meaning is what is being emphasized. They are used as tools for the creation and development of musical understanding. And, of course, you will not make the mistake of thinking that the understanding of music is a purely intellectual process, separate from appreciation and feeling. For to understand a "musical highlight" is to gain a clearer realization of its expressiveness, and a surer capacity to execute it adequately.

General Procedures: III: Cooperative Discovery

This means having the children discover a new song as a whole, from the notation, with the help of the teacher. It differs from the "highlights" procedure, because now the entire song is used.

This procedure is based entirely on very simple, straightforward, commonsense considerations. The first is that to pick up the score of an unfamiliar piece or song, try it out, discover that the music is charming, and go on to realize more and more of its charm, is a pleasing and rewarding experience. Everyone who has done such a thing, knows that this is so. The second consideration is that this discovery of charming music from the notation is a very good learning experience. One can get a great deal out of it. The third consideration is that children may not be able to make much of the notation of a new song unless they are helped, but that they can often make a great deal out of it with the right sort of help. Surely nothing could be more straightforward, more sensible, or simpler than that!

This procedure of cooperative discovery should never take on the guise of a set lesson, planned as a series of sacredly fixed "correct" steps. Should the singing be accompanied? Should the teacher sing along with the children? Planners of set lessons have cut-and-dried answers to such questions. But to make this procedure work properly, cut-and-dried answers must be avoided. The experience of discovering music is all that is wanted. Anything you find that you must do to help the children make the discovery will be well done.

Nevertheless, a great many helpful suggestions can be made. For the most part they are suggestions only, to be accepted, disregarded, or modified, just as you see fit, or as your circumstances dictate. Only the first three of them are absolute requirements; but these you *must* accept, if the job is to be rightly done. You will readily understand why this is so.

1. The idea of *discovery* is crucial. Everything turns on that. You present the notation of the song to the children with the suggestion that everyone work together to find out how it goes, what it is like, whether it is enjoyable. You may not present the thought in just these words, but it must be conveyed somehow. Above all, you must avoid presenting the material as a study song, on which everyone will be required to do some hard and careful analysis—although hard and careful analysis may come in before the end.

2. Another crucial factor is the *choice of music*. You must choose it, above all, for its interest and worth. You must try to choose music which you think the children will enjoy. Of course anyone can make a mistake about this, and you will make some too. But still, you must try. Then you must choose music that is not only interesting and valuable, but simple in structure; for otherwise the children may be defeated, and no good will come of the experience. Interest and worth, combined with basic simplicity, are the two characteristics of the music you must use. They are *requirements*, because if there is to be an experience of discovery, there must also be something worth discovering. Here is another great contrast with the conventional study song, which may be simple, but which often has little interest or charm. The songs you use for this procedure should be the most interesting and valuable of all.

3. In general, your job as a teacher is to keep things moving, to give help where help is needed, so that the children will not bog down. Above all, you must resist the temptation to turn the experience into a set lesson. At all times your business is to help the children to discover the music that is in those notes, not to have them spell the notes out one by one. Keep them moving, even though sometimes you have to carry them through. This is the third and last of the absolute requirements, and now we come to the optional suggestions.

4. Some teachers who use this procedure let the children

hear the song once before developing it from the notes. Others do not. There is no fixed rule, and perhaps the best suggestion is—sometimes. In any case, a pre-view does not short-circuit the experience of discovery, and may, indeed, help. It is quite allowable, as it would not be with a conventional reading-study song. A recording, or the piano, or your own singing may be the means. This is worth trying, if it is something you can do.

5. It will often help the children to examine the notation before starting to sing. You can guide them in looking for familiar or readily identifiable melodic or rhythmic patterns.

6. Either the teacher or one of the children will have to give the starting tone, using pitch-pipe, piano, or a melody instrument.

7. As to the teacher singing along with the children, which, of course, is strictly forbidden in the conventional reading-study-song procedure, there is no fixed rule. Everything depends on how matters move. Probably the teacher will find it well to pick the singing up when it lags or falters.

8. As to setting the tempo, some feel that this should be done at the beginning, after which the singing should be pushed right along, regardless of mistakes and hesitations. Probably this may sometimes be a good plan, but I doubt if it should be made a universal rule. The attitude to take is that the children are trying out a musical experiment, in which case the full indicated tempo may not be very important at first. As the children feel their way, and begin to get hold of the music, the proper tempo can develop.

9. Some teachers who use this procedure recommend developing the song on some easy-to-play instrument before it is sung. There is considerable to be said in favor of this, because the instrument tends to make the approach to the music more definite, and to reduce vagueness. It is certainly a practice to try out, and perhaps to use extensively.

10. As the singing begins to take shape, the teacher may be-

gin to put in a simple chorded accompaniment on the autoharp or the piano. This, again, is a break with the conventional study-song procedure, which calls for strictly unaccompanied singing. But the chorded accompaniment helps to pull the singing along, to provide cues, and to furnish an interesting and pleasing harmonic foundation.

11. There is no sharp break between this procedure and the one previously discussed, i.e., the "highlights" procedure. The "highlights" procedure may often merge into the cooperative discovery of the entire song, whenever it seems interesting to do so.

General Procedures: IV: Independent Discovery

When children have gained assurance and competence from numerous experiences of cooperative discovery, these may merge more and more into independent discovery. The difference is that there is now much less help given by the teacher. Suitable music of the previous type must still be used. The experience must not be turned into a formal reading lesson. The teacher need not refuse all help whatsoever, for the difference between cooperative and independent discovery is only a matter of degree. Sometimes, however, children in the upper grades who have sufficient background may find it an interesting and beneficial challenge to be asked to see what they can do with a song without any help at all.

It is at this point that we come nearest to the conventional reading-song procedure. This requires that all reading be done without accompaniment, and certainly without any previous notion of the music. The teacher must not sing along with the children, and naturally, singalong records are entirely excluded. All the teacher does is to give the starting tone, signal for the singing to begin, and leave the children to rely entirely on the notation, or the syllables, or both.

This is, in every respect, bad practice in the teaching of music reading. (a) It almost inevitably involves note-spelling and note-pointing, which, indeed, as a usual thing, are directly taught. This is entirely different from studying the notation to discover its musical meaning. (b) It is untrue to much that is common and legitimate in musical experience, for instance, the reliance of choir members who are hesitant readers upon others to help them along. There is no reason why similar help should not be given in a teaching situation, if the aim is not merely to get through the song, but to learn from doing so. (c) It implies that music reading is, and should be taught as, a tool skill or segregated special ability, and nothing more. What should be done, on the contrary, is to develop meaningful connections between the eye and the music, i.e., to develop musical understanding.

These considerations should be well heeded, because they convey a warning. The discovery of music from the notation with very little help should indeed be exactly what the words imply—a true and genuine discovery of music. It should never be attempted until the children are evidently capable of benefiting from it. Or if the attempt is made, and leads to nothing but failure, it should not be repeated, and full cooperation by the teacher should be supplied. Otherwise the outcome will be nothing but note-hunting, note-spelling, note-pointing, and all the value of the experience will be lost. Independent reading as such is not a fetish. It must come in its own good time. What we are working for, no matter what the procedure, is always the vital connection of ear, eye, and understanding.

General Procedures: V: Intelligent Study of the Notation

This is, or should be, involved in all the procedures previously discussed. But it is so important, so potentially valuable, and so neglected, that it merits separate attention.

What does it mean to study the score intelligently, to look at it intelligently? Any musician should be able to answer this question; but perhaps I had better present my own reply. A musical score is not a wilderness of notes, any more than a page of print is a wilderness of letters. The letters come together in constellations or groupings, which convey meanings. To look unintelligently at a page of print is to see letters. To look at it intelligently, is to see meaningful groupings. So, too, with music. The notes of the score also come together in constellations or groupings, which convey meanings; but in this case, the meanings are musical effects. To look unintelligently at the score is to see only the notes. To look at it intelligently, is to see meaningful groupings. To study it intelligently is to see these meaningful groupings better and better, and to understand them more and more completely.

That is the ability that we want children to develop. When they look at the notation of *The First Noel*, they should see, not notes, but scale passages. When they look at the notation of *The Volga Boatmen*, they should see, not notes, but a pattern of rhythmic pulsation. When they look at the notation of *Greensleeves*, they should see, not notes, but a minor tonality. So on, at any length you like.

We should emphasize this intelligent looking and studying in many connections. It should often accompany listening. It should go on when "highlights" are emphasized. It should go on in experiences of cooperative discovery and independent discovery. We should emphasize it with familiar music, with music that is being heard, with music that has just been heard, with music that has not yet been heard or performed, but soon will be. Children will need help and guidance, just as they do with any learning. There can be discussions of what they have noticed, or think they have noticed. They can execute or listen to the musical effects about which their eyes have told their minds. The intelligent observation and study of the notation is not always an independent procedure, although it can sometimes be used as such. Rather it is an element in many other procedures. But however it is done, it is one of the best of all ways of making the symbols meaningful through the music, and of making the music meaningful through the symbols.

In music education generally, as carried on in studios and conservatories and in schools, there is not nearly enough of this musically intelligent observation and study of the score. When even trained musicians hear about an eminent conductor who can assimilate a new composition from the score alone, they are apt to be filled with amazement. This is a sure sign, not of the difficulty of the process, but of the grievous defects of ordinary musical training. Such intelligent observation and study is entirely feasible and practicable. It should be a familiar experience. It is certainly a rewarding one. And it can begin quite young.

Note that the intelligent observation and study of the score does not mean a mere concentration on detail. It does not mean quizzing on key signatures, time signatures, note lengths, and so forth. It centers always on musical content and musical meanings, and specific details are always dealt with and apprehended in musical contexts.

General Procedures: VI: Extensive Reading

If we want to establish skilled and rapid reading, there is only one way to do it, and that is by extensive reading, i.e., by reading large amounts of music. This is a reason why we cannot do very much along this line in most elementary schools. In the elementary school we can do much to develop that understanding of music which is the basis of reading, as well as being valuable in itself. Extensive reading comes as a culmination of this process of development. Opportunities can be created in small ensembles, both vocal and instrumental, in music clubs, in informal music groups, and by individual suggestion, and often in connection with rehearsals. Such activities belong mainly at the secondary level; and there they provide the proper *milieu* for the development of reading as a tool skill. If the foundation is laid, and proper opportunities are provided, there is every reason to believe that the skill will manifest itself. If the foundation is laid and the proper opportunities are not provided at the secondary level, then the music specialists in the secondary school had better stop complaining that children come to them unable to read, and begin to blame themselves. It is not the business of the elementary school program to carry reading very far as a tool skill. It is the business of that program to develop the musicianship, the musical understanding, out of which skilled and rapid reading can quickly emerge.

General Procedures: VII: Writing What One Creates

This is a procedure which certainly should not be overlooked. But it is necessary to be clear about how to use it. When an individual or a group composes a piece of music, there is a natural wish to preserve it, and to communicate it to others. Thus we have a positive motivation established immediately. The desire is to communicate a self-originated musical idea. Let us keep this in mind.

Everything is falsified, and the natural motivation is negated, if what is sometimes called a "creative lesson" turns into a music-writing lesson. For one thing, the creative impulse becomes unreal and distorted; because the idea now is to make up some music for the sake of writing it down, rather than to make up some music for the sake of expressing some feeling or intimation. For another thing, the writing is almost sure to be note-wise, in effect the writing of notes rather than the writing of music.

But when we are dealing with a genuine, expressive, self-originated musical idea, we have a very excellent opportunity for establishing the relationship between sound and symbol. The child creates a phrase, with a certain rhythm. What he must do is to catch this pattern of tone and rhythm as a whole, for its vitality and meaning reside in its totality, and not in its components. It may be excellent practice to capture it in the form of a rough graph, or curve, or diagram first of all, and later on to get its detail pinned down in standard notation. This makes clear the very fundamental and important truth that phrases can be analyzed down into notes, but that they are not built up out of them. Let us remember that composers constantly use musical shorthand and musical jottings, to catch ideas and effects on the wing, and because they find the standard notation impeding. How much more, then, must it impede children! Incidentally, the tape recorder, which was not available to great composers in times past, can be a real help here.

General Procedures: Comments and Interpretations

Notice how well these seven suggested general procedures conform to our sixth working principle, and to all that was said in the previous chapter.

1. All of them stress, and indeed center entirely, on the musical meanings of musical symbols. All of them center on understanding the symbols through the music, and understanding the music through the symbols.

2. All of them are very simple, direct, and practical. They can hardly be called "methods" at all. Nowhere is there a series of prescribed steps, or any cut-and-dried formulae for the teacher. They simply amount to the application of common sense with a goal in mind, the goal being to help children to understand music better. They are the very opposite of pedagogical tricks.

3. The procedures are extremely flexible. One runs into another. There is no sharp demarcation between them.

4. They can be utilized in all kinds of musical situations—

singing, playing, creating, dramatization, rhythmics, listening.

5. They lend themselves readily to great differences in emphasis.

6. Most of them can be used effectively, at least to some extent, by classroom teachers, given some help and guidance.

7. Taken together, they add up to the very reverse of a cut-and-dried reading program, which must be taken entire or left alone. They are just simple, sensible, practicable ways of developing music reading in the way it obviously should be developed.

8. They are by no manner of means the only possible procedures, or the only good ones. Any procedure which establishes a linkage between ear, eye, and understanding—which improves the learner's understanding of music—is a good procedure for the teaching of music reading.

Specifics

Clefs, key signatures, time signatures, measure bars, sharps, flats, note lengths, lines and spaces of the staff conjoined with letter names, and suchlike items, are here called *specifics*. They are often called "fundamentals"; but this is a gross misnomer. They are not the true fundamentals of music at all. They are, precisely specific symbols used in the standard notation. Hence, the term here chosen.

The teaching and learning of specifics goes on in connection with the general procedures already discussed. But nothing has yet been said about it directly. It is, however, a matter of great importance; and a clear understanding of what is involved is much needed. Since this book is not intended as a teacher's manual, I shall not consider the teaching of all the specific symbols of the notation. Instead, I shall confine myself to a few typical instances, to make the general approach clear. The principle with which this chapter opens applies, not only to general procedures, but also to the teaching of specifics. However we may deal with and present them, and there are many possible ways, they must always be taught and learned in such a fashion as to enhance and improve the learner's understanding of music.

The essential point to keep in mind is that every specific symbol of the musical notation stands for a *musical concept*. This is something that is rarely explained, and still more rarely understood. But it should be understood, for its practical consequences are very striking.

A concept, musical or otherwise, is a generalization that applies to a range of phenomena, an identity that is found in all of these phenomena, a common characteristic in which they all share. The word "dog," for instance, stands for a concept. There are a great many kinds of dogs; and they differ tremendously in size, appearance, behavior, and so on. But they all have in common a certain characteristic, which is their "dog-ness." This characteristic is found in all of them, or they would not be dogs. This is the concept to which the word "dog" refers. It enables us to think of all dogs as, in a basic respect, the same kind of creatures. And it even has a practical usefulness, for it enables law-makers to pass laws referring to all dogs, veterinarians to devise treatments for dogs in general, dog-catchers to look for any kind of dog while ignoring cats. In general, it enables us to think of and deal with all dogs of all kinds as sharing in a common dog-ness. They may be large, small, fierce, mild, woolly, or bald, but we think and act on the assumption that a dog's a dog for a' that. The point I am bringing out is that a concept is exceedingly useful. This is true of concepts in general, and of musical concepts in particular.

Now a concept, of course, has a meaning. Its meaning is the range of things to which it refers. The meaning of the word "dog" is, precisely, all dogs. The word and its related concept, taken together, provide us with a useful device for thinking about, dealing with, and referring to all dogs—not merely all the dogs we know, but all the dogs there ever were, or ever could be. So wonderful is this thing called a concept!

How do we learn the meaning of a concept? By experiencing the things to which it refers, and by coming to notice their common characteristic or quality. We learn the meaning of the word "dog" by dealing with dogs; and the more kinds of dogs we deal with, the more completely we understand the word and its related concept. If we had never seen anything but chihuahuas, our notion of dog would be limited; and when we met a great dane our understanding would suddenly expand. As a matter of fact, if we keep our eyes open, our understanding of many concepts is constantly expanding and growing. For we learn to understand concepts by dealing with the things to which they refer.

We do not learn to understand concepts by memorizing verbal definitions of them. You might find it very puzzling to frame an exact definition of "dog"; but still you understand very well what the word means. Moreover, if you worked out a very good verbal definition of "dog," and told it to someone who had never seen a dog, he might come away with a very odd notion of what a dog really is. Verbal definitions certainly have their uses; but they are not much use for getting hold of the real meaning of concepts. One might say that they tie the meaning up neatly after we have come to understand it. All this may seem rather a long way round in approaching music, and the teaching of the specific symbols. But now I shall hope to show that the journey has been worth while.

1. To pick out one instance of a musical specific, let us consider *time signatures*. Let us remember that any time signature stands for a musical concept, that its whole meaning lies in its musical applications, and that in order to learn it one must understand it, rather than memorizing it by rote. To make matters still more definite, let us begin with the 6/8 time signature.

Some children are dealing with the well-known *Dogie Song*.

Perhaps they listen to a recording of it. They sing it; they move to its rhythm; they use instruments to point it up at interesting places. The teacher who is working with them makes sure that they notice one particular thing about it, namely, its very distinctive lilt. This swinging, to-and-fro rhythm must be noticed, or the music will not be understood in one very important respect. It must be brought out in the performance, or the music will not sound as it should. Looking into this rhythm-pattern a little more carefully, the children can realize that it is made up of successive pairs of threes, with the second of each pair slightly less accented than the first. Then the teacher points out that there are symbols in the notation that tell one to notice and produce this rhythmic effect. One of these symbols is the 6/8 designation found at the beginning of the song; and besides this there are the bar-lines which set off the pairs of threes. So the children come to see that the notation tells them something important about how the song must be sung, and how it ought to sound, if it is to be satisfactory. Furthermore, they learn that the word name for this arrangement of symbols is, "six-eight time."

Now the children understand some of the meaning of the musical concept called six-eight time, just as a person who had seen a poodle would understand some of the meaning of the concept labelled "dog." But, in both cases, the understanding is limited. How should it be extended, improved? Surely, by further experience. Soon the children will have some more music in six-eight time, perhaps *Drink to Me Only with Thine Eyes,* and *When Johnny Comes Marching Home.* The feeling of the rhythm is not quite the same in each of these two songs, and in both of them it differs somewhat from the rhythmic feeling in the *Dogie Song.* Nevertheless, there is an identity. There are still those pairs of threes, although emphasis, accentuation, and speed will differ. Now the concept of six-eight time is much better understood, because it has been experienced and noticed as an identity occurring in different contexts or applications.

A different, and indeed a contrasting way of proceeding, would be to begin by explaining the symbols themselves—what the eight means, what the six means, what the bar lines mean. The explanation would have to be made by using words and numbers, with one or two specially constructed or selected illustrations included. This is a very common approach, but it is not a good one. What is very likely to happen is that children will understand the *verbal* meaning of the concept of six-eight time, but have almost no understanding of its *musical* meaning. They understand it as meaning a certain arrangement of numbers, not as meaning a certain kind of lilt. Moreover, when the concept is understood only verbally or arithmetically, the learner is almost sure to assume that its effect is exactly the same, no matter what the setting. But, as every musically sensitive person knows, the actual effect of the six-eight pattern differs, in subtle but important ways, in different pieces of music, even though there is, of course, an underlying identity. So the learning of the six-eight concept by starting with the arithmetic of the symbols is mechanical, not musical; for the true musical significance of the symbols and the concept is never understood.

Naturally, the arithmetic of the symbols must be learned and understood at some point. Probably the "6" of the time-signature will be understood first. Just when the significance of the "8" will become clear depends on the learning and understanding of another set of specifics, namely, the duration values of the notes. But the arithmetic should always come after the experience, for otherwise the arithmetic will not convey its true meanings. In just the same way, a careful verbal definition of "dog" could only be meaningful after a person had dealt with and experienced many kinds of dogs. The value of the arithmetic—and it is a very great one—is that it generalizes experience, and defines it with precision. But there must be something to generalize, something to make precise. When there is, then the study of the arithmetic of the time signature promotes the growth of musical understanding. But when the arithmetic is taught in advance of actual experience, actual application, then the learning has very little to do with music or musical effects, and musical understanding is not helped at all.

2. As a second example of the teaching and learning of specifics, let us consider *key signatures*. The nature and significance of key, and the true musical meaning of the symbols that indicate key, are some of the worst-taught things in music education, both in the studios and the schools. The usual practice is to decide that a certain number of key signatures "ought to be known," and then to have them memorized simply as symbols, i.e., so many sharps, so many flats. Such learning is purely verbal, not musical. It is no wonder that when students so taught encounter their first courses in theory, they discover with dismay that the content of music is a mystery to them, and that they have almost no understanding of it.

It is essential to see that the key signatures all refer to an underlying concept, the concept of key. Moreover, this is a musical concept, and its meaning is a set of effects or relationships which occur regularly in an enormous amount of music. Like any concept, the concept of key can only be truly learned by being understood; and it must be understood in a musical sense, i.e., in terms of its musical exemplifications. Until the concept of key is so understood, the teaching of key signatures is bound to be a futility.

Children develop an understanding of the concept of key by dealing with it in music, and by having their attention called to it as a factor in the beauty and expressiveness of music. I believe that children can begin to sense key direction and key tendency surprisingly young. I have known of kindergarten children to stand erect and motionless in a rhythm activity while a V_7 chord was sounding, and then flop on the floor when it resolved to the I chord. No one told them to do this. They just felt it so. Therefore we have a good deal to go on, and need not think of key relationships as artificial conventions that must be forced upon children.

The thing to do, obviously, is to bring out key relationships again and again in the music that the children use and enjoy. To notice such relationships is not an artificial imposition; it is something that really makes the music more interesting. I have already recommended the movable *do* syllables as the best device we have for this purpose, although ordinary numbers will also serve. The syllables should not at first be learned as a complete system. They should not even be used throughout entire songs. They should simply be applied here and there, wherever a happy and striking example of the effect of key relationship appears. If this is done, children will readily gain a grasp of the system as a whole, for it is really very simple, being, in effect, nothing but the numbers from one to seven.

Granted this approach, the introduction of key signatures simply means taking a concept that has already been formed, and that has been expressed in one set of symbols, and translating its expression into another set of symbols. The transition need not come at some pre-determined stage, nor need it come all in a moment. Indeed, it should not. First we use gesture-symbols and picture-symbols. They do not lend themselves well to symbolizing key relationships. Quite soon we introduce both syllables and notation, not abruptly or wholesale, but little by little, where they can highlight musical effects, and also without abruptly abandoning the simpler but still meaningful symbol-systems. The notes tell one thing, the syllables another. That may be the first impression, although we do not necessarily make it explicit. But gradually it becomes evident that the notes—or rather the notation—can tell what the syllables tell. The notation does it less directly, and with more complication than the syllables, but also with more generality. So a meaning, or a concept that has first been vaguely felt, and that has been made precise by the use of the syllables, is brought into contact with a still more adequate and elaborate system of symbols, and thereby comes to be still better understood. The usual bridge between syllables and notation (and, more particularly, key signature) is the rule for finding *do*. It is a good bridge, and can help understanding. But, like every other symbolic device, its value depends on a grasp of the underlying musical concept itself. Also, like any other symbolic device, it should not be taught as a routine in advance of understanding. It can, and probably should, be usefully taught after the concept of key has already been established, after it has been defined and clarified by means of the syllables, and after the children have begun to sense that the notation also can tell them what relational effects and tendencies are involved in a piece of music.

This analysis, by implication, answers many problems. What key signatures should be taught in the grades? When should each be taught? This does not matter very much; because what really matters is to develop a musical understanding of the concept of key. Should most of the music for a beginner be in the key of C major? Certainly not. We are not teaching this or that key pattern, but the general musical concept of key. Will objective tests, or "puzzle tests," in which respondents are asked to match key signatures against their names, to fill in missing sharps and flats, and so forth, reveal much about a child's musical understanding? Not at all at the lower levels, and only a little at the higher levels. A person may have a very fine, precise sense of key relationships without much skill in spelling out key signatures. On the other hand, a continuing musical development must certainly result in precise knowledge and exact skill.

3. What has been said about the teaching and learning of time signatures and key signatures applies essentially to all the specifics. It applies, for instance, to the teaching of note lengths (quarter notes, eighth notes, etc.). These also are musical concepts, and must be dealt with as such. Notes of various lengths, including sixteenth notes, can properly be introduced almost

from the first. Attention can be called to them where they are of particular musical importance and interest. They can be noticed and responded to in a wide range of musical settings. Little by little, their exact arithmetical definition can be clarified.

Specifics: Their Order of Presentation

The problem of when to present various items and undertakings has been mentioned several times throughout our discussions. It has a somewhat special bearing on the treatment of specifics.

1. Specifics should always be presented in musical settings in which they play distinctive and striking parts. The right time to present six-eight time, four-four time, the key with four sharps, sixteenth notes, dotted quarter note followed by eighth note, and so on, is when the item is musically appropriate. This, in substance, is the position here taken. But it needs some qualification and explanation.

2. The mode of presentation is very important, and has a bearing on the order of presentation. When first we call attention to the sixteenth notes in a passage, we do not organize a complete lesson, or make a complete explanation. We try to make something clear—but only enough to make the immediate passage better understood musically, and therefore more satisfying and effective. The concept of sixteenth note is already involved, but as yet it is comprehended only in a very limited and specific sense. We may do very little verbal explaining. We may not even use the term "sixteenth note," and rely only on the notational symbol. Everything we present, everything the children understand, is right as far as it goes; but it does not go very far. This way of dealing with the mode of presentation, closely connected with the order of presentation, is similar in the case of all specifics.

3. The sequence of presentation, too, must be considered. No

specific is presented once and for all, and then passed by for ever. It is presented again and again in many settings, so that its musical meaning as a concept becomes clearer and clearer. An instance has already been given in the treatment of the 6/8 time signature. The same plan of operation applies everywhere. This constant return for the sake of wider understanding and clearer insight, for the sake of a better and better comprehension of musical concepts, is one of the most distinctive features of a developmental music program.

4. Even though the first three points are accepted, a difficulty may still be felt. We develop an understanding of the specifics from musical settings. But might we not choose and arrange our musical settings chiefly for the sake of playing up the specifics in some pre-determined order? This would tend to falsify the whole procedure. It would mean music for the sake of specifics, rather than specifics for the sake of music. The almost certain result would be a more or less devitalized program. We choose our music for its spirit, its charm, its interest, its artistic value, its beauty. We develop our musical concepts, our musical understanding, from this music. This is not at all a piece of idealism. It is a perfectly practical plan. Given fifty or sixty well-chosen, musically vital songs and pieces suitable for the third grade, one can develop from them all the musical learnings, all the musical understandings, that any third-grade group can possibly be expected to accomplish—and, indeed, many more.

5. Does the plan here presented mean that specifics will only be taught "incidentally"? If the incidental teaching of specifics means that children will be expected to pick them up hit or miss without emphasis on our part or concentration on theirs, the answer is decidedly no. We have, in fact, a very carefully organized plan indeed, and a careful and meticulous control. Specifics are emphasized explicitly and strongly, but they are emphasized when and as needed. They are taught, not incidentally, but meaningfully.

6. Does our plan mean that children will not get a complete systematic grasp of the specifics? If a complete systematic grasp means a knowledge of all note lengths, all time signatures, all key signatures, all rest values, then the answer is, probably they will not get it. A great many musicians lack such a complete, systematic knowledge. The point, however, is, that a complete and systematic grasp is something one moves toward, not something one gets at the start and keeps from that time forward. The reality of musical understanding, not the fiction of a complete, comprehensive memory knowledge, is that toward which we aim.

Questions for Discussion, Thought, and Study

1. In many cases, the general procedures described in this chapter will have the effect of giving one a deeper and better appreciation of the music that is being used. Show how this is so.
2. If one or other of these procedures were being used, would it always be necessary to set matters up so that what would be in effect a music reading lesson was being conducted?
3. Pick out three songs which you would consider suitable for the procedure of "cooperative discovery." For what reasons did you make your choice?
4. From a number of songs pick out "musical highlights" which might well be used to establish connections between eye and ear. Once again, what were your reasons for your selections?
5. Many sound-patterns outside what is ordinarily thought of as music have conspicuous tonality relationships between their tones. Instances are the chiming of bells, various calls, etc. See if you can bring together a number of such instances, and show how the use of the syllables points up these tonality relationships; e.g. what syllables do the chimes "sing" when they sound the quarter-hour?
6. The syllables have sometimes been called artificial devices. Do you think that this is true? Is it also true of the notation? Of any system of symbolism, including the English language?

7. Do you find any disadvantages in substituting the word "specifics" for the more familiar word "fundamentals"?
8. Give yourself a little self-education in the intelligent study of the notation. Take a few children's songs, or indeed any other music you like, and examine them carefully and thoughtfully without singing or playing. Indicate by pencil marks, parentheses, circlings, and so forth, the groupings of symbols on which your attention centers.
9. Bring the discussion in this and the preceding chapter into relationship with what was said about the nature of a good learning experience.

Readings

Beatrice Perham, *Music in the New School*. Chicago, Neil J. Kjos Music Co., 1937. Chapter 7, "The Specific Skill of Reading Music."

James L. Mursell, *Music and the Classroom Teacher*. New York, Silver Burdett Company, 1951. Chapter 9, "Musicianship."

CHAPTER SEVEN

Singing and Musical Growth

The Principle

In a program planned to promote musical growth, the unique values and potentialities of singing will be clearly recognized, and they will be utilized to the fullest possible extent.

This seventh principle calls for a brief explanation. There are two media in general, for the performance of music. One is the voice. The other is mechanical. There are, of course, many kinds of instruments. But all of them are machines. Psychologically, they differ much less between themselves than all of them together differ from the voice.

Each of the two media of performance has characteristics that are peculiar to it. Each has its own potentialities for promoting musical growth. Each calls for a type of educational treatment peculiar to it. This is true, even though both voice and instrument have one vital thing in common, namely, the fact that it is a medium for music-making. In this chapter we deal with the special characteristics and potentialities of singing, to which our principle refers.

Our principle does not assert merely that singing must have a place in a developmental program. It does not assert that singing is the basic type of music-making. What it does assert is that singing has unique values and potentialities; and it implies that when these are understood, we are led to important practical decisions.

Unique Values and Characteristics of Singing

What, then, are the unique characteristics and values of singing? That, obviously, is the question with which this discussion must begin.

1. Singing is universal Everybody sings. In this respect it is unique—different from every other kind of music-making.

At first sight, this statement may appear questionable, and perhaps even violently untrue. But, if one considers it with care, doubts disappear. Not everybody sings well. Not everybody sings tunefully. Not everybody sings with good tone. Not everybody sings in such a way as to please others. Not everybody sings in such a way as to please himself, except in a very limited sense. But it seems very probable that there is not a normal human being in the world who does not sing in some fashion, some time, somewhere. He may not sing in public, or in company, or in any formal way. But he hums, croons, chants bits and snatches to himself at odd moments, or when preoccupied. Children do so. Adults do so. Singing, in this inclusive sense, seems as universal as talking. The proverbial man from Mars would, no doubt, consider man a tool-using creature, and a talking creature. But also he would consider him a singing creature.

This is well worth having in mind as we deal with the problems of music education. When we really take it in, it cannot but have a great effect on our point of view. Instead of regarding the singer as exceptional, and singing as an ability that must be acquired by careful guidance and long practice, we should consider it odd that this universal behavior-pattern so often gets blocked, that it remains quite rudimentary in many people's lives. Granted that singing is a universal human behavior-pattern, it should obviously be channeled in musical directions without any great difficulty, for the start is always there. When this does not happen, something must have gone wrong, something must have been mis-handled. There must have been road-blocks along the way, impediments, errors in treatment. When the universal impulse to sing fails to develop, either no positive influences at all have been brought to bear, or the wrong influences have been brought to bear. Since many attempts are certainly made to get people to sing, and since these attempts often fail, one has to conclude that somewhere along the line there has been a clash between imposed musical standards, and a natural, universal impulse.

2. Singing is a highly personal act. In this sense, too, it is unique; for in this respect it contrasts with all types of instrumental performance.

Sometimes it is said that singing is unique, because everyone has his vocal instrument with him at all times. This is true in a loose sense; but it is a misleading statement. The voice is, strictly, not an instrument. It is part of a personality, physical and mental. It responds instantly to mood, feeling, self-distrust, self-confidence; and it does so when we sing and when we speak. There is some shade of truth in talking about the "vocal mechanism;" or at least it is a convenient expression. But a mechanism embedded in the very tissues of our bodies, sensitive to every wave of nervous impulse, affecting in turn everything in our nervous constitution, signalling what is in our hearts and minds even against our will, and often without our knowledge, is certainly a unique mechanism, different from all others, even if properly a mechanism at all. A fine musical instrument has capacities which the voice lacks. But even the most mediocre voice has capabilities which the finest instrument cannot even begin to possess; for the voice is part and parcel of the personality, whereas the instrument is not.

All this, again, must deeply affect our point of view and our practice. We must realize that it is not the voice, but the person, that sings. We must think of ourselves not, in the first place, as developing voices, or teaching singing, but first and foremost, as developing singers. Since this may have somewhat of a professional suggestion, it is better to say that we must think of our work as that of *helping people to capitalize their innate ability to sing*.

This is a consideration of the very highest importance, with very far-reaching implications. First, it suggests that many, and perhaps most, of the roadblocks in the way of the development of singing are personal rather than technical, at least in the earlier stages. This does not involve any disparagement of the proper management of the voice, or of specific attention to the vocal action. But it does indicate that the basic purpose of all voice teaching should be to open the road toward completer fulfillment of a natural impulse, and the removal of impediments to such fulfillment.

Secondly, we are reminded that the person who does, in fact, achieve a satisfying fulfillment of this universal, highly personal impulse to sing, gains many great values. He has the means for a unique and intimate form of musical pleasure that can be life-long. He has a sense of functioning, of personal achievement. The highly personal ability to sing, when not limited or frustrated, carries with it a rich reward of personal values.

3. In singing, words and music coalesce. Language conveys what have been called "discursive" meaning, or, perhaps less precisely, "intellectual" meanings. It can describe events and objects; it can explain, expound, convey a definite narrative. Music, on the other hand, conveys emotional meanings, or emotional values. In any artistically authentic song—and this can certainly include the simplest of children's songs—the music projects and enhances the emotional significance of the text. Here is one very important respect in which the vocal medium differs from any instrumental medium.

Obviously this unique characteristic has numerous and far-reaching implications. For one thing, it indicates that in developing the natural ability to sing, it is very important to stress the sense and emotional feeling and content of the words of the songs. A singer should not merely weave an abstract pattern of tone; he should, at the same time, sense and feel what he is singing about. Otherwise he is, in effect, ignoring one of the basic and unique characteristics of the medium. He is, so to speak, not using singing for its natural and intended purpose.

Furthermore, the vocal medium is of peculiar value in helping to bring music into relationship with wide ranges of non-musical experience. The songs of a people, or of a culture, represent it very significantly, because they fuse both intellectual and emotional meanings, both text and music. One of the many reasons why singing has an important place in our program, is that it so naturally provides a bridge between music as an expressive art, and the cultural experiences and content out of which music arises.

4. In and through singing we feel music as a continuous flow, to an extent and with a clarity that is hardly possible in and through any instrumental medium. Any musical instrument tends to proceed note-wise, or step-wise, and to emphasize and call much attention to separate notes. Singing, on the other hand, tends to move tune-wise. It has been demonstrated as a well-established fact, that even the most highly trained singer, even the coloratura soprano, always sings in a more or less continuous curve, sliding into and away from the separate notes, rather than enunciating them as sharply separated entities, in the fashion of an instrument. This is not avoidable, and it is not necessarily a defect. It is due to the natural tendency of the voice itself. This feeling of continuity is what is largely indicated by saying that a performer "sings with his instrument." For singing brings into great prominence the all-over general shape of melody and phrase. So it brings one closer to certain extremely important musical realities that any instrument, including the variable-

pitch instruments. This, in substance, was what Schumann had in mind, when he said that everyone should sing whether or not he has a good voice, *because of what it will do for the ear*.

Such, then, are the unique values and potentialities of singing, to which our seventh principle refers.

Implications

Singing, then, has certain special, and indeed unique characteristics, as a medium of musical performance. It is psychologically different, in many respects, from any and all kinds of instrumental performance. This special character of singing not only justifies its place in our developmental program, but also goes far toward indicating what that place should be. It will be well to point out some of the broader implications bearing on the proper use and place of singing, before turning to more detailed discussions.

1. Singing has many immediate values in the classroom. It can, and should be consciously used to promote and foster a sense of social togetherness, sharing, and companionship. This should be definitely kept in mind as we organize our singing experiences with children. It can, and should, be consciously used to bring experiences of significant success. This, too, should be definitely kept in mind in our work. That children should have successful experiences with singing is important in general, because of the high positive value of such experiences, and because of their favorable influence on growth and adjustment. More specifically, experiences with singing can greatly affect a child's whole attitude to music.

A very striking and fairly recent experiment, carried on under classroom conditions, revealed this clearly. In a first-grade group, children were selected whose attitude toward music seemed to be one of indifference or even hostility. The suggestion was that they lacked "musical talent," in some vague sense of that dubious phrase. They were taken in small groups of three or four, and given intensive help and encouragement in singing. All of them soon became able to sing, and all of them enjoyed doing so. But they did not merely acquire a new special ability. Their whole attitude toward music, and toward a whole range of musical experiences and activities, was completely changed. Whereas before they were either indifferent or negative, they now became enthusiastically and positively interested. One might say that their inability to sing, which was an inability to enjoy and experience music in the most direct, natural, intimate, and highly personal of all ways, was a roadblock that prevented any musical development. But, on the contrary, when they were successfully helped to discover their ability to sing, a strong influence making for musical growth immediately became effective.

2. Establishing and developing the ability to sing is one of the best means we have of insuring a continuing use of music throughout life. It is, indeed, perhaps the very best single means we have for this purpose. No doubt it is possible for a person to remain interested in music, and to discover more and more of its significance and value by dint of listening to it, reading about it, hearing it discussed, and so forth. This is practicable today as it was not fifty years ago, because of our wonderful modern facilities. But to be able to make music oneself brings a new cogency and vitality to a person's relationship to the art. Let us remember that musical growth, like every type of personal growth, depends upon purpose; that without purpose it will surely cease; and that granted effective purpose, it may well continue. The continuing wish, and will, and purpose to perform music for oneself, then, seems to be a factor of prime significance in securing the continuation of musical growth.

Therefore, in organizing singing in school, we should be encouraging singing out of school—out of school now, and out of school later. This thought cannot but have a profound effect on our procedures. We will wish to teach children that they can sing, and also to teach them how to sing. But this is not all. We will also wish to reveal to them what to sing, where to find vocal materials, how to use and enjoy them. We will wish to equip them to use singing as a life-long and rewarding resource. Why, for instance, should we advocate part-singing as well as unison singing at the upper grade levels? There are, no doubt, good reasons that are purely musical reasons. Moreover, we may want to build up effective singing organizations for performance and display, which is a perfectly laudable desire, granted certain conditions. But above all, part-singing can be a very intriguing and rewarding lifetime activity, so that people who can share in it have something of lasting value.

3. The ability to sing is very important and valuable for those whose development is toward specialization in an instrumental medium. In singing, one feels the flow and continuity of music with unique clarity, and with unique intimacy. The common way of talking of instrumental tone as "singing" tone is not an accident, nor is it merely a metaphor. What is referred to is certainly not the tone quality itself, but rather the sense of the moving, moulded, total shape that is so distinctive of the vocal medium. Yet many instrumentalists are virtually vocal "monotones." They lack vocal confidence, and have never had close experience with music carried on the voice. Certainly they lose something as musicians; for while the highest reaches of art song are as exacting as high instrumental virtuosity, musically significant and rewarding singing can be achieved and maintained without too much difficulty, and doing so is very rewarding and delightful. An instrumentalist who is able to use his singing voice, is equipped to explore whole continents of musical beauty; and also he has a feeling for music itself that nothing else can supply.

4. It is sometimes said that music reading is better developed by means of the instrumental rather than the vocal medium. Teachers constantly report that the children who really become

able to read are usually those who are taking music lessons, and probably piano lessons, outside school. No doubt this is a fact, but it needs interpretation. The school music program may be very limited and superficial, whereas lessons outside, which usually call for a good deal of practicing, may be comparatively intensive. The teaching of music reading in school may be confined largely to rather routine study-song lessons. Then, to be sure, the superiority of those taking outside lessons will probably be very marked. But if music reading is treated as the understanding of visual symbols in a musical sense, and if such an understanding is built into a comprehensive and sequential program involving a wide range of experiences, then the distinctive necessity of outside lessons will become far less apparent. Moreover, people who say that the only children who learn to read are those who take outside lessons, usually think of music reading chiefly as a tool skill. Piano study of the ordinary kind will usually produce this tool skill, though probably at a low or at best a very moderate level. But it certainly does not usually produce anything much that could reasonably be called musical understanding. The young piano student usually spells out the notes on the keyboard, which, of course is itself a diagram or symbolization of the musical system. He becomes able to do this after a fashion, but not usually at all well. This is more than most children ever get from the conventional study-song procedure; and so a few individuals will stand out conspicuously against the general low level of achievement. But the idea that musical understanding cannot be developed from vocal experience, or that it cannot be developed well, is entirely erroneous; although a much wider range of experience, extending beyond singing, is certainly needed for a development that will be effective and rounded.

5. What has been said about the unique characteristics of the vocal medium has definite implications about how singing should

be taught. These will soon be considered more specifically, but their general bearings may suitably be indicated here.

Let us remember that singing is a highly personal act, involving not only the use of the vocal mechanism, but the whole physical, mental, and emotional make-up of the personality. Let us remember, too, that singing appears to be a "natural" human act, in the sense that it manifests itself spontaneously and universally—in which case, the widespread inability to sing even passably well seems to indicate that the trouble lies with various inhibitions or blockages. Putting these two thoughts together, we have to conclude that singing depends very greatly indeed on encouragement and stimulation, on attitude and confidence. Attitude and confidence are, no doubt, important in connection with instrumental performance, and in connection with acquiring the ability to perform. But the very act of song itself depends upon these factors. Singing must be invited and encouraged, rather than forced or imposed. Singing, and learning to sing and to sing better, must be a pleasure first and foremost, rather than a task; although of course hard and serious work has its place as time goes on. One can, perhaps, practice on the piano to some moderately good purpose, even against one's will and inclinations, for a short time, at any rate. Or at least, even if the practice is fruitless, the instrument itself will still work as well as always. But singing is produced by an "instrument" only in the metaphorical sense. It is not produced merely by the vocal machinery, but by the whole personality. And if we have hostile attitudes, rebellion, lack of confidence, lack of desire and will, the very "instrument" of song itself is affected, and probably reduced to impotence.

This is the general conclusion about teaching procedures that is to be derived from our account of the unique characteristics of singing. We shall follow the indicated line of thought out in some detail. On this basis, you may think of three fundamental requirements for the management of singing in your program. First, you must make a *proper choice of songs*. Second, you must organize effective *singing situations*. Third, you must be ready and able to offer *specific help and guidance* in overcoming vocal roadblocks, and in solving vocal problems, when needed.

Choosing Songs

No one can give you complete, hard-and-fast directions for choosing suitable songs. Nevertheless, a number of helpful suggestions can be made. Before coming to them, however, I would like to stress the extreme importance of making a proper choice of songs. You will find that an attractive, musically interesting, singable song will do far more to make people want to sing, and even to make them able to sing, than any teaching method or device. So the choice of songs is vital. Now for the suggestions on how to go about it.

1. You should have a large number of simple unison songs, that groups and individuals enjoy singing. These are songs "just for singing," but do not think for a moment that this makes them unimportant, or puts them beyond the realm of serious business. One of your basic aims will probably be enjoyment, and here is a fine chance to promote it on quite a large scale. Moreover, the free, confident participation that such songs suggest and encourage is one of the most potent influences there are for making people *singing people*. And the pleasure, drive, and enthusiasm of free, confident singing is, without a doubt, a powerful force for musical growth. So never feel one bit apologetic over having a large number of unison songs—so long as they are good ones. This free, confident singing should go on in all grades, and it can be done with varying degrees of reliance on the notation, all the way from none at all to complete reading. Many such songs are suitable for several grades, and most of them spill over

the grade subdivisions. This makes them specially suitable for assembly use. It can be a fine musical experience for several grades to learn some such songs in their own rooms, and then come together in assembly to sing them as a whole-school group. Instances of such songs would be *Marching to Pretoria, Sailing, All Night All Day, Anchors Aweigh.*

2. You will want songs, both unison and otherwise, from many and varied areas of human experience, such as work, patriotism, war, peace, home life, the outdoors, adventure, romance (perhaps?), and so on. Remember that, from the first, children should feel and know that music speaks of many aspects of life, that it does not, as it were, exist all by itself in isolation.

3. Some radio and television songs (but *not* singing commercials) are suitable to use. They link up school with life and interests out of school. And, above all, children know them, like them, enjoy singing them, and can get much real value from them.

4. Folk songs, of course. It is, perhaps, a little hard to say just what a folk song is, and often even harder to tell whether any given song is a real folk song. For instance, is *Waltzing Matilda,* a genuine Australian folk song, that just "grew" among the sheep shearers; or did some one person compose it? Leave such questions to experts and musicologists. It will, perhaps, be better to think of *folk-song-type* songs, which makes matters more vague, but still says what you are really after. What you want are plenty of songs that people in different places have sung, probably for ages, without self-consciousness or any conscious concern for art. Many, many people have enjoyed such songs, and this is their greatest recommendation. A word or two of warning, however, may be in order. Do not think that just because a song is a folk song, it is therefore good. There are plenty of dull and deadly folk songs, so you must still use your judgment. Also, I am sorry to say, there are such things as fake folk songs, manufactured

by somebody to teach the dotted quarter note or some such, and given the folk song label. Finally, do not be so carried away by the idea of folk songs that you go in for almost nothing else.

5. Songs which call for some sort of social interchange when they are sung, can be excellent. One type is the familiar verse-refrain arrangement, with a soloist or small group singing the verse, and everybody coming in on the refrain—such as *Two Wings, Swing Low Sweet Chariot,* or *The Orchestra.* Then there are still more informal and varied patterns, such as question-and-answer songs, or songs calling for responses from different parts of the room. All such songs make for free, confident singing, and invite participation.

6. Ballads and story-type songs should certainly be included, such as lumber-jack songs, coal-mining songs, railroad songs. They connect music up with many phases of life. Their words are interesting, and they lend themselves to interesting variations and shifting social patterns when they are sung.

7. You must always consider the suitability of the words. A lullaby, or a song about a pet kitty might go very well in the first grade, but very badly in the fourth. A love song is a doubtful choice anywhere in the elementary school. There is, of course, no fixed rule. You must know your children, and decide what words will be suitable on the basis of your knowledge. Also, of course, you must never forget that singing depends very much on attitude, and that attitude, in turn, depends very much on the suitability of the song. What I have said so far on this point has been negative; but there are positive things to say too. Have songs that make a good contact with the interest and experience of the children, such as *Mary Had A Little Lamb,* or *Peter Peter Pumpkin Eater,* or songs for Easter, Christmas (of course), and suchlike fine occasions. Always keep your eye on the comprehensibility of the song, from the children's viewpoint. This means attending not only to vocabulary, but also, and even more, to sentiment.

8. All the songs you use should have musical interest and expressiveness. This, indeed, is the supreme requirement in a program planned to promote musical growth. But there will be some songs specially chosen for their musical worth and beauty, and perhaps for nothing else. For the most part these would be simple, manageable art songs, an instance of which might well be *Jesu, Joy of Man's Desiring*.

9. So much for suggestions about the songs to choose. Now for a word or two about the kinds of songs to exclude.

A. Have nothing at all to do with songs specially constructed for instructional purposes. They usually have no musical value; and if so, they have no educational value either.

B. Avoid songs with a pattern so complicated that it defeats the children, because their minds cannot grasp it. *Adeste Fideles*, for instance, breaks down in the first grade for this reason.

C. Avoid art songs that may be great, but that are musically and emotionally too mature or too advanced.

Always remember that encouragement and attitude are the essentials, and that the choice of songs has a great deal to do with them. So has what I have called the "singing situation," and to this I now turn.

The Singing Situation

You will find the concept to which I have attached the term "singing situation" very useful in your thinking and planning. By the singing situation I mean the entire situation, social, personal, and emotional, in which the song is presented and sung. Strictly speaking, of course, the song itself is part of the singing situation; but I think it is convenient to consider the song separately, which I have done. Also it may occur to you that there are physical aspects to the singing situation, such as standing, or sitting, or the seating arrangements, or the use of a music room instead of a classroom, or, for that matter, even the acoustics of the room. On the whole, however, it seems to me that these physical factors are important because of their social, or personal, or emotional effects; and so I will not consider them separately.

No one, of course, can give you a complete account of prescription for a good singing situation. But, as with the choosing of songs, many helpful suggestions are possible.

1. Create situations in which children feel free to join in when and as they will, more or less regardless of vocal limitations. The old-time congregational singing in church—which, fortunately still goes on—was often a very good singing situation indeed, and certainly had a considerable musical effect. A well-managed community sing is another instance of a good singing situation. I have had classroom teachers ask what to do with "monotones" and hesitant singers, apparently expecting to be given some special trick or some clever teaching procedure. The best answer, by far, is to organize a good singing situation which will tend to draw the hesitant ones in; for while no one can be forced to sing, most people can be incited to sing. So build up a group momentum; make yourself a good song leader; use singalong records—use them of course if you must, but use them often even if you can get along without them. This, I am sure, sounds very un-lesson-like, and so, indeed, it is. But it can add up to an excellent and effective learning experience.

2. Carrying the idea a little further and making it more definite, non-singing activities can help singing. Rhythmic activities, dramatizations, and playing instruments, can involve many hesitant singers in singing almost before they know it; whereas formal tone matching can produce a vocal thrombosis that will last a lifetime. In our developmental program, rhythmics, dramatizations, and so forth will not be run in watertight compartments. They will be used, among other things, to encourage and stimulate participation in song.

3. The use of simple instruments, of both tonal and rhythmic type, can help to carry singing along. "Taking up instruments" certainly need not, and usually should not, mean a total quietus on singing. The right thing, most of the time, is not instruments *or* singing, but instruments *and* singing, with children taking turns on the instruments, or with one or two sticking only to instruments for quite a while, and then merging into song at will. Here is another reason why the familiar rhythm band looks rather dubious. It is quite a definitely segregated activity.

4. Accompaniment on the piano or the autoharp can help carry the song along, and can add interest and richness to the singing experience. Unaccompanied singing has often been made rather a fetish in certain quarters, and considered the only proper procedure. But it stems from a "task-wise" or "lesson-wise" point of view that is usually poison to singing, which depends so much on enthusiasm, confidence, and the sheer will to sing. At the same time, you must be careful not to let the accompaniment overpower the singing. Also, it is not good for the accompanist to be out of touch with the singers, as easily happens when the teacher sits at the piano with her back to the children.

5. Emphasize and bring out the spirit and meaning of the words. Be sure, first of all, that the children really understand the words. Obvious, you might suppose; but not always done! And beyond understanding, help them to catch the spirit, the feeling, the emotional flavor of the words—the quality in the words on which the music itself really turns. The point is that children should feel that they are singing about something, saying something, feeling something, expressing something, projecting something—not just making sounds with their voices. You will often be amazed how much this will help singing. And yet, there is nothing so very amazing about it. Music is the expression of feeling. A song is feeling embodied in tone and rhythm. Singing is the projection of this feeling. It is, essentially, a meaningful utterance, and should be experienced as such.

When it becomes just the making of sounds with the "vocal instrument," we are going against its essential nature.

6. It can often help with the singing situation for children to invent words, alter words, perhaps invent whole new stanzas. These practices help to get everybody into singing, with the feeling that they are really expressing something, saying something, not just sounding the "vocal instrument."

7. It will often help the singing situation a great deal for children to choose the songs to be sung. Arrange matters so that this is possible for them. Give them chances to look through their song books, instead of doling out songs as if they were doses of medicine to be taken only on prescription. Build up lists of favorite songs, and put them on a chart. Suggest that they might run across songs out of school, which could be brought in and used.

8. Be sure that the social situation in the classroom is flexible, free, natural, and geared to the song. Children may sometimes gather round the piano or the phonograph. One or two may change records, or several may take turns doing so. Small groups may go off into different parts of the room, to sing questions, answers, echoes, etc. By all means encourage solo singing, and here again follow the turn-about rule most of the time. Sometimes, too, a song of unusual beauty and appeal, perhaps a simple art song, may call for the attentive singing of the whole group, with everyone in place, attending to the leader or accompanist up in front.

9. Assembly programs, of course, can be grand singing situations, and can reflect back to the singing in the classrooms. It is strange but true that some practical school people never seem to think of connecting singing in the classroom with singing in the assembly. But this spells nothing but lost opportunity. When suitable classroom songs are used in the assembly, the singing there is likely to go better. And to sing in a big group a

song that has been used in a smaller group is to realize new possibilities in the song.

10. Do not, for a moment, hesitate to help the children along with the singing. You can do this by singing along with them; or, if this seems difficult, you can use singalong records. The idea that the teacher should never sing along with the children, which has been very firmly implanted, comes from the theory that one learns to sing by struggling, by hesitating, by succeeding very meagerly and perhaps not at all. It is a ridiculous theory; for one learns to sing by singing enthusiastically, confidently, pleasurably, and with a sense of succeeding. Still, you should not always sing along with the children. When to do so is a matter of judgment, and depends very much on your knowledge of the children, and your sense of the situation.

11. Your own attitude is enormously important in making a good singing situation. Perhaps it is the most important thing of all. I have seen a teacher make what seemed to me a very formal lesson rewarding because she herself sang so beautifully and with such evident pleasure. What a pity that she did not realize that her own singing was worth infinitely more than all the little bits and pieces about which she was so anxious! Perhaps you yourself can't sing like that. Perhaps you must rely largely on some such device as a singalong record. Even so, your attitude can shine through, like the sun breaking through the clouds. If singing with your children, and helping them to sing, is a painful duty or an anxious chore, neither you nor they will get very far. But if it is an evident pleasure to you—and it certainly can be—then your pleasure will radiate out, and be transformed and transmuted, by some magic, into joyful singing, sincere and beautiful singing, and a joy in music that may well be lasting.

12. Now for some things to avoid.

A. Avoid assignment to "singing seats," if not always, then

ninety-nine times out of a hundred—and perhaps not even then. Singing seats work directly against spontaneity, and tend to make singing a task and a chore. The idea of putting the good voices at the back of the room, so as to spread the tone, is nearly always all wrong. We are not trying to get a good class tone as such, but to get everybody to sing, and to sing happily. A hesitant singer is not encouraged when someone three rows back sings quite well. He is much more likely to keep still, or perhaps to make his mouth go, so as not to be dragooned into a nice drill on tone matching.

B. Avoid insisting always on a fixed posture. Posture is not of the first importance in the early stages, when all we want is free, spontaneous participation. It becomes important, like any other point of technique, when real and desired musical effects depend upon it.

C. Avoid any rigid rote-note classification of singing activities. All singing should be by ear, as we have seen; and symbols can and should be introduced gradually and flexibly for the sake of the music.

D. Avoid anything that may humiliate, discourage, or antagonize hesitant singers. What these people need is not the application of some clever instructional trick, but encouragement and incitement. Encouraging help and stimulation are the only constructive answers.

Special Vocal Help and Guidance

Up to this point in our discussion, the proper treatment of singing has been represented as wholly a matter of encouragement and motivation; and it has been intimated that the proper use of the voice depends upon attitude. How should you go about getting children to sing? By choosing interesting and appealing songs, and by organizing good singing situations. That has been my answer so far.

You will find the answer a good one. It will carry you a long way, and prevent you from making many mistakes. With young children, that is about all there is to the business of singing. Moreover, the answer applies far beyond the years of early childhood. No matter how expert and highly schooled a singer becomes, enthusiasm, eagerness, confidence, and the will to sing remain not merely important, but altogether essential. This is because, as we have seen, singing is a natural act involving the whole personality, which means that it can never cease to depend on the orientation and attitude of the person.

But all this leaves specific training in the proper technical use of the voice entirely out of the picture. Can we afford to leave it out of the picture, to do nothing about it, to rely on nothing but good songs, and good singing situations? If not, what ought we to do about it? That is the question which we must now consider. I do not believe for a moment that we can afford to ignore specific voice training—or, as I much prefer to phrase it, specific vocal help and guidance. And I also believe that we already have some good clues as to how this training should be managed, how this help and guidance should be given.

1. The first point that comes to mind is that successful vocal functioning is very important. A child who sings happily, confidently, and with satisfaction to himself (at least for the time-being), already has a good hold on music, a promising start toward musical growth. But if, at a certain age, the child abandons singing, a powerful musical impulse has vanished; and besides that, he probably will not have singing as a resource in later life. Now by far the most common reason why children abandon singing is that they do not develop as singers. They begin to compare themselves with others; and, indeed, other children often force such comparisons on them. Also they begin to judge themselves. The conclusion they reach is that they are not much good; and so they give up singing. This has a very

clear lesson for all of us. Since singing itself is very important (as we have already seen), it is very important to help children to make enough improvement so that singing will continue to seem attractive and worth while to them.

2. Suitable songs, and dynamic singing situations are quite enough for an excellent start. They will carry children far beyond this good start. They will always be valuable, always necessary. But if there is nothing more, the singing impulse of many children is almost sure to dry up. It will dry up because, at a certain level of maturity, social standards, comparative standards, and standards of self-judgment begin to have an effect. And that effect will be to kill the impulse to sing, unless there is a real and promising improvement. The experience of success and achievement is a very simple affair at first; but as children develop, attitudes become more and more exacting and self-critical. This is the reason why specific vocal help and guidance—or, if you will, specific vocal training—is necessary. Without it, many children will lose the early singing impulse.

3. But what sort of vocal training, what sort of special vocal help and guidance should be given? When should it be given? How should it be given? These are the questions you want answered; and they seem quite puzzling.

If you turn to the voice teachers, whose problems are more concerned with adults, you may find their suggestions puzzling. Many have developed concepts, devices, and procedures to develop, bring out, and control the singing voice. These are primarily directed to students in high-school select choral groups and those taking private studio lessons. However, vocal teachers really do get a great many learners to sing, to sing well, and to improve. How can you pick out the practical ideas for elementary grades that will serve your purpose? The ideas that we have already formulated in this book will give you some excellent clues.

4. The first thought that comes to mind is that *conscious*

control of the voice must evolve. If you have followed our previous discussions, this is an idea that you might very well expect. To encourage children to sing freely up to a certain age, and then suddenly to subject them to vocal drills and the routines of technical voice training is certainly contrary to our notion that development must be continuous. But merely to say that conscious control of the voice must evolve is not sufficient. You naturally want something more explicit, something in the way of a bill of particulars. Let me try to supply it.

When children in the first grade sing a pleasing song happily, and under the encouragement of a good singing situation, their minds are on the music, its interest, its charm, its content. They may be using their voices all right, but there is no consciousness of doing so, no conscious control.

How should they begin to gain this conscious control? Certainly not by being suddenly told to attend to their diaphragms, to attend to their breathing, and to try to get their voices up in their heads. Even if these three suggestions were good vocal advice, they would be premature. Instead of helping children to sing better, these suggestions might make them anxious and puzzled, and make them sing worse and begin to dislike singing.

Remember that the children have been guided in their singing by the music, and particularly by its general effects and meanings. Their consciousness of the music has been guiding their voices, and guiding their voices quite well. All right! The first thing to do is to sharpen up their consciousness of the music, so that it can guide their voices still more specifically.

A. You can emphasize tone-quality. You can emphasize it in and through the song itself. Indeed, you should. Do not think in terms of, or work for some predetermined kind of "good tone," and in particular do not make a fetish of hushed tone. Good tone-quality is expressive, and depends on what is being expressed. A voice should sound differently in *Sweet and Low* and in *The Marseillaise,* just as it should sound differently when murmuring loving words and when scolding the dog. Help the children to realize and feel, ever more clearly, what they are expressing. Now and then call attention to the kind of tone they are producing. Call attention to the kind of tone more and more frequently as they get older. But never lose touch with the expressive intention. Sometimes it is said that children will damage their voices unless they sing with a hushed tone. The idea that many potentially good voices are endangered by elementary-school singing is, to put it mildly, quaint. But the impulse to sing is certainly impaired or destroyed in many children by artifical imposed restrictions. No one, of course, will advocate unmusical yelling. But the way to avoid it is not to forbid yelling but to emphasize expressiveness.

B. You can emphasize pitch control. In doing so, remember that what you want is to have children carry tunes rather than match tones. The musical response of young children is primarily tune-wise rather than note-wise; and singing itself is also primarily tune-wise. That is, we tend to sing tunes as wholes, rather than as separate notes. You can emphasize the exact pitch line, the exact rise and fall of the melody, matching it here and there against separately sounded single notes when necessary. Thus children's attention can be sharply concentrated on pitch, at first occasionally, and later more and more extensively. Conscious attention to pitch will do much to affect the vocal action.

C. You can call attention to phrasing. At first children can sense a phrase as a musical statement, continuous and flowing within itself, and with a beginning and ending. The notion that the phrase must be carried on the breath can be made clear gradually. Thus little by little the conscious control of breathing can be developed.

5. So far you will have been working for vocal control and effective vocal action largely through a better and clearer grasp of the music itself. But in and through this development

children will have been brought, little by little, to a consciousness of the voice itself and its management. As children grow older, explicit attention to vocal management becomes meaningful for them, on the basis of much previous experience of the kind indicated. It is at this level that some, at least, of the procedures and devices of voice teaching have their place.

But, as we have seen, the name of such procedures and devices is legion. Which should be chosen and utilized? My answer is: Choose the simplest, the most direct, the most obviously sensible. In guiding and helping young people in the controlled and conscious use of their singing voices, I will suggest that four factors should receive attention. These are (i) freedom of the mouth and jaw, and no obvious straining and tightening of the muscles in the neck, (ii) a posture suitable for effective use of the vocal appartus, (iii) conscious control of breathing, and (iv) intentional and deliberate projection of the voice.

In any case, if you can show young people how to sing with a free mouth and jaw, to take a posture that liberates and supports the vocal organs, to carry phrases on the breath, and consciously to project their voices, you are on solid ground. These things indubitably happen in good singing. If you emphasize them, you cannot go far wrong, and young people will develop the vocal competence that has so much to do with their overall musical growth.

6. One last point will round off this discussion. The explicit teaching of voice control, voice production, vocal technique, or whatever you like to call it, should always aim at freeing up a natural function, removing roadblocks, enabling a person to succeed with something that it is in his nature to do, making possible a continuing development. Such instruction is not the teaching of an artificial skill or set of tricks. It is, essentially, a continuation of the singing situation, with everything becom-

ing more particularized, and more and more subject to conscious attention. What should come from it is a sense of advancing achievement. But from beginning to end, from the lowest level to the highest, the key words in developing the ability to sing are encouragement and attitude.

Part-Singing

No discussion of singing in relation to musical growth can be complete without at least some reference to part-singing. Part-singing is one of the most delightful and intriguing forms of musical enjoyment. It should always be experienced as such. It should never be handled as a problem-like, and probably baffling, task; or its values will be destroyed.

This means that part-singing should be developed gradually, rather than being introduced as a new departure at some predetermined grade level. You can inaugurate the beginnings of part singing with quite young children, perhaps in the first or second grade. Once in a while, during the singing of a familiar song, you can add some brief musical fragment along with the singing. You can use your own voice, or a simple melody instrument, or, for that matter, the piano. The whole simple idea is for children to be aware of some musical embroidery going on as they are singing their tune, and for them to find the experience interesting and enjoyable. At first the fragments can be quite short, and even a single note will often do. Wherever possible, help and encourage individual children to put in these little musical additions or (if you will) comments. Out of these super-added fragments can grow true descants, which again may be either instrumental or vocal. Another interesting possibility is, from time to time, to add a pedal point below the melody, so that children become aware very early that the musical embroidery can be either higher or lower than the main tune. Always it is important to guide the children so that they will *listen* to what goes on; and this calls, of course, for soft singing as well as conscious attention.

The use of rounds is another natural lead into part-singing. Rounds can be introduced and managed in various ways. Sometimes it may be well to have the round learned first as a unison song. Or the class may listen while two individuals sing the round or play it on melodic instruments. Or the class may sing in unison while the teacher sings or plays the second part of the round. (This statement, of course, assumes a two-part round.) Or some of the children may play the second part of the round on instruments while the others sing in unison. These are some, but not the only possible, ways of working to the point at which the class is divided into suitable groups for the singing of the round as intended.

Yet another contributory experience can be the use of a second part following the first one in parallel thirds. The second part can be played, or sung by some individual, or by a group.

All these are leads into true part-singing. If they are introduced early and used extensively, they can greatly enrich early singing experiences, and go far to solve the vexed problem of when and how to introduce part-singing proper. Many teachers in the upper grades and junior high school complain that their children do not want to sing in parts. I have been asked to produce, on the spur of the moment, some magic remedy for this difficulty. Probably a skilled and resourceful teacher can do a great deal to overcome it. But the point is that the difficulty should never have arisen. Children should have discovered very early how pleasant and interesting it can be to have musical embroidery for a tune, and also how easily such embroidery can be supplied. The word "fun" is tossed about far too freely by music educators. But the word is perfectly legitimate and accurate to describe exactly what many valuable part-singing experiences should and can be.

Questions for Discussion, Thought, and Study

1. Not so very long ago, the ordinary elementary-school music program was virtually a program of singing. Why do you think this was? What comments and evaluations would you make, in the light of this chapter, and also in the light of what has already been said in this book?

2. What reasons do you find in this chapter for believing that tone-matching drills, i.e., drilling children to duplicate single tones, are not a desirable practice?

3. One often hears about what is called "voice training." What misleading suggestions, both theoretical and practical, does this idea convey? What phrase would you suggest as a substitute?

4. It is often said that music reading is more readily taught in connection with the use of instruments than in connection with singing. Is there any truth in this claim? Is there anything to be said for a different opinion?

5. Should the use of the syllables be confined to singing? Give reasons for your answer.

6. Review and consider the assertion by Schumann, that everyone should sing even if he has not much of a voice, because of what it can do for his ear. What are some of the things that singing "can do" for a person's "ear"?

7. One of the main points made in this chapter is that the voice should not be thought of as an instrument. Review the reasons for this assertion. What are some of its implications and practical consequences?

8. Some music educators contend very strongly that children should, at all times, sing softly, and with what is sometimes called a "hushed tone." What might be the reasons for this? What do you yourself think of the idea?

9. Do you think that there is any serious danger that children may damage their voices by singing in school?

10. Bring together all the suggestions you find in this chapter and elsewhere in this book for dealing with children who hesitate to sing.

Readings

Paul W. Mathews, *You Can Teach Music*. New York, E. P. Dutton and Co., Inc., 1953. Chapter 2, "The Common Sense Way to Singing": Chapter 3, "Let the Singing Begin."

These chapters contain many helpful ideas and suggestions.

Emma D. Sheehy, *There's Music in Children*. New York, Henry Holt and Company, revised edition, 1954. Chapter 4, "Singing."

Once more, many excellent suggestions, interestingly presented.

James L. Mursell and Mabelle Glenn, *The Psychology of School Music Teaching*. New York, Silver Burdett Company, 2nd edition, 1938. Chapter 11, "Singing."

A systematic account of the act of singing, with practical implications.

James L. Mursell, *Music and the Classroom Teacher*. New York, Silver Burdett Company, 1951. Chapter 6, "Singing."

Anne E. Pierce, *Class Lessons in Singing*. New York, Silver Burdett Company, 1937.

CHAPTER EIGHT

Instruments and Musical Growth

The Principle

In a program planned to promote musical growth, the essential function of experiences with instruments will be to make musical response richer, deeper, wider, more precise, and more dynamic.

How easy it is to take instrumental music for granted, as an obvious part of a complete music program! But it is always the obvious things, above all, that are most worth questioning. If you accept instrumental music "because it is there," or because "everyone admits" that children should have the chance to learn to play instruments, and that bands and orchestras are desirable, you can hardly have any well-thought-out ideas about how instrumental music should be handled. All you can say is that instruments should be taught and used in your program as they are elsewhere; which is not very satisfactory. But, if you can see *why* instrumental experiences belong in a developmental program, then you can also see *how* such experiences should be planned, organized, and managed. Here is the point of our eighth principle. It tells us why instrumental experiences belong in a program planned to promote musical growth.

The use of instruments can contribute much that is valuable, even essential, to musical growth. It opens up a whole range of new musical possibilities. It helps learners to grasp and understand music more adequately and more precisely. And, for a great many children and young people, it is very interesting. These are the reasons why it belongs in the program. These are the functions which it should be planned, organized, and conducted to discharge.

It is clear immediately that this answer to the question *why* points straight to answers to the question *how*. For instance, consider the bearing of our eighth principle on the ordinary piano lesson, or violin lesson, or clarinet lesson. Such lessons usually concentrate on the playing of the instrument, and nothing else. The learner goes over some exercises and studies; and the teacher makes some criticisms, and assigns some further studies. Then a piece is reviewed, and the teacher makes corrections and suggestions, and lays out more work of the same kind. Very little, and indeed probably nothing, is said about the content of the music itself, or about its tradition, or setting, or meaning. I do not think that this is an unfair picture; and if your experience has been different, you are a very lucky person. But according to our principle, lessons of this kind are almost pitifully defective. A child who is studying an instrument should be widening his musical horizons, discovering new musical possibilities, coming to understand music more precisely, becoming more and more interested in music. Instead of having piano lessons, or violin lessons, or clarinet lessons, he should be having *music* lessons. That is a sample of the many practical outcomes of our answer to the question: why instrumental music?

Again, this eighth principle helps our thinking at a point that is both crucial and practical. Like most music educators, you have probably said from time to time, that you are not trying to train concert performers. Very right! Very true! But this, after all, is a negative statement; and a negative statement cannot point to or indicate a positive program. You are not trying to develop concert performers? Very well, then what *are* you trying to develop? Poor performers? Clumsy performers? Bad performers?

I cannot imagine that you will accept any of these answers; and you should not accept them, for they are wrong. What you should be trying to do is to develop musically discriminating, musically sensitive, musically intelligent, musically interested performers—performers who are growing musically through the use and study of instruments. That is the right answer. As to skill, you will feel that so long as your learners are really growing musically, growth in skill which is part of the picture, will also take place. For you are putting music first, and skill second.

Some hard-boiled instrumental men may think this point of view a little too fancy and high-flown for "human nature's daily food." After all, they do want to turn out decent bands and decent orchestras, and this means developing decent performers. Are they wrong in this desire? Not a bit of it! But what they need to understand is that the shortest and surest road to skill with an instrument is always the musical road. An enormous number of what look like technical difficulties are not technical at all. They arise because the learner does not know the precise musical effect—and above all, the precise rhythmic effect—he wants to produce. Blind learning is always slow, always doubtful, always liable to fall short. Intelligent learning always tends toward efficiency. So the wise instrumental supervisor will work for a program that stresses musical intelligence from the very first; and will see to it that when pupils study instruments they are not merely learning to manipulate machines, but to bring musical intelligence to bear in new, more precise, and intriguing ways.

So much for the general bearings of our eighth principle. Now let us go on to its more detailed applications.

What Instruments Are and What They Offer

Our eighth principle tells us that instrumental experience belongs in our program because of its effects on musical growth;

and it goes on to say, at least in a general way, what those effects can be. These growth-producing, developmental effects are possible because of the nature of musical instruments, and because of their distinctive possibilities.

Here I am going to ask you to think about what may seem quite an odd question. *What is a musical instrument?* My guess would be that you have never asked this question, for it is certainly not a common one. I believe, however, that you will be surprised to find how worth-while the question is, and how much an answer to it can tell you about what ought to be done with instruments in a developmental program.

Very likely your first thought would be to answer the question by the method of "pointing." Here are the brasses, here are the strings, here are the woodwinds, here is the percussion family, here is a piano, here is an organ, here perhaps are a few more. *These*, you say, are the things that we call musical instruments. Certainly your answer would be quite true so far as it went. But it would not be sufficient. It would not be general enough. The true general answer is that *a musical instrument is a mechanical device for making musical sounds.*

Obvious, did you say? Very well! But consider what the answer immediately begins to do to our thinking. Our standard instruments are beautiful and intricate machines for musicmaking; but they are instruments, not because they are beautiful and intricate, but because they are machines. A kazoo is a machine for making musical sounds. So are half-a-dozen bottles containing varying amounts of water. So is a steam radiator with a stick resting on it. So, for the matter of that, are hands that one can clap with, and knees that one can slap. They are crude, they are simple. But they are, in some respects, just as genuinely musical instruments as a Stradivarius violin, and have many of the same psychological characteristics.

Rattles, drums, gongs, whistles, and suchlike, have been used the world over for ages. The eminent psychologist Wundt thought that music may have begun when some primitive human sat himself down in the shade of a tree and twanged out various notes on a catgut string, holding one end in his teeth and the other in his hand. Whether or not this person was really the first musician, he was certainly an instrumental performer, and just as genuinely so as Rubinstein or Menuhin (only not quite so good). All such simple instruments have very limited possibilities. But all of them share many of the distinctive values of musical instruments along with the aristocracy of the breed, such as Stradivari, Steinway, and Erard families. So our answer to the seemingly odd question: What is a musical instrument, already warns us not to be snobbish, not to make judgments in advance, not to despise some music-making machine because it is crude and simple. Any music-making machine can contribute something to musical growth. It can contribute something that cannot be derived from singing, because the voice is precisely *not* a mechanical means of making music, as I have already insisted. Musical instruments contribute to musical growth because of certain basic characteristics and possibilities common to all of them. When we see what these characteristics and possibilities are, we will also come to see a good deal of how to manage instrumental music in our program.

1. Let us begin by considering the *musical values and characteristics* of musical instruments.

A. Musical instruments tend to make music precise and definite. This they do in several ways.

First, instruments make music precise and definite through their acoustical characteristics. It is perfectly possible to have vocal music without any defined notes at all, and certainly without anything in the least like a fixed scale. Modern musicians may find it hard to accept, but the indubitable fact is that there has been an enormous amount of music in the world without any scales and even without any notes. Such music consists simply of tunes. Some of these tunes are handed down through generations; others are invented by individuals who treat them as their personal possessions, and keep them as deep, dark secrets, because they are supposed to have magic potency. But when an instrument is being used, one cannot slide around at will. One is immediately limited to certain possible sounds. Hence definite scales arise. Many East Indian scales are bell scales or marimba scales. In some parts of the world music is made with bugle scales. Our own diatonic scale is originally a harp-player's scale, and arose as such in ancient Greece.

Second, instruments make music precise and definite through their manipulative requirements. An instrument is a machine, and one must do certain definite things to make it work. One presses, or blows, or scrapes, or hits, or tweaks in a certain way, and out comes a note. So the use of instruments forces a person to think of music as made up of notes. Here again is a contrast with the voice, whose whole tendency is to make a person think of music as a tune.

Third, the use of instruments tends to make rhythm more clear-cut and definite. This is really implied in what has already been said, but it is worth noticing separately. An instrument tends to bring to attention attack, release, and small differences of accentuation. It has a strong tendency to sharpen up the rhythm, to define the pattern.

I need not do more than merely mention the educational significance of all this. When a child uses or studies an instrument, his grasp of musical shape and pattern—that is, his understanding of music—can be made more precise. If this does not happen, he has been badly taught, and his instrumental experience has been allowed to miss fire. If precision does improve, his musical growth is carried forward, and he is then studying his instrument in the way that promises most for a rapid development of skill.

B. The use of instruments greatly extends the possibilities of tone quality or tone color. Thus a whole vast range of sound effects becomes available for music. Instruments can be used to imitate sound effects, and to represent the rumble of thunder, the swish and whistle of wind, the pattering of rain, the clatter of horses' hooves, the lowing of cattle, the notes of birds, and so forth. Often their tone quality is meaningful, or referential—the trumpet for war, the bugle for the rousing sense of morning freshness, the flute for soothing, bell tones for calling. And also each instrument has a tone quality peculiar to itself. Thus one of the great educational or psychological advantages of instrumental experience is that it can call the attention of children to tone quality and its almost endless variety as one of the expressive factors in music. Clearly we should plan and organize instrumental experiences in our program with this effect very definitely in mind.

C. Instruments give great prominence to harmony. Instruments capable of producing chords were developed early in the evolution of music, instances being the harp and the organ. And certainly harmonic instruments fill a very real need in the musical growth of children. The present autoharp is the latest of a long line of harp-like instruments, and has a long and honorable ancestry. It provides a very convenient way by which children can sense chords as colors or tonal effects, which is the proper beginning of awareness and understanding of harmonic content. This color-sensing of chords is the source of an understanding of the difference between major and minor, for major and minor triads can be sounded, tried out experimentally, and then explained as far as seems desirable. Also the autoharp makes it easy for children to begin to realize that most melodies have harmonic implications, and can be enriched by a harmonic background. Piano, of course, can be used for these same purposes, and can go much further than the autoharp. But its limitation is that it is much more difficult to play.

So to sum up at this point, instruments can give precision to musical responses, they can put the spotlight on tone quality, and they can put the spotlight on harmony. These are the considerations to have in mind, so far as the musical values of instruments are concerned, when you plan how to use them in your program. To anticipate a little, the suggestion certainly is that instrumental experience should be universal, that every child should have a chance to use instruments, and to use instruments of various types, and that much work with instruments should have the character of experimentation or improvisation.

2. Besides these musical values, instruments have some very distinctive and striking *personal and social values*.

A. Instruments offer a means of musical participation that is an alternative to voice. This in itself can be quite enough to save for music many children who sing hesitantly or not at all, who are embarrassed by singing, and who, in spite of every approach you can think of, still do not like singing. You would be highly unrealistic to think that you can reach everybody, no matter how well you teach. So it is very good business to have at least two strings to your musical bow, and not to stake too much on singing as the sole or even the dominating medium of performance.

B. The ability to play even a simple instrument acceptably can yield a very definite and satisfying sense of achievement and success.

C. Because all musical instruments are machines, even the simplest of them set up mechanical or manipulative problems and challenges that many children find extremely fascinating.

D. No one has to tell a youngster that if he is going to play an instrument even passably, he is in for some serious study. Thus the instrument itself tends to impose the discipline of hard work for a desired goal. The same thing, of course, is true of the voice, at advanced levels. But we certainly do not expect or even desire intensive vocal study with elementary school children; whereas intensive instrumental study seems quite natural and proper for many of them. All we have to do to get many youngsters to work hard at instrumental study is to provide the right conditions (which certainly include suitable and appealing music), and to show them how to practice to good effect by setting up and concentrating on musical goals.

E. Pride of possession, and a sense of respect and responsibility for one's own property and the property of others, are values that can and should be deliberately cultivated in connection with instrumental experiences.

F. The ability to play an instrument tends to carry considerable social prestige, and very fortunately and rightly so. A non-singing boy in the lower grades who makes himself a virtuoso on the melody flute is rewarded, not only by a real musical achievement, but also by the admiration of the other children. Later on comes the ambition to belong to the junior band, the senior band, the orchestra; and if special costumes and field formations help to build the motivation up, there is nothing wrong with that, for we are dealing with human beings, not trying to develop musical purists. Moreover, the ability to play an instrument gives a person what it takes to shine in almost any company. And if he can even do something with two instruments, his lustre is greatly increased!

G. The ability to play a musical instrument tends to carry forward through the years, and to make music a life-long resource. This is not a value unique to instrumental music, because vocal performance opens up the same possibilities. However, it should certainly be considered as you plan for the use and study of instruments in the program. It is quite true that the future-use potential of various instruments differs a good deal. A tuba player will not have nearly as many chances as a pianist to use his skill. But even so he will have some. And, as we shall see, this is an argument in part for diversification of instrumental experience, but above all for using instruments and instrumental study as a means of continuing musical growth, rather than as an end in itself.

This is a very impressive array of musical, personal, and social values, and I hope you will give careful thought to each and every one of them. Taken together, they are a very decisive answer to the question: Why have instruments and instrumental experiences in our music program? If you are ever asked this question, or if you ever wonder about it yourself, there is your reply—a far better one than saying merely that instrumental work is generally recognized, or carried on elsewhere in good school systems.

But you have here something much more than an answer to the question *why*. Also you have the necessary starting point for an answer to the question *how*. Each and every one of these distinctive values and possibilities, afforded by instrumental experience, indicates something of how the use of instruments must be planned, organized, and carried on. For such values and possibilities are not to be realized by chance or by magic. They are all practically attainable, but their attainment calls for planning and thought.

Extensive Instrumental Experience

A very clear implication of what has been said is that instrumental experience should be very widespread. The whole argument has been that the use of instruments can make contributions to musical growth that are not obtainable from vocal music alone. Hence, if your program is planned and organized for musical growth, you will want all children to have the experience of playing instruments.

There is a very convenient term for this universal and inclusive plan. It can be called *extensive instrumental experience*. That is what you want. The word "extensive" has been used in this general sense in educational discussions in connection with other subjects; but it has never yet been applied to music. Some years ago there was quite an important movement in favor of what was called "extensive reading." Extensive reading contrasts with the detailed or intensive study of a textbook. It means covering a great deal of material, perhaps rather superficially, instead of covering only a little ground very thoroughly. No one denies that intensive reading—i.e., careful detailed study of a small amount of material—has important values, and is often necessary. But the point has been made, and well established, that extensive reading has many important values too.

I am suggesting that the word "extensive" can be taken over into our own field, and used in our thinking about the music program. Here its meaning is almost the same as when used in connection with reading. Extensive instrumental experience is experience with instruments for *all children,* with instruments of *several types,* but *without long and intensive study.* As you cast your mind back to our discussion of what instruments have to offer, you can readily see that this kind of experience can be very valuable. No one doubts that intensive instrumental study is valuable too. The only point I am making is that extensive experience, in the sense just explained, certainly belongs in our program.

There is one great and obvious obstacle to extensive instrumental experience. This is the technical barrier. As everyone knows, it takes years to gain a reasonable proficiency on most standard instruments. True, the time required has been much exaggerated, and has been extended beyond all reason by inept teaching. But even with the best of teaching, the road to the mastery of any standard instrument is long and hard. This, of course, is why musicians, both amateur and professional, tend to specialize as pianists, violinists, and so forth. It is the reason why extensive instrumental experience seems an impossibility to many musicians.

However, the technical barrier can be overcome, and even almost entirely removed. This makes extensive instrumental experience a practical possibility. There have always been some very simple and easy instruments, such as zithers and what used to be called "penny whistles," which latter were rudimentary flutes. But now such instruments are available in abundance, and in great variety. Many of them are melodic instruments, of which some are percussive (such as bells and marimbas), and others are wind instruments of the flute type. The designations of these instruments (melody bells, tone bells, tone flutes, song flutes, flutophones, etc.), are nearly all of them trade names, and their meanings are not always any too clear and precise; so reference to them is sometimes difficult. Then, besides the melodic instruments, there is the autoharp, by far the most important harmonic instrument. The autoharp is essentially a zither, or modified harp, with bars that can be pressed down to produce a number of different chords. The instrument is very easy to play, although recently some very impressive models with a great many bars have been produced. Then again, there are rhythm instruments of various kinds, including drums, rattles, rhythm sticks, and the like. Rhythm instruments will be discussed more at length in the next chapter.

So we have at hand some quite remarkable resources. The question, naturally, is how to use them for the purpose of providing fruitful extensive instrumental experience.

1. First and foremost, the proper designation is important, because it does a great deal to slant both thinking and practice. Various labels have been proposed for these simple instruments, of which such a surprising profusion exists. Sometimes they have been called "social instruments." But this does not really set them off, and seems to have little meaning; for, after all, any musical instrument has social possibilities. Sometimes they have been called "pre-orchestral instruments." But this suggests something positively wrong. The study of the standard instruments

should always be thought of as emerging from the program as a whole, and forming part of the program as a whole. The simple instruments are not intended specifically to prepare for the standard instruments. For instance, the point of introducing the melody flute in the grades is not to prepare children to study woodwind; and the point of using drums in the lower grades is not to prepare tympanists for the high school orchestra. The value of the simple instruments is to provide for extensive instrumental experience, which helps so much with musical growth in general; and, to repeat, the intensive study of standard instruments emerges from general musical growth. All in all, I am convinced that by far the best designation for these simple instruments is *easy-to-play* instruments. This says just what they are. It tells at once their point and purpose. They are devices for getting round the technical barrier, and for making extensive instrumental experience possible.

2. Never, under any circumstances, allow yourself to think of easy-to-play instruments as poor substitutes for standard instruments. Never think of them disparagingly. To be sure, they have musical limitations. But also they have very positive values of their own, and a very important place in the scheme of music education. Children can learn a great deal about music from them, because they are, in fact, musical instruments, with most of the psychological values and possibilities common to all instruments, and because they set up no technical problems to speak of. This is their advantage. It is a great one, and can be obtained in no other way.

3. Children should have opportunities to study, examine, try out, experiment with these easy-to-play instruments—to discover their tonal possibilities, both as to pitch and tone quality, and to understand how they produce sound. A variety of such instruments should be available, and there should be plenty of opportunities for guided experimentation with them. You will see how important this is if you remember that one of the distinc-

tive values of instrumental experience is that it makes musical responses definite because of the acoustical character of the instrument. I have seen a situation in which song flutes were provided for every child in a third-grade group. First there was some singing. Then the instruments were passed out, a suitable piece of music was chosen, and the children proceeded to play. Obviously some of the greatest values of extensive instrumental experience were being lost. You might almost make it a rule never to use simple instruments as if you were managing and conducting an orchestra of young children. The purpose is not simply to play these instruments, but to learn as much about music from them as may be possible.

4. Children should have as much opportunity as possible to choose which instruments to use with this or that piece of music, and when to use them. Which instruments shall we use with a song about a clock? With a shepherd song? With a yodel song? You can see the point of this suggestion when you recall that one of the great values of instrumental experience is that it plays up tone quality as an expressive element in music. When children are asked to think, experiment, and decide in such situations—to choose which instruments to use for this or that effect —they are thinking and deciding about tone quality. But if a teacher tells the children which instruments to use, or, worse still, provides the instrument she considers suitable, and no others, then there will be little active attention to tone quality, and consequently, little learning about it. Once again please notice the great difference between the proper use of simple instruments, and the use of standard instruments, which is, of course, pre-determined by the orchestral score.

5. Always remember that two related values of using instruments are that it tends to arouse interest, and that it offers an alternative to singing. This suggests that you should use simple instruments freely, flexibly, imaginatively, in as many ways as you can think of. For instance, you can use them to bring out

the melody of a song while it is being sung, before it is sung, or after it has been sung. You can use them to highlight striking and interesting effects in a song, here, as always, stimulating and guiding the choices of the children whenever possible. You can use them for playing descants, second parts, or in connection with rounds. You can use them for extemporized introductions or codas, with songs that lend themselves to such treatment. Often this plan will go particularly well with songs where a procession advances from far away, passes by, and recedes. You can use them for producing a large variety of sound effects. So far as the autoharp is concerned, it is always a good idea to give children plenty of opportunities to experiment with it, and to encourage them to choose the best chords to go with their songs. Undoubtedly you will need to give help and guidance, so that children will not become baffled and discouraged. One simple indirect way of helping is to suggest autoharp experiments in connection with songs calling for only a very few basic chords. Always remember that what you are after is the experimental discovery of music, not a "show off" performance.

6. If any children seem to show special interest or aptitude in connection with easy-to-play instruments, by all means encourage them. Try to arrange things so that such a child can take an instrument home for practice. See if you can get in touch with his parents, to raise the question of purchase. Give the child opportunities to show his skill by playing special parts, short solos, or by demonstrating the use of the instrument to others. Keep in mind the thought that interest is very important, and that it is often catching.

7. The question of making simple instruments at home or at school naturally comes up. Projects of this kind are entirely feasible. Also they have some quite definite, down-to-earth values. They can be a way of adding to the stock of available instruments when purchase is not possible. They call for some rather intensive and careful study of acoustical characteristics.

For some children they constitute a rewarding manual activity. However, the making of simple instruments is not a panacea. There are some situations where is can be very rewarding. But there are other situations where time and energy can be more advantageously spent in other ways.

8. There is a close and natural tie-up between extensive instrumental experience and music reading. This tie-up is favored because of the definiteness which is a striking characteristic of all music-making machines. Most of these simple instruments produce a certain set of tones, and no others. The production of each tone calls for a definite, clear-cut manipulation. Hence the effect of the instrument is to call attention very strongly to constituent tones. This is certainly a help, and instruments should be used for the development of music reading. But it also indicates that the teaching of music reading should by no manner of means be confined to instrumental experiences. The flow, the relationships, the melodic and phrase pattern of music are just as important as its separate constituent notes; and these factors are featured better by the voice than by any instrument.

There is also another way in which the use of instruments can help with reading. A great many instruments provide for a visualization of music. This is true of the piano with its keyboard, the flute with its holes, the layout of the marimba, the arrangement of a set of melody bells from high to low, and so forth. Music reading, as we have seen, depends altogether on understanding music; and the mind can be helped to grasp musical relationships by the use of the eye. Instruments provide visual symbols which help to make musical relationships clearer and more comprehensible.

9. So far I have been dealing with easy-to-play instruments, which are very important and valuable. But please do not think that extensive instrumental experience is limited to them. Children should have opportunities to examine, and so far as possible, to explore standard instruments as well. Pictures of

standard instruments are much less valuable that the instruments themselves. Children should see them, have them demonstrated, hear them played, learn their uses and the effects they can produce, and have chances to handle and sound them. Experiences of this kind are good promotional and recruiting opportunities for instrumental study. But they are more than this, for through them children can learn a surprising amount about music, and learn it in a very interesting way.

The above points indicate fairly clearly what is meant by extensive instrumental experience. Never consider such experience as trivial or superficial. People sometimes speak condescendingly, not to say disparagingly, of easy-to-play instruments, because they are musically limited. Why should a child use an autoharp, they ask, if he has the chance to practice on a Steinway grand piano? Personally, if I could arrange a child's music education to my liking, I would get him to using autoharp, melody bells, a marimba, a melody flute, drums, and maracca, as well as his voice—and also to practicing on the best concert grand piano available. I am quite sure he would learn a great deal about music from each of these media, and that each medium would give him something that none of the others could yield. The piano would have a noble quality; but it would be so difficult that my learner could think of little else than the problems of making it sound. The autoharp would teach him chords, and he could transfer these to the piano. The melodic instruments would teach him how tunes are put together. The use of his voice would teach him flow, and continuity, and phrase. The drums and the maracca would play up the vital factor of rhythm, although something more would be needed here. This would be a many-sided, repaying music education; and through this wide and varied range of experiences I would confidently expect that the child's musical growth would move onward toward favorable outcomes.

Intensive Instrumental Study

In contrast to extensive instrumental experience, intensive instrumental study means specialized work, usually on a single instrument, aimed at competent performing ability. People often think of this as the only kind of instrumental work, and when they talk about the place of instruments in the program, they have in mind intensive study and nothing else. That this is a mistake we have already seen. And it is a serious mistake, because extensive instrumental experience is very important and very valuable—so much so that a music program which does not provide adequately for it is sure to have a reduced effectiveness.

It is not my intention to go into a detailed discussion of intensive instrumental study; but I must try to indicate with sufficient clearness its relationship to the thinking presented in this book, and its setting in the developmental program as a whole. This is very important, because the teaching of instruments often seems pretty much like an isolated specialty, and is often carried on almost as a program within the program, with very little relationship to anything else.

I have talked to a good many earnest and able instrumental teachers who are aware of this isolation, who sense something wrong in it, but do not see what to do about it. I try to point out that technique should be developed out of musical situations, that all good technical study is music study, that the learning of an instrument should be part of a child's total musical growth, and not the acquisition of a special skill unrelated to everything else. Usually they are inclined to agree in principle; but they do not see how to apply these ideas in practice. Whether the considerations I am about to present add up to a totally satisfactory answer I must leave to the judgment of others. But I am sure they do indicate some constructive lines for thinking, planning, and acting, which can lead to adequate solutions.

1. *Intensive instrumental study should emerge out of the general program, and should proceed in a continuing setting of broad musical experiences.* This is my first suggestion, and I think it is the crucial one.

The besetting weakness of a great deal of instrumental study, both in studios and schools, is narrowness. Music study itself is virtually made identical with learning piano, violin, clarinet, and so forth. There is a strong natural pull in this direction, because the intensive study of an instrument is difficult, and also very intriguing. A youngster easily comes to feel that there is something solid about practicing his instrument; that this is what gets him somewhere; that this is about all that really matters. Unfortunately, too, a good many teachers of instruments aid and abet this feeling, because to some extent they themselves share it. Also it is possible that the general program is so superficial, or so mechanical, or so lacking in real musical content and significance, that it does not command the respect of serious-minded specialists.

But whatever the reason for it may be, narrow specialization of this kind has many unfortunate consequences, among them being the fact that it actually works against effectiveness and rapid progress within the specialty. Almost any top-ranking virtuoso will agree that a first-rate clarinettist, or violinist, or pianist should also be a broad-gauge musician, and indeed must be if he is really to attain the highest level in his specialty. But by the time this becomes clear to young people, if it ever does, the opportunity is past, and the awakening has come too late. All of us, therefore, including instrumental teachers, should remember that the learners for whom we are responsible will certainly be missing something of genuine and life-long value if intensive instrumental study means narrow specialization and nothing more. On the other hand, great benefits will accrue if we plan our work so that intensive study emerges from the general program, and goes on in a continuing setting of broad musical experiences. Let us see what some of these benefits are. To make everything as specific as possible, let us center on the case of Bill, a fourth-grader, who is just starting the study of clarinet.

A. Bill's musical development up to this point will have much to do with his approach to his instrument. If he has had only sporadic experiences, or if he has had nothing but a sequence of mechanical lessons on the so-called fundamentals, he is all set for narrow specialization. For him, clarinet study and real music study will mean just about the same thing. But let us say that he has already developed a considerable responsiveness to music as an art. He has dealt with many kinds of music, and has felt their appeal. He already has a kind of built-in awareness that music arises out of and expresses human experience. He may not yet be an independent reader, and probably will not be; but he has achieved some real understanding of what music is, how it is organized, and what makes it expressive, by coming to understand the musical significance of eye-symbols. Moreover (and this is very important indeed), his feeling for rhythm and rhythmic patterns is already shaping up. Clearly, he is in good condition to approach the study of clarinet not simply as a machine to be manipulated, but as a new and intriguing means of making music.

B. Moreover, it will be very valuable for Bill to continue with his broad, general musical experiences. There are still new musical realms to be explored, new kinds of music to be enjoyed and appreciated. Bill still has much to discover, much to learn, about the content of music itself. The clarinet study on which he has newly embarked will contribute to these other, more extensive experiences; but it certainly cannot be a substitute for them. Then, more specifically, a continuing contact with other media of performance will be very valuable for him. The clarinet is not a harmonic instrument, and many quite good clarinet players have only the most rudimentary notion of harmony, decidedly to their disadvantage. This need not happen to Bill; for the autoharp will still be used in the general program, and chording on the piano is also possible. Anyone who has ever seen even a first-rate woodwind player tied up in knots over the simplest problem in keyboard harmony knows how much this can mean. Furthermore, we shall certainly hope that Bill will keep right on singing. Singing experience can do so many things for any musician, for any performer—some of the most valuable of these things being the least tangible—that we cannot doubt the value to Bill of a continuation with the vocal medium. The whole effect and tendency of these broad experiences, once again, will be to lead Bill always to regard his clarinet as a means of music-making, not a tricky piece of mechanism.

C. Of course the way Bill is actually taught the clarinet itself will be a factor of the utmost importance. I shall have more to say about this a little later on. Here I will only remark that the controlling thought of Bill's teacher should be to have him study the clarinet as a means of realizing intended musical effects. This idea needs some explaining, and even some qualifying, but for the moment I will postpone its further consideration.

D. A functional relationship between the general program and specialized intensive instrumental study is the true solution, and the only good solution, to the problem of recruitment. What made Bill decide to take up clarinet in the fourth grade? Who advised him to do so? Who urged him to do so? On what grounds was this advice given? Let me say once and for all that no hand-and-fast snapshot test can ever pick out the right people for intensive instrumental study in the fourth grade or any-where else. Growth over a period of time is always the best in-dicator for these decisions, which, of course affect the future. From first grade on, his teachers have been watching Bill. His classroom teachers have known him intimately in the intimate circle of their grade groups. The music specialist has known him in the longer sequence of his development through several grades, and has a special knowledge of the crucial signs that indicate the right musical future for him. The story has been told by his reactions to a range of vital, and above all sequential, musical experiences and challenges. The direction of his interest has been considered of great significance. Now the time has come when an opportunity for clarinet study is available. Bill's attention is called to it, and his case is called to the attention of the woodwind teacher. So a decision based on cooperative insight is reached. Of course things may not work out as hoped. That is always possible in human affairs. But the chance for a fruitful outcome is excellent, for no better scheme of guidance is possible. In years to come, Bill may well be grateful that the decision to study clarinet was made, because he knows that it has had a beneficial effect on his whole life.

2. *Specialization should constantly feed back into and enrich the general program.*

Bill should undoubtedly continue on with vital, broad musical experiences. But as his specialization advances, his relationship to the general program will begin to change. As soon as possible he should be encouraged to use and display his growing skill in class, in informal groups, in connection with projects, comprehensive units, and so forth. This will be excellent for Bill, both musically and personally; and it will be valuable also for his fellow students. I know of a few situations in which highly skilled instrumental performers have been forbidden by their teachers to have anything whatever to do with the musical activities of the school. Apparently these youngsters' virtuosity was a plant too rare and precious to be profaned by common use. I am sure that such advice was disastrous, artistically and personally. Contrast this with yet another situation, in which a whole program of work with small instrumental ensembles was set up, being made possible by mobilizing student leaders. Perhaps Bill will never render this kind of service, either because he will not become good enough on his instrument, or because the opportunity will not exist. But if he does render it, his musical and mental health and growth will certainly benefit.

3. *Expert and enlightened instruction in the special medium is of the utmost importance.*

If Bill gets into the hands of the wrong kind of clarinet teacher, then indeed the outcome is likely to be sad, in spite of anything that anyone else can do. The wrong kind of teacher is *narrowly specialized,* so that he sees nothing but the clarinet, and *mechanically minded,* so that he emphasizes nothing but manipulative technique. The right kind of teacher has a *broad human outlook,* so that he sees Bill's clarinet study in the total setting of his development as a person; has a *broad musical outlook,* so that he sees Bill's clarinet study in the total setting of his musical development; and has a *musicianly approach,* so that he works for technical skill in a setting of musical intention and musical expressiveness.

One of the practical problems of Bill's teacher will be how to get him started on his instrument. I have had teachers of clarinet and other instruments talk to me about this. There must be a considerable amount of sheer physical accommodation. There must be exercise material, designed to help Bill to manipulate his instrument, and for the most part this material will not have musical value. Does not this mean that the relating of technique to music is, to some extent, impossible? I think not. I think the answer lies largely in the background with which Bill approaches his intensive instrumental study. Musically, Bill is not at a zero point. He has sung, he has listened, he has played easy instruments, he has acquired some general musical insights, and some insights into rhythm. This means that he can see the point of what, on the surface, look like mechanical routines, without being thrown off the track by them. He is already able, to a considerable extent, to orient himself to remote goals. So what might be, and probably would be, almost meaningless drudgery for a person without any background at all, can be acceptable nourishment for him. Let every instrumental teacher remember this: *There is all the difference in the world between starting a learner with no musical background and intention, and starting a learner who has appreciable musical background and genuine musical intention.* There, I am convinced, lies the answer to this vexing and troubling problem.

But the fact that mechanical exercise material for the primary physical adjustment to the instrument can be used without damage so long as Bill himself is already growing musically, and is continuing to grow, is no excuse at all for divorcing technique from music one moment longer than is absolutely necessary. Just as early as possible Bill should be developing his technique in and through the study of music. The contour and movement of a melody, its rhythm, its phrasing, its dynamics, its demands for attack, release, and tone quality are musical problems. They should also be used as technical problems. When Bill works for technical control and dexterity, he should not be working for them as ends in themselves. He should be working for control and dexterity always for the sake of producing desired musical effects. The clarinet is a machine, and an intricate one. As such, it makes certain demands upon Bill's nerves and muscles; and these demands must be met. But as soon as this basic adjustment has been gained, he must study his instrument, and acquire skill with it, as a means of making music. If this happens, his musical growth, which has been inaugurated and carried forward by a broad program of musical experiences, and is still being carried forward by such experiences, will also be advanced in and through his increasing mastery of his special medium.

There are many other things that could be said about specialized and intensive instrumental study. Group instruction, properly used, can be very fruitful. Competent teachers find movement-study very valuable, which means that they carefully analyze the movement-pattern required by the instrument, and emphasize it in their work, instead of relying on un-analytic technical practice. But the essentials are to develop intensive study out of a background of musical growth already inaugurated, to see to it that over-all musical growth continues, to relate specialized achievement to the general program as closely as possible, and to deal with the acquisition of the special technique as the study of the medium in relationship to musical effects that are envisaged and desired.

4. One further point calls for notice. This is the bearing of Bill's clarinet study upon his future living. For him, as for everyone else, we want our music program to reach forward into the future, providing lasting values. But is the clarinet a wise choice with this long future in mind? Probably he will have plenty of chances to play it while he is in school. But what happens then? If Bill were studying one of the brass instruments, or the tympani, this question might be more serious still, for then he would almost certainly have few opportunities to use his medium. No sincere person, with Bill's true interests at heart, can shirk this issue; for none of us can be very happy at the idea of sacrificing Bill's long-term musical future for the sake of gaining a recruit for the high school band. On the other hand, it seems asking a great deal to say that we ought to limit our instrumental offerings to instruments like piano, strings, and accordion, for which future uses are not too improbable.

I think there is at least a partial answer to this dilemma, and perhaps not such a bad answer, after all. If we are actively concerned with Bill's continuing, over-all musical growth, we cannot be accused of exploiting him. Twenty years from now, he may not be an active clarinet player. But he will probably be actively interested in music; and he will have music as a life-resource. Indeed, his clarinet study will have contributed to this outcome, so long as it is centered always on music itself, and leads to a deeper and clearer musical understanding, more discriminating musical taste, and a stronger musical interest. But if we allow

Bill's specialization to shut out everything else, and if his clarinet study centers on nothing but dexterity with the instrument, then we are almost certainly exploiting him. We are giving him something that he is very unlikely to be able to use, or even to continue to want to use, something that is very likely to be transitory, rather than a permanent resource for better living. Skill on the clarinet? Yes, that can do something for Bill—at least for a time. But a growing and living grasp of music, which he can gain, at least in part, as he gains that skill, is a lasting value that will go with him through all the years ahead.

Questions for Discussion, Thought, and Study

1. Some musicians feel quite strongly that the use of simple instruments is a waste of time, or mere play and triviality. How would you go about showing that it has real substantial values?
2. If a decision were made to introduce the use of instruments, would it be a good idea to purchase one instrument of a certain kind, perhaps a song flute, for each child in the class, and then, on certain occasions, have everyone play some assigned music on the chosen instrument?
3. What values might there be in arranging for children to make instruments either in school or at home? Would you consider this an important kind of creative activity?
4. Most of the simple instruments used in the elementary school are much easier to play than standard instruments. Is this an advantage or a limitation?
5. Where would you draw the line between sound effects, which might be introduced during a dramatization, and instrumental effects proper? Is there really any essential distinction? In considering this, go back to the definition of a musical instrument given in this chapter.
6. Teachers often find that children greatly enjoy using simple instruments. Is this, in itself, a strong argument for using them?
7. The bars of the autoharp have the names of the chords printed on

them. To what extent would you call the attention of the children to these names? How and in what connection would you do so?

8. Any chord may have two names. For instance, the chord G-B-D may be called either the G chord or the I chord. Do you see any parallel here between calling a note by both a letter name and a syllable name? Which of the two chord names would you use? Why?

9. Show how a musical background can affect a child's approach when he first begins to study a standard instrument. In reverse, show the effect of the lack of such a background.

Readings

Satis N. Coleman, *Creative Music for Children*. New York, G. P. Putnam's Sons, 1922.

This book deals at length, and in a very practical way, with the making and playing of instruments. It is the best on the subject.

Beatrice Perham, *Music in the New School*. Chicago, Neil J. Kjos Music Co., 1937. Chapter 4, "An Environment for Music."

Deals with the use of instruments in a wide setting.

Emma D. Sheehy, *There's Music in Children*. New York, Henry Holt and Company, revised edition, 1954. Chapter 2, "Children and Instruments": Chapter 3, "The Piano."

Two chapters full of excellent ideas, sympathetically presented.

James L. Mursell, *Music and the Classroom Teacher*. New York, Silver Burdett Company, 1951. Chapter 7, "Making Music with Instruments."

CHAPTER NINE

Rhythm and Musical Growth

The Principle

In a program planned to promote musical growth, there will be, from the beginning and throughout its course, explicit emphasis on developing a feeling for and a grasp of rhythm.

This principle calls attention to a great need, and also to a serious lack, in present-day music education. As to the need, there cannot be much doubt. You will almost surely agree that a feeling for and grasp of rhythm ought to be developed. Whether you would be able to give full and convincing reasons for your belief is another matter, into which I shall have to go very soon. Beyond this, you may feel that, in your own program, some quite effective things are being done about rhythm, particularly in the lower grades. This is so in a great many places, and very likely it is the case with you. But it is with the follow-up—with what happens beyond the lower grades—that the really serious question arises. In many situations, an excellent start is made in dealing with rhythm, and good success is achieved. But about the fourth grade a lag sets in, and the sequence of development seems to falter and stop. When this happens, our ninth principle is being violated. And the result is that we are turning out a great many learners who are rhythmically immature, and whose whole musical responsiveness is thereby compromized.

Our principle tells us that there must be an explicit emphasis on rhythm all through the program. It implies that growth in feeling for and grasp of rhythm must continue throughout the program. What this means, in a practical sense, I shall try to explain in the present chapter.

The Importance of Rhythm

Everyone agrees that rhythm is very important. To say so is a truism. But just why is rhythm important? Just how is it important? Just what will a good sense of rhythm do to anyone's musical responsiveness, whether he is a child or an adult, a beginner or an advanced musician? These questions are not very often raised. However, I recommend them to you. You will find that the answers will reveal to you, most impressively, the great significance of rhythm in music, and the urgency of developing a keen feeling for it.

1. Rhythm gives life, sparkle, reality, expressiveness to the performance of music. Many people, even many musicians, fail to realize what a decisive effect it has. They hear a song sung, or a piece played, and they know that something is wrong. The notes are correct, but somehow the piece does not "get across." It may sound gushy and sentimental, or dull and flat, but the listeners find it hard to diagnose the trouble. Amazingly often the weakness is that the rhythm of the music is not being realized or brought out. On the other hand, one may hear a performance that sounds masterly, effective, impressive, and yet have difficulty in telling what makes it so. Amazingly often the secret—if such it can be called—lies in the precise and subtle rhythmic grasp of the performer. Performing musicians often try their very best to make music sound expressive and beautiful. They make many dynamic changes and shadings, and introduce much *tempo*

rubato. But they are haunted by an uneasy feeling that somehow the rendering does not come through as it should. Nine times out of ten at least, the trouble is that they have not clearly grasped, firmly held, and effectively projected the rhythm. It is impossible to over-emphasize the importance of rhythm, as a factor in musical beauty and expressiveness. Unless one grasps the rhythm, one has not grasped the music. Hence rhythm should be explicitly stressed from the very beginning of our program, and it should be featured at all levels throughout it.

2. A grasp of and feeling for rhythm adds immensely to the pleasure of listening. When a person listens to music, he may get nothing but a confusing jumble of sounds. This is true, not only with children, but with many adults as well. But if one grasps and senses the rhythm, everything tends to come out clearly, to fall into place, to "say" something.

If you want an every-day but very impressive demonstration of the importance of rhythm in this connection, watch a group of people who are listening to music. Unless they are hopelessly baffled, you will certainly notice many of them tapping, nodding, swaying, moving their heads and limbs and bodies. Their movements may not be very closely related to the music, and probably will not be, for unfortunately most folks are rhythmically immature. But it is as though they were reaching out for the rhythm as well as they could, obeying a sort of natural urge, and somehow getting closer to the music by so doing. Of course any large and very noticeable movement-response to music is considered a social *faux pas,* but incipient movements are so common that they seem irrepressible. They are, as I have suggested, a reaching out for something in the music—for something that is vital—for something that it is a pleasure to grasp. This happens as a common and familiar affair, with people who have no trained and developed sense of musical rhythm at all. If then, over the years, we can help people to develop a really fine and keen responsiveness to rhythm, we will have opened the way to a whole realm of enticing musical pleasures. And there is no reason why this cannot be done, if we go at it properly.

3. It is quite astonishing, and to anyone who has not had experience, almost unbelievable, how much a sense of the rhythm of a passage can do to carry one over its technical hurdles. Many and many a difficulty that seems purely manipulative is almost entirely caused by lack of rhythmic grasp. I have known cases where students have worked for weeks, even for months, to master some passage, and have met with more or less complete failure and frustration. Then, when they clearly sensed the fall of the beat, and the arrangement of phrases on the beat—which is the same thing as saying when they clearly sensed the rhythmic pattern—the difficulty evaporated in fifteen minutes. I have watched a high school orchestra labor for an hour over a short phrase that persistently refused to come out right. The director seemed to have no idea of the source of the trouble, or of how to clear it up. All he could do was to go over and over the notes. As a visitor I had to hold my tongue, but I was on pins and needles. To me it was as clear as day that these young people had no guiding sense of the rhythmic structure that held the notes together; and I am perfectly sure that, if they had been given that sense, a change like magic would have taken place.

The instances I have just given are from fairly advanced work, but the idea applies right down the line. If you want your children to make a song sound like something, if you want them to move along through it with assurance, confidence, and the pleasurable sense of succeeding, be sure to help them to catch and realize its rhythm.

I feel so strongly on this point that I would like to add an illustration from outside of music. You have probably taken lessons in social dancing; and if so, another probability is that you have had some difficulty in remembering and executing the steps. When your instructor is carrying you along, all goes fairly well. But without him you lose confidence, and easily become confused. Much of your trouble is that your mind is on the separate steps, and on the proper way to make them. But, if only you will turn your mind to the rhythm that holds the steps together, you will be surprised to find how readily difficulties clear up, how quickly you become confident, and how well you are soon dancing. It is just the same with music.

4. A live feeling for rhythm facilitates music reading. When a person reads music, he should, above all, *move along*. He must not get caught in anxious note-spelling, or bog down over small details, or break down because he has made an error. Above all, he must push forward. This all-important onward drive depends a great deal upon his grasp and sense of the rhythmic pattern of the music. To a good reader, the symbols for rhythm—time signature, measure bars, note lengths, etc.—are not so much mathematics. They tell him at once how the music must swing and move. This is one reason why it is so very necessary to develop an understanding of the musical meaning of the rhythm symbols if we take the job of teaching music reading seriously. The good reader does not spell. He moves. And his grasp of the rhythm tells him how to move.

5. Rhythm is one of the best and most natural starting points for musical creation.* This is true all the way up the line, from first-grade children to the greatest composers. When jazz players extemporize, the whole performance is held together by a living core of expressive rhythm, which everyone in the ensemble feels and projects in various ways. We know that the music of a great many of the finest art songs has stemmed largely from the rhythm of the words of the poem. Beethoven has told us that the whole of one of his sonatas evolved from a persistent rhythm pattern that went on and on in his mind.

* By musical creation here, I mean the making up, or composing, of songs and pieces. As I shall point out later on, it is rather unfortunate to tie the word "creation" up to these activities, for creativeness has a far wider meaning. Still, one has to bow to accepted custom!

Here, certainly, is a very broad hint that you can apply in working with children, and that you can pass on to classroom teachers who ask how to help children to make up original songs. The music can often flow very naturally from the rhythm of a poem, either made or chosen by the children. Or it can flow from natural rhythms and non-musical rhythms, such as the beat of marching feet, the rising and falling rumble of machinery, the coming and going of the wind, the ticking and striking of a clock. The rhythm is sensed and felt. It clothes itself in tone. The music is brought into being.

All the thoughts presented under these five points should deepen and strengthen your belief that rhythm is very important in music. Perhaps, indeed, you may be led to feel that it is far more important than you supposed. Anyhow, you can see very clearly that, if a person fails to develop a grasp of rhythm, his musical growth is sure to be stunted and crippled. The reason is that he is failing to grasp, and, as it were, to identify himself with, one of the most vital factors in music.

What Is Rhythm?

Having established the importance of rhythm, we must now consider how to teach it. I shall approach this subject by raising a question that may, at first sight, seem remote, but that is really very pertinent and very practical. This question is: *What is rhythm?*

Instead of approaching this question step by step, I shall give my complete answer first, and then explain it as clearly as I can. I will define rhythm as *an expressive pattern of accent, duration, and pause.* You will see at once that there is nothing "fancy" about this definition. It is very definite, very clearcut; and perhaps you may think it almost disconcertingly realistic and businesslike. It brings what is, in many people's minds, a very vague concept, right down to earth.

There is endless talk about rhythm, and many fine and flowery things are said about it. It has been called the "life of music," or the "soul of music," and some folks have even spoken of it as the basic principle of the whole universe. Perhaps you know what such talk means; but I certainly do not. To me it seems to get precisely nowhere. It does not even begin to tell me what I should do—and what I should avoid doing—from day to day, in teaching rhythm properly. But surely that is just what a good definition ought to do. The definition I have set up does, in fact, tell us what we ought to do in teaching rhythm; or at least it indicates the sort of thing we ought to do, naturally leaving the details to be filled in. My definition has only a few words. Yet within its brief compass is the germ of a whole working plan of action. But before we begin to consider what this plan of action is, we must consider the definition itself, taking it point by point, so as to understand its meaning.

1. First, the definition says that rhythm consists of *accent, duration, and pause*. Let us look at this idea. Take any piece of music, or any passage in any piece of music that you please. Strip all the tone from it, and leave only neutral sounds. What will you have? Some of these neutral sounds will be accented. Some will be longer and shorter than others. There will be pauses of various lengths, usually quite brief, between groupings of these sounds. This is the rhythmic structure of the passage or the piece. You say that the effect of the rhythm is not the same when it is embodied in tone, and when all the tone is stripped away? Of course you are perfectly right. Music, as we experience it, is an indivisible whole. No element, no part of it can be separated out without changing its character. But, since our minds are finite, we must think about, consider, and even deal with the parts or elements in this indivisible whole one by one. The melody of your passage will not sound quite the same if the accompanying harmonic background is taken away. But still you must sometimes think of and work at the melody without the

harmony. The harmony of your passage will not sound quite the same without the melody. But still you must sometimes study the harmony independently. The same is true of the rhythm. When you separate it out, you change its character. But sometimes you must separate it out, consider it, study it, deal with it in isolation, for all that.

Did it ever occur to you to wonder why there should be a subject called "harmony" in the music curriculum, but not a subject called "rhythm"? Is it because harmony is important, and rhythm is not? No! Is it because harmony is complicated, and rhythm is very easy? No, again! The reason is that musicians and musical scholars have been able to identify, define, and single out the harmonic component in music, but have not done so with the rhythmic component. So harmony is pulled out of its live setting, displayed before our eyes, analyzed, studied, and taught. But rhythm is not. The result is that many musicians are quite good at harmony, and dreadfully bad at rhythm. Why would they not be, when they have never studied it, or been taught a single worth while thing about it?

This is the advantage of our definition so far. It tells us exactly what the word "rhythm" means—exactly what the thing called rhythm is. It tells us exactly what we should be trying to teach—namely a sense of the patterns of accent, duration, and pause that occur in music. And a clear-cut idea of what we are trying to teach is the only intelligent basis for making decisions about how to teach it.

2. But our definition goes a step further. It says that rhythm is an *expressive* pattern of accent, duration, and pause. Let us follow through on this new idea.

Please take a few sentences of ordinary prose, from an editorial, or a news story, or a textbook, just as you like. Read these sentences aloud, and notice what you do. You read a series of words. Some of these words you stress. Some of them you say quite fast, while you tend to dwell on others. You make brief pauses between groups of words, i.e. phrases and sentences. Certainly there will be accent, duration, and pause in your reading. But will there be rhythm? Well, that is partly a matter of definition; but personally I would say not. I would say not, because the pattern itself—the pattern of accent, duration, and pause—says nothing, conveys nothing, expresses nothing. It is not, in itself, an expressive pattern; and this to me indicates that it is not truly a rhythm pattern.

Now try the experiment of reading a short poem aloud. Again you notice a pattern of accent, duration, and pause. But in this case the pattern has a beauty, a value of its own. The poet intended it to be so; he chose and arranged his words for this very purpose. Instead of making just a hit-or-miss pattern of accent, duration, and pause, as the prose writers did, the poet made an *expressive pattern*. That is why I would say that the poem has rhythm, whereas the passages of common prose do not.

Of course, if you dislike putting this limitation on the meaning of the word "rhythm," I cannot quarrel with you, although I do believe it makes for clear thinking, and hence for intelligent action. But the point to get hold of, and to remember always, is that there is a world of difference between a hit-or-miss, or merely practical pattern of accent, duration, and pause, and a pattern framed and fashioned to express something. What I want to insist on is that the patterns of accent, duration, and pause that we find in music are, through and through, and essentially, *expressive* patterns—that they must be considered such, understood as such, taught as such, if we are not to go straight up the wrong alley. I would like to confine the word "rhythm" to such expressive patterns. But if you find this too much to swallow, and prefer to talk about certain kinds of rhythm as "expressive rhythm," I will go along with you—so long as you will agree that *the rhythm of music is always expressive, never mechanical, never mathematical in essence*. But I still like my own definition of rhythm far too well to give it up!

3. Now that the nature of rhythm in general has been considered, a further question comes up. Is there anything distinctive about *musical* rhythm? Yes, indeed there is.

Think of two pieces of music, both in 4/4 time—*Men of Harlech,* and *The Doxology,* let us say. Both have the same kind of underlying beat. But they do not have the same rhythm. The rhythmic patterns of the phrases are quite different in these two songs. And so, if we stripped away all the tone, and had nothing left but accent, duration, and pause, conveyed in neutral sound, the two rhythmic arrangements would be different.

The point is that musical rhythm is always made up of at least two elements. There is the rhythm of the underlying beat, which Germans call the *Takt.* And there is the rhythm of the phrases, which overlie and twine about the beat. Here is a simple comparison that will clarify the idea. You have in your garden two trellises, each exactly the same. On one of them you train a Virginia Creeper, and on the other a climbing rose. In each case the underlying structure will be the same, but the total effect will not. The rhythm of the beat in music corresponds to the trellis. The plant trained on the trellis corresponds to the phrase pattern. So all music, or almost all music, has at least a double rhythm, that is, a combination of beat and phrase.

This is so even if the music consists of nothing but an unaccompanied melody; for the melody moves along with the beat, and is made up of phrase rhythms that are superimposed upon and twine about the beat. Some music, and in fact a good deal of it, has an even more complicated rhythmic structure. If we put an accompaniment against our melody, the accompaniment is likely to have its own pattern of phrase rhythm, although it follows along with the underlying beat, just as the melody does. In elaborate contrapuntal music, like some of Handel's works for double chorus, there may be a great many patterns of phrase rhythms moving along together, all coordinated by the underlying beat. But there is no need for us to go deeply into these complexities. The main thing to get hold of is that musical rhythm is very rarely a single rhythm. Nearly always it consists of a beat rhythm with phrase patterns superimposed on it.

Perhaps you may find yet another illustration interesting and helpful. If you have ever been far out to sea in a storm, you may have noticed that the waves do not all come from the same direction. The reason is that there will nearly always be more than one wave system. A storm that has passed over, or a distant storm, will make long, heavy, regular swells, travelling away from the wind that produced them. The wind that is blowing in the place where you are does not entirely beat down these swells; but it makes its own waves, which move in the direction it is blowing. So there will be at least two (and often more) wave patterns running. You will not notice these different patterns unless you look for them; because what you tend to notice is the total effect. But the different patterns are there, nevertheless. That is just how it is with musical rhythm.

There are quite a number of things that I must point out about this fact that the rhythm of music always involves a combination of at least two elements. I hope you will pay careful attention to them, because they all have a vital bearing on the teaching of rhythm.

A. First, not all rhythm is repetitive. People often think that there cannot be rhythm unless the same pattern is repeated again and again. This is really a very great mistake, and quite enough to throw the teaching of rhythm completely out of line. A steady drum beat is, of course, a repetitive rhythm. But one could use a flute to weave all kinds of flowing, shifting rhythmic patterns about it. When we try to teach rhythm by stressing nothing but the beat—which, as a matter of fact is not seldom done—we are not teaching rhythm as it actually is; and so our efforts are sure to fail. In other words, our learners will never really get hold of the rhythm of music, because we are not presenting it to them properly.

B. Please banish from your mind any idea, or any vestige of an idea, that the beat of music is basically a matter of arithmetic. I make quite a point of this, because people so often talk of the beat or *Takt* as the *meter,* and make a distinction between meter and rhythm. This way of speaking is quite all right if you always remember what you should really have in mind. But the word "meter" can easily be misleading. The beat is not mechanical. It is not arithmetical. It is a very essential part of the living, expressive whole that we call the rhythm of the music. In dealing with any piece of music, all the way from the simplest of songs to the most complicated of symphonies, a firm and certain grasp of the beat is of the very highest importance. Unless the beat is grasped, sensed, and brought out, the music will never sound satisfactory. I have known children in school, and music students in studios work away at pieces of music, without ever seeming able to get them to sound the way they should. These people try this and try that, but the music won't come out right. Very, very often the reason is that they have not sensed and brought out the beat.

C. Now let me carry this last idea further, and generalize it a bit. We have seen that musical rhythm is always (or very nearly always) a combination of the steady repetitive rhythm of the beat, and free-flowing, varying phrase rhythms. This rhythmic plan is one of the most valuable resources we have for making music expressive. For instance, it is this rhythmic plan that makes syncopation possible; for a syncopated passage is simply one in which the phrase rhythm does not coincide with the beat. Notice the practical implication. *If you want to teach syncopation properly, you must see that children have a clear grasp of the beat. Otherwise the whole effect of syncopation is gone.* But syncopation is only an extreme case of the complicated, shifting relationships that can be established between the rhythm of the beat and the rhythm of the phrase. Phrase rhythms can twine about the beat in all kinds of changing, subtle, lovely patterns, as, for instance, they do in the *Londonderry Air.* Or they can coincide solidly and square with the beat, as they do in most of the *Hiking Song*. This combining, shifting, inter-weaving of beat and phrase is one of the most valuable resources that composers have. And if performers or listeners, whether children or adults, are not aware of it, they are missing one of the most vital elements in musical beauty and expressiveness.

D. So, if we are to teach rhythm properly, we must help children to develop a real sense, a real grasp of this entire pattern, in which beat and phrase are combined to make a living, organic whole. Never for a moment must we let ourselves think that we are teaching rhythm properly when we only stress the beat. And above all, we must never dream that we are teaching rhythm properly when we try to teach the beat as a matter of arithmetic, by stressing nothing but time signatures and measure bars.

E. One last remark must still be made. There is no such thing as non-rhythmic music. Some people seem to think that marches, dances, and peppy tunes generally are the only kinds of music that can properly be called rhythmic. This is entirely and completely untrue. The softest, gentlest, dreamiest of music has in it a pattern of beat and phrase—a rhythmic pattern. And if this pattern is disregarded, the effect of the music will certainly be lost.

All this discussion of the nature of rhythm has been very necessary. Many teachers try to teach rhythm without really understanding what it is. But when they do so, they are almost certain to teach it wrongly. An understanding of just what one is trying to convey is always the first step toward planning good procedures. But now we are ready to consider how rhythm should be taught, how children can best be helped to develop a feeling for and grasp of rhythm.

Developing Rhythmic Grasp: I: Expressive Bodily Movement

1. The first and most essential approach to rhythm is by way of bodily movement. This is because of the relationship between

rhythm and movement. Extensive research has done much to clear up this relationship.

It has been seriously questioned whether what we call our sense of rhythm is actually identical with the feeling of bodily movement. After all, one can grasp a rhythmic pattern quite well even when one is lying perfectly still. But what is quite certain is that the best way to grasp a rhythmic pattern is by way of movement. Indeed, some experiments have even indicated that, if a person does not feel a rhythm in his muscles, he never gets hold of it at all. From muscular feeling and movement to mental grasp is always the right order. Indeed, it is the only order that will really work. For if a person starts off with the intellectual or arithmetical representation of a rhythmic pattern, it is very probable that he will never grasp its reality at all.

I have been told by an experienced dance teacher that she finds trained musicians unusually bad pupils. In fact, she says that she usually has to tell them whether a given dance tune is in 2/4, 3/4, or 4/4 time, because they simply do not sense it from the music. Now of course these musicians could tell you in a moment what the 2/4, 3/4, or 4/4 time signature meant. That is, they could give you a nice explanation in words or in figures. But when they are up against the real thing, which is the musical pattern itself, they cannot tell t'other from which. And they have no idea how to move to the rhythm without a helpful word from teacher, because the music itself does not cue them in. So, if you have the least notion of teaching rhythm by starting with arithmetic, you had better forget it. Rhythm is simply not taught and learned that way.

You may be quite ready to agree that the right approach to rhythm is from movement to understanding where children are concerned. Undoubtedly this is so. But it is the right approach to rhythm for everybody—for persons of eighty just as much as for persons of eight. This is so because of the nature of rhythm itself.

2. Research tells us that by far the best approach to rhythm is

by way of movement, and even suggests that this may be the only possible approach that will really get us anywhere. But it goes beyond this. It gives us some very useful information about the *kind* of movement to choose.

For getting a feeling for a rhythm pattern, *large* movements are better than small ones. Swinging of the arms, swaying of the body, free movements of the legs will give one a far better sense of the rhythm than tapping with one finger. Then again, *free-flowing* continuous movements are much better than short, broken jerky ones. Some people may find this a little hard to understand. But the reason for their difficulty probably is that they tend to think of rhythm as a series of sharp raps or taps— one, two, three, four—one, two, three, four—and so on. Here is a very serious misconception, to be gotten rid of; for rhythm is not like that at all. It is a continuous flow; and its patterns are like the patterns you see on the surface of a moving stream. Then thirdly, *coordinated* movements are much better than isolated ones. A coordinated movement is one that involves several parts of the body—say arms, trunk, and legs, all moving together, instead of just forearm, or hand, or finger.

So rhythm is best sensed and grasped by means of large, free-flowing, co-ordinated bodily movement. But there is also another requirement, which is vital. *The movement must be expressive*. It must catch, convey, realize, the spirit of the music itself. The reason is that rhythm itself is expressive, not arithmetical. So a person never really gets hold of it in and through movement that is arithmetically accurate, and nothing more. Expressive movement is essential.

You can very easily see that this must be so. To convey and feel the rhythm of *Long Long Ago* by means of the spectacular antics of a drum majorette would be monstrous, even if the movements coincided exactly with the arithmetic of the musical rhythm. Or again, anyone who undertook to display and feel the rhythm of a military march by dreamy swaying would look extremely silly, even if he swayed precisely in time to the march. These, of course, are extreme cases; but they help us to see the point. The rhythm of music is part of its expressiveness, and it can only be caught and sensed by means of movements which are themselves expressive.

3. All that has been said so far points straight to classroom procedures. Expressive bodily movement should be tied up closely to singing, playing, and listening. It is the very best means we have of helping children to get hold of the rhythm of the music they sing and play, and to which they listen. To set up rhythmic activities by themselves may be quite all right at times. But our contact with rhythm should not begin and end with any kind of separate, segregated activity. Moving to music always helps one to feel and sense it better. That is the point to have in mind.

Of course children should have sufficient opportunity to listen to and get a general familiarity with any piece of music whose rhythm they are going to experience in and through expressive movement. If you are using a song that is already well known, the problem takes care of itself. But if you are using a new song or piece, then the children must have time to get at least some impression of it, to experiment, to make up their minds. Teachers sometimes make the mistake of calling upon children to move to music that is almost brand-new to them. But this defeats the entire purpose of the procedure, which is to bring out certain things in the music, so that the children can realize them better.

Always go as far as you can to let the children themselves decide what to do in making their movement responses. This is the only way in which they can learn. Never for one instant let the thought come to you that what you want is a nice, pretty picture of movement, a sort of juvenile ballet. That would immediately defeat everything. You will, of course, need to help them, both by the arrangements you make, and also, when necessary, by making suggestions. For instance, you will have to wrestle with the problem of floor space; and if your classroom has fixed seats, this will probably mean using the dais, and perhaps shifting the blackboard. The children should listen, decide little by little and perhaps one by one what to do, try out this and that, watch one another, make improvements. You may find that suggestions about walking, skipping, running, jumping, flopping down and rising up will help matters along. But remember that your job is to help matters along, not to force them to go your way.

Always, always, always, however, you should emphasize expressiveness. What does the music say? What does it suggest? What does it tell us to do? These are the questions to put right in focus. To this extent, indeed, you must control the situation, for it is imperative. But, on the whole, let coordination, and the movement picture, and also precision develop as they will, coming in with suggestions of your own to open up unconsidered possibilities, and to prevent children from becoming frustrated. Make the whole situation flexible. For instance, some may move while others sing or play instruments. Singing, playing, and moving should merge into one another informally, and without prearrangement. Some individual children may be invited to suggest movement patterns, and to demonstrate them. And so on.

4. How far up the grades should the experiencing and sensing of musical rhythm through expressive bodily movement be continued? This is a question to which American music educators, by and large, do not seem to have found a good *practical* answer. The *theoretical* answer is as plain as day. It should be continued all the way through the grades, all the way through high school, all the way through music study at the level of the college and the conservatory. As a way of developing musical sensitivity and perceptiveness, there is nothing to compare to it. It is a type of developmental experience enormously more valuable than the labored effort to produce a correct harmonization of melodies in chorale style. Yet the often fruitless study of harmony is re-

spected and stressed, while the realization of rhythm through movement is likely virtually to terminate somewhere about the third or fourth grade.

The trouble is that, about that level, youngsters begin to find free, large, expressive movement to music rather childish. They become uncomfortable and self-conscious, and this kills the value of the activity. Children's instinctive judgments on a matter like that are usually pretty right; and in this case, unfortunately, they are right. Free, expressive movement is always an incomparable means of perceiving a rhythmic pattern. With young children, the movement need not be very precise. It can be spontaneous, extemporized. Indeed, it ought to be. First and second grade children will get hold of rhythm very well in terms of movement-patterns of this order. But there must be a development, an evolution, of rhythmic grasp.

No doubt you can see well enough what this means. It means *first*, increasing precision, so that the bodily movement becomes more and more exactly coordinated with the musical rhythm. And *second*, it means increasing subtlety and finesse, so that finer and finer points in the musical rhythm are brought out, sensed, and realized in the pattern of movement. When this evolution, this development toward increasing maturity is not provided for, and does not take place, a time will certainly come when children will consider the whole activity babyish, and from that point on they will have none of it.

What is often done as children grow older, is to introduce movements of a more formal, patterned, and controlled type. Instead of inviting and encouraging children to do anything that the music tells them to, action songs, play-party songs, folk dances, square dances, and the like are used. Undoubtedly these will work all right, in the sense that the children will accept and enjoy them. Undoubtedly, too, the children get something out of them. But whether these activities really lead to a finer, more precise, surer, and better grasp of musical rhythm is quite another matter. My personal conviction is that they do not. The reason is that an invisible but fateful line has been crossed. In the lower grades the children are led to think about and notice the music, and to use the music as their guide. But later on they are led to think about the figures and steps of the dance, the doings required by the play-party song. Whereas at an earlier stage, a genuine realization in movement of musical rhythms goes on, now a transition has taken place, and children are doing dances and enjoying little social revels, with music as an obbligato, not as a controlling guide.

I am sure that some of my good friends in music education will be very much annoyed at this discouraging analysis. If they can refute it, no one would be better pleased than I. Some of them are much devoted to play-party games, folk dances, and square dances. I quite agree that these are charming, and in many respects valuable activities. But if we let ourselves think for one moment that they really bring children's rhythmic responses to greater maturity, more precision, more subtlety, I am convinced that we are fooling ourselves.

As a matter of fact there is available a practical answer to this problem. It is embodied in the system known as Dalcroze Eurhythmics. Dalcroze Eurhythmics is an elaborate plan for the realization of musical rhythm in and through bodily movement. It is worked out in great detail and specificity, with very definite procedures. It begins simply enough. But no one familiar with it can think that it keeps children very long on a babyish level. In some places in this country it is taught and used. But its widespread introduction into our schools has presented serious problems.

The difficulty is not that it is not an admirable system, or that it will not do the trick of effective rhythmic development. It is an exceedingly admirable system, and it will do the trick. The obstacle is that Dalcroze Eurhythmics is highly specialized. It calls for various rather unusual procedures and techniques that must be carefully learned. Moreover, its exponents tend to cling very tightly to the precise teachings and methods of their revered master, Emil Jaques-Dalcroze.

Yet this excellent system can be made, and indeed has been made, much more adaptable. Its procedures have been simplified without sacrificing its essential values, so that it can be used in many classrooms. When it is so used, it goes far toward solving the most refractory outstanding problem of rhythmic development. It offers something much more effective as a means of rhythmic development than folk dances, square dances, and play-party games. But without some such organized procedure we are in the unfortunate position of having made an excellent beginning in conveying to children the realities of expressive rhythm, while lacking any adequate and effective follow-up.

Developing Rhythmic Grasp: II: Rhythm Instruments

A considerable variety of easy-to-play instruments are usually spoken of as "rhythm instruments." These include rhythm sticks, rhythm blocks or tone blocks, jingle clogs, cymbals, tambourines, drums of various kinds, and so forth. These instruments can be important and valuable as means for developing rhythmic grasp, when they are properly used.

However, there is a caution which you need to have in mind, because it leads to important practical consequences. The designation of these instruments as rhythm instruments is somewhat unfortunate, and can be quite misleading. There are two reasons why this is so. First, every musical instrument is really a rhythm instrument when properly understood. The factor of rhythm is just as important when one is playing a melody flute or a violin as when one is using a drum. In the second place, rhythm instruments are not mere noise-makers, as the designation easily suggests. They are true musical instruments, and should always be treated as such. The tone quality produced by rhythm sticks depends on how they are struck and held—whether they are held tightly or loosely, whether they are struck on their ends or near the middle. A drum sounds quite differently when struck in the middle of the head, on the edge of the head, on the side, with a hard drumstick, with a padded drum stick, and so on. Children should never use these instruments to produce a mere clatter. Always the conscious purpose should be to produce a musical effect. The reason is that, although we can, and often must, consider rhythm in isolation, we never experience it in isolation. Rhythm is one of the contributing factors to the organic, integrated, expressive whole of music. It should always be developed in a musical setting, and emphasized for the sake of musical values.

In this connection a very interesting piece of research once indicated that the members of the first violin section of a famous orchestra seemed to have a definitely more accurate and refined feeling for rhythm than the members of the percussion section. Yet the members of the percussion section were playing what would certainly be called rhythm instruments.

2. The great value of the rhythm instruments is that they tend to point up and sharpen up rhythmic response—to make it more precise, more definite, more discriminating. One might say that they operate to *underline*, or to *italicize* the rhythm pattern. This is the purpose for which they should be used. We have already seen that rhythmic development means a gain in precision and exactitude, and a gain in finesse and subtlety. This is just what the rhythm instruments can contribute, at least to some extent.

Children should have ample opportunities to examine and explore these instruments, to find out their possibilities, to realize the quite considerable range of effects they can produce, and of course to learn their names. They should be used in connection with music, usually in connection with singing. They can embellish and add interest to a song in many ways. They can highlight any striking or important rhythmic effect that it contains, such as the ticking of a clock, the tinkling of a cowbell, the swish of the wind, the sudden pattering of rain. Sometimes, if the underlying beat is a striking factor in the effect of the song, it can be featured by instrumental means, either throughout the whole song, or in some part of it. The point always is to use these instruments selectively, to feature, or, as it were, to underline, striking rhythmic effects. As one consequence of this, the children should always be led to decide, with the help and guidance of the teacher, what instruments to use, when to use them, and how to use them.

One real practical advantage of rhythm instruments is that most of them are very simple, and can be satisfactorily made at school or at home. As a matter of fact, pencils, rulers, books, and the classroom radiator can serve to underline the rhythmic content of music. So also can clapping hands, tapping feet, slapping knees, for these also are instruments in the broad sense of being mechanical agencies capable of producing musical sounds.

It is very probable that the use of rhythm instruments can be continued much further up the grades than the free, expressive rhythmic bodily movement that succeeds so well at the lower levels. The instrumental accentuation of rhythm can become very precise, and it can bring out delicate and subtle rhythmic effects. When it is properly handled, older children are not likely to consider it as a sort of infantile play. It can be a real challenge to insight, and can obviously add both to the interest of music, and to the understanding of it.

As a final comment here I wish to point out that the proper use of rhythm instruments is basically very simple. All that a teacher needs is to see clearly what these instruments are for, to have a few concrete and workable suggestions; and from that point on she can develop her procedures readily and with confidence. So the use of these instruments is entirely within the capacity of classroom teachers who feel themselves musically limited. And there need be no doubt that their use is well worth while, that it really gives the children something worth having, that it really contributes to musical understanding and musical growth.

Developing Rhythmic Grasp: III: Rhythm Symbols

The chief rhythm symbols are time signatures, measure bars, and note lengths. I shall mention them here quite briefly, as they were discussed in a previous chapter. Always the main thing to keep in mind is that one should not approach rhythm through symbols. One introduces the symbols to give names or labels to what one has already sensed and felt, and to lead to a better, clearer, more general understanding of what one has already sensed and felt. Nothing could be more completely wrong than to think one is teaching rhythm when one is teaching the arithmetical meaning of the rhythm symbols without any reference to music itself. Moreover, there is no fixed or "best" time to introduce any of the rhythm symbols. The moment to bring in any one of them is the moment at which it will help to clear up a rhythm pattern occurring in a piece of music.

I must add, however, that the use and teaching of the rhythm symbols is essential for rhythmic development. It is certainly true that children may be able to recite the definition of 4/4 time, or of half notes and eighth notes, without the slightest idea of how music in 4/4 time, or music using half notes and eighth notes, is supposed to sound. But when children have had experience with music in 4/4 time, and with music involving half notes and eighth notes, then the introduction of the symbols with their related concepts, gives them a new, deeper, more generalized understanding of this experience. It is just this deepening insight, this increasing precision, this widening generality, that we have in mind when we talk about growth in musical understanding.

There is one interesting point about the rhythm symbols that deserves to be mentioned, because it can clear up some confusion. Our symbols for musical rhythm all indicate precise subdivisions of time. An eighth note is exactly half of a quarter note. The 6/8 time signature indicates six equal eighth notes to the measure. And so on. But research has conclusively shown that, whenever rhythm is present, there is always a distortion of time. Accented notes are always lengthened a little bit. Unaccented notes are always shortened a little bit. There is always a brief pause between rhythmic groupings; and the length of the pause is not always the same. This, let me repeat, has been conclusively proved again and again, and never contradicted. Precise electric timing devices have been applied to the performance of the most expert musicians, who have been instructed to play just as evenly as they could. But these lengthenings and shortenings and pauses always, and without exception occur, even though the performer may not be conscious of them. They are an essential part of the rhythm itself, *for rhythm is not arithmetical, but organic and expressive.*

Yet these lengthenings, and shortenings, and pauses are in no way indicated by the rhythm symbols. What the symbols indicate is arithmetically even timing, which is just what never occurs. There is always a distortion of timing. Without it, music would not sound right or feel right. It only becomes objectionable when it gets out of control, passes beyond bounds, and becomes inartistic. So the rhythm symbols must always be interpreted, rather than taken with slavish literalness. To understand and use them properly requires, not arithmetical knowledge, but artistic judgment. They are intended to tell one how the music ought to sound. This is another and decisive reason why they should always be taught and learned primarily in and through their musical applications, and not primarily in terms of their arithmetic. Putting this in words that may be more familiar to you, it means that rhythm comes before time, and that the symbols which seem to indicate nothing but time values should be understood as really indicating rhythmic effects.

Developing Rhythmic Grasp: IV: Some Errors to Avoid

To round this chapter up I will present a brief list of errors to avoid in developing rhythmic grasp. All of them have already been mentioned in one way or another. But you may find it helpful to have them all brought together.

1. Avoid an arithmetical approach. This is the teaching of the arithmetical meanings of the rhythm symbols first, rather than introducing them to clarify expressive rhythmic effects.

2. Avoid a mechanical approach. In using expressive bodily movement, do not *tell* children to walk, run, skip, jump, stand still, and so forth. Help them to interpret the rhythmic element in music in and through movement. No doubt they will walk, run, skip, jump, stand still, and all the rest of it. But they will do these things because the music tells them to, not because you tell them to, although it is all right to help with suggestions.

3. Do not concentrate on the *Takt* or beat, and its symbols, to the exclusion of everything else. The beat is vitally important. But it is not nearly all there is to rhythm.

4. Do not be so carried away by sentiment that you ignore the rhythm symbols. They are not merely valuable and helpful. They are essential for clear understanding and effective musical growth. They are frustrating and harmful only when they are taught out of relationship to their musical meanings.

5. Do not become ensnared by a mere noise-making approach to rhythm.

6. As a last remark, I feel bound to repeat that there is one great and lamentable gap in our procedures for promoting the development of rhythmic grasp. We are not doing what we should in organizing and carrying on expressive bodily movement. We begin well, but all too soon comes a sad falling off.

This is something to which all music educators should give thought, for it is a serious weakness. Thus I end this chapter on a note of pessimism. But it is only a modified and conditional pessimism, for the weakness can be overcome.

Questions for Discussion, Thought, and Study

1. This book has dealt in general and at length with the nature of growth or development, and has shown how our conception of growth applies in many situations. In the light of all that has been said, what, specifically, would rhythmic growth or development mean?

2. Some people say that rhythm cannot be taught. Why do you suppose they have such an opinion? What do you yourself think of it?

3. Why is it not enough to provide experiences of expressive bodily movement for comparatively young children?

4. In this chapter it has been intimated that square dancing and folk dancing do little for rhythmic development. Consider carefully just how people do, in fact, react during such activities. In the light of your analysis, make up your mind whether you agree or disagree with the above statement.

5. If we sense rhythm through movement, might we not expect that lessons in ballroom dancing would help to develop a feeling for rhythm? Do you think that such lessons really have this effect? If they do not, why not?

6. There has been considerable argument among music educators about whether we should begin by teaching time or rhythm. What would it mean, as a matter of practical procedure, to begin by teaching time? Would you regard it as wise to do so?

7. If even the best musicians never conform strictly to the time values indicated in the notation, does this mean that there is no need for them to be aware of these time values?

8. Would it be right simply to disregard time values, or to take any liberties with them that one might wish?

9. Do you think that there are any legitimate uses for such devices as the metronome, counting out the beat, beating time, etc.?
10. Have you ever found that a grasp of the rhythm of a passage helps you in dealing with its technical problems? Why should such a thing be possible.
11. Explain the proper uses of rhythm instruments. Why should they always be treated as *musical* instruments?
12. Consider carefully the bearing of what is said about rhythm instruments upon the use of so-called "rhythm bands."

Readings

Beatrice Perham, *Music in the New School*. Chicago, Neil J. Kjos Music Co., 1937. Chapter 6, "Music and Rhythms."

A chapter full of valuable suggestions.

Paul R. Mathews, *You Can Teach Music*. New York, E. P. Dutton and Co., Inc., 1953. Chapter 5, "Everyone Has Rhythm."

Practical material for all teachers.

James L. Mursell, *Music and the Classroom Teacher*. New York, Silver Burdett Co., 1951. Chapter 4, "Expressive Bodily Movement."

Emil Jaques-Dalcroze, *Rhythm, Music and Education*. New York, G. P. Putnam and Sons, 1921.

Emil Jaques-Dalcroze, *Eurhythmics, Art, and Education*. New York, A. S. Barnes and Company, 1935.

These two books are invaluable. They are collections of essays, ranging widely over the field of music education, but with special attention to rhythm. You will find it very repaying to browse through them.

CHAPTER TEN

Listening and Musical Growth

The Principle

In a program planned to promote musical growth, listening will be cultivated in connection with all musical experiences and activities, as an essential factor in them.

This tenth principle says that, in all our dealings with music, listening of one kind or another should always be going on. Listening is not a separate, segregated musical activity. It is not something we do sometimes in dealing with music, and not at other times. It should go on all the time.

Consequently, we should not think of our program as made up of a number of separate, segregated activities, namely, singing, playing, rhythmics, creative activity, with listening included as one of the list. Listening should go right along with singing, playing, rhythmics, and creative work. It should penetrate and infuse all musical activities and experiences. Learning to listen in this inclusive sense is vital for musical growth.

Of course there should be times when children listen, and do nothing else. It is very important for them to become able to listen in this way more and more intelligently and discriminatingly. Listening includes this type of situation and response, but goes much further, and includes much more. There are many ways of listening, and all must be recognized, emphasized, and cultivated, if we wish to promote musical growth to the best effect.

This is what our tenth principle says; and I am sure you will agree that it is saying a great deal. It is the thought with which I am going to deal, and which I shall try to develop, in this chapter. At the outset I think I must give you a word of warning, and perhaps almost of apology.

The thought that there are many different kinds of listening is a familiar one. Writers on the psychology of music, and on music education, have set up a number of classifications of types of listening. I do not find any of them very satisfactory from a practical point of view; so in this chapter I am going to use a classification of my own. But this has created a difficulty. I have found it impossible to avoid using some terms and some concepts that I am sure will seem strange to music educators, because they have never before been used in connection with music education. I hope that, even if some of the types of listening that I am proposing seem peculiar, you will be patient, and willing to stay with me long enough to find out what I am driving at. For it really seems to me that this chapter presents a way of thinking about listening that clarifies our ideas, and that has real practical usefulness, even though it may be disconcertingly novel.

Having said this, I now turn to consider various types of listening, the discussion of which makes up the main body of this chapter.

I. Normative Listening

The first type of listening which I think we should consider is what I will call *normative listening*. So, at the very start, I am using a term that is a stranger in music-education circles. What does it mean?

We say that any body of doctrine is normative when it tells

us what ought to be done. Ethics, for instance, has often been called a normative science, because it tells us how we ought to act. The subject called Principles of Teaching is normative, because it tells us how we ought to teach. In these cases, and in all similar ones, norms or standards are set up, which is the reason for using the word "normative".

Now there is one very important, very widespread type of musical listening that does exactly this. It is the type of listening that shows us how to sing a song, how to play a piece, how to interpret a passage, how to improve a performance—the type of listening that reveals to us what we ought to do musically, in many and varied situations. I call this type of listening "normative", because its essential function is to set norms or standards, to provide models, to establish and define goals. And I think it valuable and helpful to use a special word as a label for this type of listening, because it really is a special type of listening with requirements of its own, though it is not usually recognized as such.

To show you that the use of this unfamiliar term is not just a piece of word juggling, let us apply the concept of normative listening to the well-known business of teaching a "rote song." In teaching a song "by rote", the teacher first presents the song as a model; and then the children try to sing it. This is a very clear-cut instance of normative listening. If we see that this is so, and always remember it, quite a number of advantages come our way. The ordinary teaching of a "rote song" always seems to me a very objectionable procedure. But all these objections disappear if we think of ourselves as teaching the song by means of normative listening.

To make matters as clear as possible, I will set off my objections to the ordinary rote song procedure by numbers, and show in each case how the objection is overcome by a changed point of view.

(i) The very word "rote" strongly suggests emphasis on crude and even slavish imitation. This is just the emphasis that we ordinarily find in practice; but it is an entirely wrong emphasis. When the children listen to a song they are going to sing, they should listen to it musically, and they should be helped to do so. Enjoyment, insight, and discrimination should be emphasized, not mere imitation. The song should not be a model to be copied, but a guide and stimulus for the children to create their own interpretation. All this is emphasized at once by saying that they learn the song by normative listening, rather than by rote.

(ii) When we say that children learn a song "by rote", the suggestion is that they are learning it in a special way, i.e., by using a musical model. In particular, the learning of a song "by rote" is supposed to be a contrast with learning it "by note". But in this there is a tremendous fallacy. All music—not some music, but *all*—should be learned by ear. All performance—not some, but *all*—should be pointed toward a musical conception. If we say that the children are learning the song by normative listening, we mean that, at their present stage, they are using listening more extensively than and perhaps differently from the way they will use it later on. For, if their musical development goes on as it should, there will never be a time when their performance will not be oriented toward a musical conception. All this is obscured when we talk about rote singing as a special kind of singing, different from and perhaps even inferior to singing "by note"—i.e., spelling out the score without any musical conception at all.

(iii) When we talk about teaching a song by rote, we think of setting up a model which is to be correctly copied just as soon as possible, with the emphasis on getting the correct notes. One might almost say that we think of the learning of the song as a one-shot task. The model is set up; the children go to work; the song is correctly learned; the process ends. But this too is all wrong. The proper learning of any piece of music is not a one-shot job. It means returning to it, thinking about it, seeing more and more in it, realizing its artistic values better and better. It is almost better to say that people should grow into competence with a piece of music, rather than to say that they learn it. Normative listening provides for exactly this condition. The children listen, sing as discriminatingly as they can, get something out of it. Later on they come back to the same song, listen again, see more in it, get more out of it, and so on.

So I hope you will agree, in particular, that it is far better to say that we will teach a song by normative listening rather than by rote, and, in general, that the concept of normative listening is really very valuable and illuminating, and not just a bit of word juggling. From this point I must go on to indicate what normative listening should accomplish, and how it should be managed.

1. Normative listening is not only for beginners. It is immensely valuable for all makers and users of music, all the way from the first-grade classroom, to the podium of Carnegie Hall and the Metroplitan Opera House stage. It is very valuable for a mature artist to hear how other performers deal with a work that he himself is studying, even though he may not follow their interpretation. The same experience is also very valuable for a high school chorus, or band, or orchestra. Notice that when mature artists, or members of secondary-school performing organizations listen to music that they are to perform, they are doing, or should be doing, exactly what ought to be done when first grade children learn a song by "rote," to use the objectionable phrase. In all such cases, a guiding musical conception is being developed; and this is immensely valuable, and immensely important.

Music teachers, and directors of high school performing organizations often ask whether learners who have the chance to listen to music on which they are at work may not simply try to imitate. What this amounts to saying is that there is a danger of the learners' trying to learn the music by rote. But this is exactly what should not, and need not happen. What should happen, and what can happen is that the learners will build up their own grasp of the work as a piece of music. This is what should happen with the advanced artist. It is what should happen with the first-grade child. It is what normative listening is for.

So normative listening belongs at all levels of musical maturity. Teachers of music, whether in the studio or the school, whether dealing with individuals or with groups, who neglect it, are ignoring a major influence making for musical growth.

2. Normative listening should reveal the distinctive spirit, and expressiveness, and charm of the music. It should not merely present the learner with a pattern of notes to be slavishly copied. On the contrary, it should set up a genuine and intriguing musical goal. Anything done to contribute to this is rightly done.

Let us say that you want to develop a Gaucho song with fourth-grade children. Probably the song does not lend itself well to the procedure of discovering the music from the notes; so the children must hear it. If you yourself can sing it with real spirit and meaning—fine! But perhaps you can get a good recording of it, with instrumental and sound effects. This will be a boon, even if you yourself can sing the song well. Remember what you are after. The first thing to do is to put the song across as an expressive piece of music. That is the norm to establish from the start. After this is done, details fall into place. But details brought in at the beginning can obscure the concept.

Should you make interpretive comments, telling something about Gaucho life, about Gaucho music, about the meaning of this particular song? Why not? The great thing is to put across the musical idea, and any comments that will help are all to the good. Should the children look at the notes while they listen, after they have listened, or not at all? You must use your own judgment. Looking while one listens can give a person something; and so can looking after one has listened. It is also quite possible that the children may get a great deal out of the song without using the notes at all, though I think that, by the time fourth grade is reached, the symbols have great importance. Anyhow, the main thing is to create in the children's minds a musical conception that will guide their performance.

Very different from teaching the song by rote, is it not? Instead of a hard and fast lesson, there is musical enthusiasm. Instead of slavish copying, there is musical understanding, and along with that, some initiative in interpretation. This will give you an idea of what normative listening should mean.

3. Normative listening can and should go beyond the general impression or the general effect of the music, although the general over-all effect is very important. But here again, beware of slavish note-wise copying. When children (and older learners, too) listen to music that they are going to perform, they can be helped to notice the shape of the melody, the tempo, the dynamics, the rhythm patterns, the accompaniment, the instruments used, the harmony. These are all factors in musical expressiveness, and they should be noticed, not simply for their own sake, but to recognize the effects they produce. Of course you will not call attention to all these factors all at once, or indeed to nearly all of them. The point is to begin somewhere, to bring out something that leads to a better grasp of the musical pattern, a clearer musical conception of the work.

Perhaps you think that I have made too little of the importance of right notes, and that this is a dangerous omission. Certainly I had no such intention. But I think that people develop accuracy through understanding, rather than through routine. The way to get children to sing or play the right notes is to get them to feel and sense the rightness of the notes, rather than simply to tell them that these are the notes to be executed because the notation says so. No person in his senses would doubt the importance of accuracy. Certainly I would not do so. But accuracy should be an outgrowth of insight, not an arbitrary end in itself.

4. Normative listening is by no means confined to singing. I have already suggested as much, but it seems well to make the point explicitly. It is very important in connection with rhythmic movement, and also in connection with dramatization. Always, in such activities, be sure to let the children hear, listen to, and consider the music sufficiently so that they can get from it suggestions about what to do. Also normative listening has immense value in connection with instrumental performance, both solo and ensemble.

5. Normative listening should by no means be confined to the pre-performance stage of dealing with new music. It is entirely proper, and even very desirable, for learners to return again and again to the model, when and as may seem advisable. Also, after there has been a good deal of try-out, the model may be presented again for the sake of picking out passages and nuances that call for special attention.

There are two specially interesting uses of normative listening that call for consideration. The first is the experience of listening to one's own performance. The availability of tape recorders and recording machines makes this possible, and the experience is often very impressive and illuminating. The second of these two uses is the experience of hearing music that one has already learned to perform, presented by an artist on radio, or television, or in person. Opportunities of these two kinds are well worth working for. If you have any chance at all to provide them, by all means take it. And also, by all means, help the children to make the most of such opportunities. Make them opportunities for self-evaluation, self-guidance, and for realizing more fully what can be done with the particular piece or song, and what musical standards really mean.

6. A great deal of listening that is not intentionally normative can readily become so. Children hear a song or a piece, perhaps

at home, perhaps at school, perhaps elsewhere, and want to learn it. This is a common experience, and has affected the musical lives and development of a great many people. By all means keep such possibilities in mind, and take account of them in your planning. Encourage children to talk about the music they have heard and liked. Raise the question whether the learning of it might not be enjoyable. In choosing music for your children to listen to, remember that some of it may carry over into performance because of their own choice and initiative. These are all very simple, unpretentious, common-sense procedures, far removed from complicated and ambitious "methods". But musical goals are established and musical growth is promoted in just such ways.

II. Interpretive Listening

In what I call here "interpretive listening"—and I think the term, and the idea it conveys, are helpful—music is related to non-musical meanings, conveyed by poetry, prose, dramatization, bodily movement, pictures, events, and so forth. These serve as interpretations of the music; and, in turn, the music interprets them.

Here a question arises. Are non-musical, or what are often called "literary" interpretations of music ever proper, ever allowable? Some people would say that they are not, and that they lead to an entirely wrong approach to music. The claim is that music makes its own impact, and conveys its own meanings, which cannot be conveyed otherwise. The practical conclusion would be that we should be willing to accept music just as it is, for itself alone, that we should learn to do so, and that we should teach children to do so.

I think this position is much too extreme. And yet there is an important warning in it, which should be heeded. It is perfectly true that music cannot tell a story, or describe an event, or present an argument. Much fine music has been written around what is called a "program", such as a dramatic happening, a series of moods, and the like. Yet if we listen to the music without being told what the program is, we would never be able to guess it from the music itself. In fact, if we were not told that there was some program, we might never even guess that there was one.

Some good instances of music deliberately intended to correspond in a general way to a "program" are found in the compositions of Richard Strauss. But a person who hears one of these works—let us say *Till Eulenspiegel,* or *Ein Heldenleben,* will certainly not know what it is "about" just from listening to it. Furthermore, some music has been written to give what amounts to quite a literal sound-picture of various happenings; one such work being the celebrated and quite dreadful *Battle of Prague,* with the firing of artillery, the cries of the wounded, and so on. But this kind of music is always atrociously bad. Even Beethoven himself could not produce a respectable piece that would actually depict events, as he proved very successfully when he tried to by writing the *Battle of Vittoria,* which is a very regrettable work indeed.

All this is perfectly true, and we must accept it and be clear about it. But there is another side to the matter. All music is certainly related to human life, and to the doings and experiences of men. Moreover, it expresses the emotional significance and the emotional values of life and experience. Sometimes the relationship is obscure or general, and we may have difficulty in penetrating down to it. Sometimes it is quite reasonably evident, as with some of the *Etudes,* and *Mazurkas,* and *Polonaises* of Chopin. But everything we know about music indicates that the relationship is there. We may not have any very clear idea of what was being conveyed in the Bach *Great G Minor Fantasy and Fugue.* Yet no one but Bach could have written it. The artist stands revealed in the work. And perhaps if it had been our good fortune to know Bach intimately, we would have gained considerable insight into the emotional significance of the work.

Furthermore, composers have often given us hints about the meaning, and therefore about the proper interpretation, of their music. Often they have done this by means of titles, such as *The Moldau,* or *The Engulfed Cathedral.* Schumann, who said so many profound and suggestive things about music, has some very interesting comments about titles. He maintains that a composer should fix on a title for a composition, *after it has been written,* because, while the music should not be created to correspond to a program, it does have a distinctive spirit and a relationship to life, which the title should hit off.

There is a little known letter of Mendelssohn which deals with this problem. A gentleman had written to him, enclosing a number of poetic interpretation of some of the *Songs Without Words,* and asking Mendelssohn's opinions about them. The composer replied that he had no objection to such interpretations, that they really did have significance, that they really were related to his musical intentions. But he went on to say that, since music is essentially a means of expressing feeling, it can do it better than any words. That seems to me to be the real answer.

But of course you want a practical conclusion. My advice, based on the argument I have presented, is to steer clear of extremes. On the one hand, never encourage people to listen to music with questions in mind such as "What's this about? What's happening now?" On the other hand, do not treat music as if it came from some utterly impersonal source, and as if it would be profaned by being related to anything so commonplace as human experience. No interpretation can convey what the music itself conveys. But a judicious and sensitive interpretation can help listeners accept music, respond to it more adequately, and get more out of it. A trained musician who sees on a concert program that he is going to listen to Beethoven *Opus* 106, has a great many human circumstances brought to mind. His recollection of them keys him in to an acceptance of the music. But a layman, to whom the opus number and perhaps even the composer's name mean very little, will be at a loss; and he will not be much helped by being told that he is going to listen to a great work which tells its own story, and perhaps even scolded for asking any further questions.

That is the general attitude I would recommend about non-musical, or literary interpretations of music. Now let me offer some more specific suggestions about how interpretive listening might be conducted.

A. It is often quite all right to ask children for "story interpretations" of a piece of music they have heard. Of course, beware of extravagances and absurdities. But remember that a good story interpretation can do something to key listeners in to the piece.

B. Another procedure that may sometimes be possible would be to ask children if they can think of, or find, some song or piece to go with this or that poem, or picture.

C. If a piece or a song has a title, by all means make use of it. It can be announced, discussed before listening, discussed after listening. If you feel brave enough, you might even ask if anyone can think of a better title. But if you use the title, *be quite sure that the children understand it*. Some dreadful pedagogical boners are made by neglecting this.

D. If an integrated or comprehensive unit is going on, suggest that children may find some music to use with it. Here is a place where the music specialist can help with the general program, by indicating to the children where to look, what to look for, what to choose.

E. A dramatization of a song or piece is, in effect, a nonmusical interpretation of it. This is another way in which interpretation can enrich listening.

F. Call attention to motion-picture music, its appropriateness, the effect it has when one is looking at the picture.

G. Suggest that children may find a poem to go well with a piece of music.

F. Include in your program music of peoples far away and long ago. Bring out the background of such music. This will help children to accept and appreciate it.

G. Some music has arisen in connection with great events. *Dixie, The Marseillaise,* and *A Mighty Fortress Is Our God,* are good examples. Do not act as though these stirring works came "out of the everywhere into here". If their human background and meaning are made clear, they will mean much more to listeners and users; and quite probably a sounder attitude towards music itself in general may be fostered.

So much for my suggestions. I am sure that there could be many more. As you see, there is nothing in the way of a teaching formula for dealing with interpretive listening. Its values are that it puts music in its human setting, makes the particular composition easier to accept and appreciate, and subtly conveys the lesson that all music has a human meaning.

III. Exploratory Listening

One of the main purposes of listening is to enable children, and older people also, to discover the great world of music, its richness and variety. One should always keep this purpose in mind in organizing listening experiences. I have called listening centered on this purpose "exploratory listening". It is a type of listening that should be definitely considered in your planning. But always remember that the expanding discovery of music, which is the controlling aim, is quite a different thing from learning facts, names, dates. It is the discovery of new possibilities of enjoyment.

Here are some suggestions for the organization of exploratory listening.

A. Try, even from the first, and just as far as possible, to bring to the children a wide variety of musical samples. By this I mean instances of many different kinds of music. Remember that the main purpose is not simply to acquaint children with any set list of compositions, but to arouse curiosity, interest, and initiative—to stimulate children to start exploring and enjoying for themselves as soon as possible.

B. Beware of preconceived notions about what children will enjoy and accept. It is very probable that many music educators think that children's capacity for musical enjoyment is a great deal more limited than it really is. A great deal depends on how the music is presented, and what is done with it. Undoubtedly it is a great mistake to use unduly long selections with young children. But the belief that children will respond, in the main, only to music that is gay, or light, or very markedly rhythmical, is almost certainly a mistake.

C. When music is presented for listening, use the very best medium you can get. This is extremely important. Good tone quality has a very great effect on the impression made by music. This seems to be particularly true with children. Research has indicated that children are very responsive to tone quality, and that they can be charmed and impressed by it when almost nothing else in the music makes much impression on them. You will have difficulty in "selling" music if you have to use an inferior phonograph; and if you cannot "sell" music, a great deal of the educative effect of your work will be lost. Impress this on principals, superintendents, members of the P.T.A., and any others who have anything to do with school equipment.

D. With older children, suggest readings about music, including books, material on record envelopes, record reviews, and the like. There are many books about music that are suitable for children; and an interested child will often surprise you by the maturity of the material he reads—so long as he is not forced to do so. Readings will open up listening possibilities that you do not have time or opportunity even to indicate.

E. Call attention to forthcoming musical programs on radio and television, to local concerts, to motion picture music that can be heard locally.

F. Encourage initiative in listening. Be practical about this. Acquaint children with sources of material, school record collections, rental record collections, etc. Be on the lookout to give children chances in school to tell about and discuss music they have heard.

G. Do not be upset if even older children do not like and accept music that you consider good, or that is universally so considered. Very few of us like and accept every kind of so-called "good" music. Probably you yourself are able to enjoy music that meant little to you five years ago. It is a matter of growth, of enlarging horizons, and forcing is impossible. The best policy is to do all you can to influence children and young people to explore, to try out music that, for the time-being, may mean little to them. You can tactfully make it clear that music that goes over one's head at first hearing often comes to seem wonderful on better acquaintance, for this is perfectly true. It is also true that great music is music that has been admired and loved by innumerable people, often for generations, and that if any of us cannot accept it, the defect—and also the loss—is ours. But there is no royal road to the enlargement of musical taste, and I can give you no sure-fire device for bringing it about.

IV. Analytic Listening

This is listening that centers on the content, form, and structure of music itself. There is some tendency to disparage listening of this kind in the intermediate grades, for it can become very academic and abstract, and is sometimes made so in what are called "appreciation lessons". I have seen objective test forms used in such lessons, which required children to indicate by checking the appropriate item, whether they were listening to an ABA, a rondo, an air with variations, a minuet, etc. This, of course, can be quite enough to stultify listening, and to defeat its purposes. But analytic listening need not, and should not be academic. A realization of what one is listening to, of what is going on musically, certainly can be a factor of interest and enjoyment.

Analytic listening is always a matter of noticing. As such, it can begin very early and very simply. First-grade songs are perfectly suitable material for the beginnings of analytic listening. Indeed, they should be used for this purpose, for children should be helped to notice and bring out simple effects that do much to make them charming.

Analytic listening, first of all, means noticing such things as tempo, the rise and fall of melody, dynamics, instrumentation and tone color, recurrence of some turn of phrase or harmony, similarity to other music, recurrence or contrast or variation of musical pattern, and the like. At more mature levels it may mean noticing themes and their treatment, connective material, over-all form, harmonic and contrapuntal content. Curiously enough, in all the quite impressive and extensive flood of advice about analytic listening, very little is said about noticing the *rhythmic* content of music, which is a very serious omission, and one of which you should not be guilty.

Here are two words of advice that you may find helpful. First, do not swamp your listeners. Do not ask them to notice too much at one time. It is far better to emphasize only a little, and to emphasize it clearly, than to try to cover a great deal and so make everything vague and baffling. One chief reason why children and young people often find analytic listening dull and un-attractive is that too much is attempted. To highlight the principal themes only may be far better than trying to explain the entire structure of a symphonic movement. The same idea applies at earlier levels also.

The second piece of advice is not to stress technical terms and concepts for their own sake. The function of such terms as sonata form, fugue, canon, rondo, air with variations, and so on, is exactly the same as the function of the visual symbols which we discussed in a previous chapter. These terms are labels by means of which we identify, highlight, talk about, and generalize experience. Introduce them always and only to make listening better and more enjoyable. Very often, with older children, they will do this very thing.

As analytic listening evolves, becoming more mature, intensive, and specific, it merges into what is called ear-training. Or at least it evolves into what ear-training ought to be. Ear-training should never be an affair of working at abstract tonal drills, or wrestling with isolated tonal problems, such as identifying and naming chords and intervals presented out of context. It should always center on the ability to grasp, in detail, the expressive musical content. The right material for ear training is not drill material, but living and expressive music.

V. Inner Listening

By inner listening I mean the ability to think or image a musical effect, quite apart from and without any outward sound. We have seen that this type of listening should be developed in connection with music reading. Children can and should be taught to look at the notation, and from it understand how the music ought to sound. In dealing with music reading I stressed the factor of looking, and pointed out that the ability to look intelligently and understandingly at the notation is very important, and that it can be developed. Here I am stressing the factor of listening, which goes along with the looking in all such cases. To repeat, I am sure that this is an ability well worth cultivating, and that, if we start early and go about it in the right way, it is not anything like so difficult as many musicians and music students suppose.

But I also suggest that inner listening is well worth cultivating quite apart from reading or the use of the notation. Why should it not be a good thing sometimes to ask children to *think* a familiar piece of music, to hear it in their minds? Then the music can be executed, and each child can inwardly compare the reality with his previous impression, after which, perhaps, there might be a discussion. Why should we not sometimes connect inner listening with normative listening? Present, let us say, a song that is to be sung, ask children to think it through silently, then proceed with the singing. Pick up a phrase that has not been adequately grasped, go over it, get the children to think it, then try it again. Or after a song has been sung, ask the children to review it in their minds, and then come up with suggestions, comments, and ideas. Musicians always speak admiringly of inner listening. But almost nothing is done about teaching it. This seems to me both needless and unwise.

VI. Receptive Listening

Receptive listening is primarily an individual affair, even though a group of people may be present. It is listening in which the individual receives for himself, in his own way, the message and appeal of music. Not much can be said about it, because it depends far more on simplicity, directness, and sincerity than upon any definite procedures. But much can and should be done about it, for it is one of the most rewarding of musical experiences. Such listening is sometimes called "passive", but I think this is a rather unfortunate word, and it seems to me to convey a wrong suggestion. For it is an experience that can and should be definitely sought, and that necessarily depends on the positive attitude of the listener.

The following suggestions may be helpful; and they may lead to discovering other suitable ways of encouraging receptive listening, and of making it fruitful.

A. The choice of music is important. This choice can be cooperatively made. You may find it a good idea to get children to build up a list of compositions that they enjoy; and then selections from the list can be made from time to time, on the basis of suggestions from individuals or from the group. You yourself, no doubt, will have to exercise leadership, which simply means suggesting music that the children do not know or may not have thought of, and trying it out. Cooperation between the music specialist and the classroom teacher can be very helpful in choosing music that will make receptive listening fruitful.

B. There should be, at most, a bare minimum of comment, exposition, explanation, and analysis. What you should aim at is a situation in which the music speaks for itself. Still, some discussion may be in order, particularly after the listening experience; for, as we all know, the sharing of a pleasure can often make it keener.

C. What has been very well called the "stage setting" is very important. Try to create a sense of expectation. Let the children settle down and prepare to listen before the music is played. Be careful that little errors and bungles do not occur, for they can spoil the atmosphere.

D. Do not think of receptive listening as an "appreciation lesson." Sometimes it should be planned and prepared for beforehand. But such experiences can occur at many times during a school day, and they have many uses, including rest and relaxation.

E. Do all you can to encourage and stimulate receptive listen-

ing out of school. Various suggestions pointing in this direction
have already been made, so I will not repeat them here.

VII. Remembered Listening

I hesitated a bit about setting up this topic, because it does not
indicate what can be considered a special type of listening in any
sense. But I decided to introduce it because it speaks of something
that we all should have in mind.

> "The music in my heart I bore
> Long after it was heard no more."*

That is exactly the point. What we should aim at, hope for, and
try for is to make the listening experiences we organize *memorable*. How can we work for such an aim? Certainly there is no
formula. But still a little can be said.

Certainly Wordsworth was not talking about a music memory test, or anything like one. So please do not go in for the
memorizing of themes, or titles, or names, or dates. Perhaps I
hardly need to say this.

What makes any musical experience memorable is its *quality*.
If you will read the poem from which I just quoted two lines,
and think about it, you will understand pretty well what quality
means. It has to do with the music itself, the way in which it is
performed, the sincerity of the performance, your own sincerity,
and the whole setting of the experience. That is almost all that
need be said, for you can follow out these few hints in your own
thinking.

Only one thing more I will add. If you can organize only a
few memorable listening experiences, you will have done the
children a favor; if you are working with a classroom teacher you

* These lines are from Wordsworth's poem, *The Solitary Reaper*. If you will
read it, you will do yourself a favor.

will have done her a favor; and you will have done yourself a favor. For such experiences can stay with people as long as they live, and shape and mould the whole tenor of their lives.

Listening Experiences

I believe that it is very important to realize how many-sided listening is, and how completely it should permeate the developmental program. It is not a segregated, special activity, but an experience with many phases, many aspects, many uses. This is the thought I have tried to convey in this chapter. It is the reason why I have set up all these numerous classes or types of listening, which could, no doubt, be subdivided still further.

But it is also very important to realize that these various types of listening are not sharply marked off from each other. One may, and indeed naturally does, merge into another, as clouds merge and change in the sky. The classification is set up only to indicate possibilities, only to indicate the immense variety of listening experiences that one should consider. Never think to yourself that today we are going to have normative listening, tomorrow analytic listening, and so on. That would be a poor way to go about the job. But do consider how widely, how variously listening can be used.

What you should try for is to help children to discover listening itself, to discover its varied possibilities, to discover music through listening, to continue on with such discoveries, to make them ever deeper and more significant. In fact, you might do worse than to seek such discoveries for yourself. Many musicians, many music teachers, are so wrapped up in technicalities and details that they never take the time to listen, or to realize in their own lives the fruitfulness of listening. I was almost tempted to say that many musicians and many music teachers get so wrapped up in the technicalities of music, that they forget to love it. But there I hesitate! Be that as it may, it is most certainly true that vital, memorable listening experiences are one of the chief influences making for musical growth, and one of the chief means of making music a life-long resource.

Questions for Discussion, Thought, and Study

1. How are the types of listening discussed in this chapter related to the teaching of appreciation? Is the teaching of appreciation limited to certain types of listening? Does it involve more than is presented in this chapter?

2. Teachers often fear that if children, or indeed music students in general, hear performances of music they are learning, they will proceed to imitate. Have you ever known this actually happening? If it does happen, is it a good reason for never letting learners hear music they are learning?

3. Would you say that what is here called "exploratory" listening can easily become "normative" listening, even though this may not be the conscious and deliberate intention of the teacher? In dealing with this question, you need to be quite clear about the meaning of these two types of listening, which is one reason for raising it.

4. Ear training is usually thought of as a drill procedure. Show that it can go on in connection with almost any kind of musical experience or activity. Show where and how ear training may take place in connection with singing, or the use of instruments, or rhythmic activities.

5. Is there any connection between ear training and the development of music-reading ability? In answering this question, check back to the various procedures suggested for the teaching of music reading.

6. Is there any place at all, at any level, for formal ear-training drills? For instance, is there any reason why children should learn to recognize and perhaps name isolated intervals?

7. Could the movable *do* syllables help a person to listen better? Could their use do anything to increase musical enjoyment?

8. Would it be a good idea to build up a repertoire of compositions that children will recognize and be able to name when they are heard?

9. Might it sometimes be a good idea to play the principal themes of a composition as a preparation for listening to it? Might it be a good idea to have these themes in notation, for children to look at while they listen?

10. Is there any sense at all in which listening can be called "creative"?

Readings

Paul R. Mathews, *You Can Teach Music*. New York, E. P. Dutton and Co., Inc., 1953. Chapter 7, "Listening."

Many interesting and helpful suggestions here.

James L. Mursell, *Music and the Classroom Teacher*. New York, Silver Burdett Company, 1951. Chapter 5, "Listening."

Suggestions both for the classroom teacher and the music specialist.

James L. Mursell and Mabelle Glenn, *The Psychology of School Music Teaching*. New York, Silver Burdett Company, 2nd edition, 1938. Chapter 5, "Appreciation."

Deals with a wider concept than listening, but applies to it.

James L. Mursell, *Education for Musical Growth*. Boston, Ginn and Company, 1948. Chapter   "Musical Awareness."

Listening dealt with in a wider setting.

PART TWO

Retrospect and Preview

In the second part of this book we have been putting up our structures on the foundations that we laid in part one. The outcome of part one was that we want a cooperative music program, aiming at human values, and achieving them through musical growth. In part two we have seen how music reading, singing, playing, rhythm, and listening will be conducted in a program like this. I have called these the special areas or aspects of the program; and in a real sense they are. Each calls for its own procedures and treatment. Yet every one of them is related to the rest. Not one of them can be well handled in a water-tight compartment. Reading, singing, playing, rhythm, and listening are all of them essential components of our program. If any one of them is missing, or slighted, or ill-directed, the program will not be complete, musical growth will be hampered, basic human aims will not be fully achieved—and the sufferers will be the children.

And now a look ahead. Although reading, singing, playing, rhythm, and listening are all inter-related, so that the program is an integrated whole, there are also certain coordinating factors of peculiar significance. These are integration, creation, and administration. You may have thought it curious that I did not deal with integration and creative activity as two more of the special areas of the program. I did not do so because they seem

to me to have a somewhat different status and meaning from
the five special areas I considered. It seems to me that we do better
to think of them as coordinating factors rather than as special
types of activity, or special areas of concern. It is in this way
that I shall deal with them in part three, along with the third
great coordinating factor of administration.

PART THREE

THE COORDINATION OF THE PROGRAM

CHAPTER ELEVEN

Integration

The Principle

The comprehensive purpose of a program planned to promote musical growth is to make music an integrating influence in the present and future living of children.

By way of explanation of this eleventh principle, three points must be made.

1. The principle indicates the true meaning of integration. It indicates that integration has to do, not primarily with subject matter, but with people and their lives.

Integration is one of the most discussed of educational topics, and also one of the most misunderstood. To a very great many teachers it means a way of organizing the curriculum, and, more specifically, a way of organizing subject matter.* The organization of the curriculum into separate subjects is by far the most familiar, and it is still the pattern most widely used. However, the various subjects are not always taught separately. They may be brought together in various ways, so that history and literature, history and science, literature and art, science and music,

* Here I follow the discussion of curriculum patterns presented in *American School Curriculum,* 31st Yearbook, American Association of School Administrators. National Education Association, Washington, D.C., 1953. Chapter 3, "Organizing the Curriculum." This is a highly authoritative survey and evaluation of modern curriculum practice.

are related to each other, and so on. This is what is called *correlation,* and it is a step away from the curriculum made up of separate subjects.

The *broad fields* curriculum is a still further departure from the subject curriculum. This is a plan under which wide areas, such as social studies, language arts, and general science are set up in place of the much narrower special subjects. One might think of it as correlation carried to its logical conclusion. But many people would consider it as a modest beginning of true integration.

The *core curriculum* is a still further advance. In place of correlated subjects, or broad fields of subject matter, we may now have units, such as The Westward Movement, Indians, Early Discoverers, and the like. Or, going still further, the curriculum may be organized about "centers of interest," such as protecting life and health, cooperating in civic and social action, expressing religious impulses, and the like. A great many people think that integration, in its full sense, means a curriculum of this kind.

But integration so understood is wrongly understood. Integration is a psychological term, with a definite psychological meaning. When we say that anyone is an "integrated person," we mean that he is "all of a piece"—all on one note—so to speak. We mean that his thinking, feeling, and acting are consistent, through and through. On the contrary, when a person is full of disharmonies and contradictions, we say that he lacks integration; and in extreme cases we have to do with a psychopathic personality.

When a badly disintegrated person is given psychiatric treatment, various measures are taken to help him to become more consistent with himself. The treatment is intended to have an integrating effect. The measures themselves are not integration, but only the means of bringing it about; for integration is the intended result—the effect on the person. The same is true of education. To say that a person's education must be "integrated" is a clumsy way of talking, and a very misleading one. After all, the subject curriculum itself is "integrated" in the sense of being organized about certain focal points. What we ought to say is that a person's education should be planned to make him a better integrated, a more consistent, human being.

Integration, then, is an effect that we want to produce in people, not a way of organizing the curriculum. The word is used more or less in this sense by those who defend the *experience curriculum,* sometimes called the *activity curriculum.* This is yet another type of curriculum pattern, organized not on the basis of subjects, or broad fields, or units, or centers of interest, but on the basis of the interests and needs of the children. So here the effect of the curriculum on the children is the central consideration. Even enthusiastic supporters of the activity curriculum, however, do not always seem quite consistent or clear. Thus a recent writer on music education who seems to be of this persuasion, talks about music in "the integrated activities program," as though it were the activities that should be integrated rather than the child. Moreover, the plan called the experience curriculum, or the activity program, is very rarely found, being confined almost wholly to experimental schools. And it presents many serious operating problems which, in the opinion of practical educators, have not been satisfactorily solved.*

So it is extremely important to realize that integration does not refer to any type of curriculum organization. What it does refer to is an effect on personality, an effect on the child—and a very important and valuable effect. If integration required an experience curriculum, then it would hardly ever take place, for the experience curriculum is a rarity. If it required units or centers of interest, then it would be possible only in a minority of

* *American School Curriculum,* 31st Yearbook, American Association of School Administrators. National Education Association, Washington, D.C. 68–70.

schools; for these curriculum patterns are less common than the subject curriculum. Some curriculum patterns facilitate it, and make it easier to achieve, than others. But it is never the curriculum pattern, but always the effect on people, that we should keep in mind. Every curriculum pattern is a means, and not an end. All this is involved in our eleventh principle.

2. The principle indicates a modest, limited, yet genuine possibility. Teachers and educational writers sometimes say that the business of education is to "integrate children." This is a very extravagant notion. There is no such thing as a perfectly integrated human being. Everyone has many inconsistencies. Perhaps it is just as well! In any case, anything even approaching the complete integration of any personality is an impossibility.

But still, something can be done—and something of no small value. We can bring to bear integrating influences. A good home is such an influence, and a powerful one. It is a center around which much of a person's living is likely to revolve, both during childhood, and later on. A good school is a powerful integrating influence; and its effect too can be life-long. The comics and television are integrating influences in the lives of many children, whether for weal or for woe. Any subject in the curriculum should be, and indeed can be, an integrating influence, leading to increased consistency in thinking, feeling, and acting.

This, precisely, is the claim made by our eleventh principle. It does not say that music can reform human nature, or make people over from the ground up. But it does say that music can be an integrating influence in the lives of many people, and that it is the over-riding purpose of our developmental program to make it so. Music becomes an integrating influence in anyone's life when it is a center of interest and concern, when it matters to him, when it affects his thoughts and plans and actions, when it colors his outlook, his feelings, his choices, his dealings with others. This is far from a fantastic possibility. One need not say that music can be the only integrating influence in anybody's life. All that the principle claims is that music can be a dynamic center of interest and concern to many people; that when this happens, it will be a good thing for them; and that to make it happen is within the bounds of common-sense practicality.

3. It must now be very evident why I do not regard integration as one of the special areas of the music program. Our intention is to make music an integrating influence in the present and future living of children; and this calls for nothing less than the shaping of the entire program. Comprehensive units may be one of the means we use; but so should the teaching of music reading, or the teaching of clarinet. The effect on people is always the important thing; and if it is to be produced, the entire program must be geared to do so. Thus integration is one of the general coordinating factors of the program as a whole, not one of its special areas.

Agencies for Intregration

Since what we want to do is to make music a real, vital, and lasting influence in people's lives, everything in the program bears on it, and everything so far considered in this book is related to it. But I think it will be helpful to review our thinking from a new vantage point, and consider what is required in our program, if music is to have the integrating effect that we desire.

1. First and foremost, we must build our program out of *convincing musical experiences*. This is by far the best way of making as sure as we ever can that music will have an immediate and lasting effect on children's lives. It is, indeed, the indispensable condition, and it *must* be fulfilled. Let me present some illustrative cases.

A partially-sighted eight-year-old boy with serious behavior problems was encouraged to make up tunes. At his first try, he was made to feel successful. Now he is having countless happy musical experiences, which certainly help to fill many otherwise lonely hours.

An underprivileged boy in junior high school has developed an intense interest in and love for music, due to the school offerings and experiences. His intelligence is not high. His social and economic background is bleak. Probably he has not much to look forward to in life. But there is no doubt that, in music, he has found something that he prizes; and one may hope and believe that it will be a resource for him in future years.

A child hears a great singer for the first time. The experience comes with the force of a revelation, for he had never dreamed that there was anything so wonderful and charming in the world. He had been taking piano lessons for some years; but here is something new and amazing. This is what music can really be! His whole attitude to it is changed. Because of this experience, music has a great and continuing place in his life.

A boy in his early teens is giving a small radio for a birthday present. (This happened a number of years ago.) Following some suggestions from the school music director, he tunes on concert programs, and becomes almost a musical addict. He gets to know a wide range of musical literature, becomes familiar with the major orchestras and virtuosi, and his interest leads him into the intensive study of music. This boy enters the musical profession, which means that, for him, music becomes a very important integrating influence indeed. But even if he had remained an amateur music-lover, the effect might well have been great and lasting.

Our whole program should be pointed straight at just such effects. Notice that they are produced by convincing musical experiences, not by routine learnings. Children should discover the varied and fascinating beauties of music through listening. They should develop the ability to grasp and enjoy music through singing and playing. They should develop the ability to understand music better and better, and so to enjoy it more and more adequately and maturely. To say that the quality and convincing character of musical experiences is a first-rate integrating influence may seem strange to those who think that integrating must mean elaborate curriculum arrangements, and far-reaching and difficult planning. Yet such is most certainly the case. If our program consists throughout of experiences of many types, but which are all of them convincing experiences of music itself, it will exercise an integrating influence on many lives. If it does not consist of such experiences, nothing else we do will fill the gap.

Let us always remember that music, in itself, has an extraordinarily powerful appeal. There is about it a sort of ineffable magic, which cannot be fully explained, but which is a most potent reality, as the testimony of uncounted millions proves. The direct appeal of music is far more powerful than any teaching procedure. What we teachers have to do is to help this appeal to become manifest, to help this magic to do its work, to avoid standing in the way by insisting on clumsy mechanical demands and procedures. Then music will do its own integrating, and create its own influence.

Everywhere throughout our program we must be concerned, above all, with the quality of the experiences we open up. This seems very simple. It has little to do with the paraphernalia of integration as ordinarily understood. It is not the only step to take. There are procedures which have real value. But it is the essential step. If we can reveal to children what music really is, and what it can mean to them, we succeed in bringing to bear an integrating influence upon them. If we fail to reveal this, then all we have will be the bare externals of integration, and no procedures or pedagogical techniques can alter the bleak fact.

2. We must work for the most extensive possible use of music in the classroom, and throughout the school. If you will go back to our principle, and remember that we want to make music an integrating influence in the living of children, this suggestion

seems obvious. Music should be one of the interesting, intriguing, appealing things that children experience in school; and the more widely they experience it the better, other things being equal. What we want is to make music a significant part of the child's school life.

Perhaps you may even think that I should have put this requirement at the head of the list, instead of beginning with the quality of musical experiences. With this I cannot agree. Just a few really impressive musical experiences can have an enormous and lasting effect. They can do a great deal to make music a lasting influence, and a powerful influence, in a person's life. Indeed, this can happen because of only one single experience of this kind. So quality and significance are always the first things to have in mind. Of course, if we can have many and varied musical experiences that are really impressive, really significant, really memorable, this will be better than having a few. But a flood of low-grade musical experiences is no substitute for quality, and may even work against integration.

Just how to get music widely used in the classroom and the school will depend a good deal on the way the curriculum is organized. But much can be done with any kind of curriculum pattern. If there is a subject-wise set-up, teachers can use music in ways that might, in one sense, be considered incidental, but that can still be very valuable. It can come at the beginning and end of the school day, at intervals for rest and relaxation, and just for sheer pleasure. Obviously it can be introduced in many ways in connection with comprehensive units and centers of interest; and whole units dealing with music and the arts can be set up. And in those comparatively rare schools where there is a fully developed activity program, the extensive introduction of music should present no great difficulty. Then there are many out-of-class possibilities, such as assembly programs, lunch-hour opportunities to experiment with instruments, and so forth. By all means some stated time during the school day should be set aside for music, because many important things cannot be done without a consecutive run of time. But even with a subject-organized curriculum, music lends itself readily to wide and varied uses.

3. We must make wide use of *socially and culturally significant materials*. Let me try to put this idea in a specific setting. Suppose that in our material for some grade we include a Chinese work song, a South African song of the Great Trek, an art song by Franz, and the Shepherd Song from the Beethoven Sixth Symphony. (Of course I mention these items only as instances of the sort of material I have in mind here.) One would say, *prima facie,* that this is a choice of good material. Also one would say that it has much social and cultural significance, for it either arises out of and expresses some of the meaning of a social background, or it conveys something of the personality and situation of a great man.

But what has all this got to do with integration, in the sense in which we have come to understand the word? The answer is very clear. Something of vital significance is being revealed— namely, that music arises out of human situations and expresses human feelings. This, in itself, is quite enough to make music more significant to anybody, and to reinforce and point up its intrinsic appeal.

Of course we might make various mistakes in using our material. We might take all such songs and pieces, and employ them as opportunities to teach the musical content—the pentatonic scale, repetitive phrases, syncopation, simple harmonic sequences, and the like; and entirely ignore anything else. We might deal with these materials simply and solely as items that occur on certain pages in a book. Certainly the musical content needs to be taught and understood. But if we ignore the social and cultural setting out of which music arises, and from which so much of its significance derives, we neglect something which strongly tends to bring the music itself to life.

Or we might deal with the social and cultural background of our materials as lessons to be learned, as facts to be memorized. Then again we would be misusing it. What we want children to feel and to realize is that music speaks with the voice of humanity. Any facts, any ideas relating to it must be presented for the sake of reinforcing its effect, and interpreting its emotional meaning.

Let us venture a glance into a by-no-means impossible future. We have managed to reveal to a child that music really does convey the emotional values of a vast range of human experience. Surely we may reasonably hope that this will tend to widen and deepen his interest in music, and to make that interest lasting. Twenty years go by. Perhaps our child, now grown to man's estate, has a record collection which is one of his chief joys, and to which he is always experimentally adding. Perhaps he plays the fiddle or the clarinet with a small, informal group of musical friends, and he suggests that they might try out something by Couperin, or a composition by one of the more formidable moderns. His awareness that music has endless variety, and arises out of an endless variety of circumstances, has a great deal to do with this exploring, questing, discovering. Music will be an integrating influence in his life, and our choice and use of materials will have done at least something to make it so.

4. We must be willing to work cooperatively in connection with *comprehensive units,* and must learn how to do so to good purpose. Music specialists who fear or oppose the use of comprehensive units are making a great mistake. This kind of curriculum organization offers excellent opportunities for music.

What we have here is, in a sense, the obverse of what was said under the previous heading. Under point number three I dealt with developing and using the social and cultural background of music, starting with the music. When music is brought into a comprehensive unit in the way it should be brought in, you start with the social and cultural situation, and then show how it has expressed itself in music.

Music certainly is relevant to a great many comprehensive units. An enormous range of human experiences, doings, and adventurings have blossomed in music. Harvest time, midsummer, springtime, autumn, labor in the woods, seafaring, work and adventure on the great plains, Yuletide, home, love, the passion for liberty, love of country, war, peace, religion—all such, and many more, have come to musical expression. Moreover, the greatest of art music has come from the heart of some man, living under certain circumstances, responding to the spirit of his day, coping with triumph and disaster. Music is not an isolated manipulation of tone and rhythm, but an expression of life. This is what makes it so naturally available in comprehensive units whose very purpose is to bring the stuff of the curriculum into relationship with life.

All this is true, and it is important. But in itself it is not enough. When music is introduced in comprehensive units, two great defects are possible, and they must be avoided. First, there is the danger of factualism. It is not enough, and perhaps not even very important, to let children know that cowboys sang the *Dogie Song*, that Indians sang *Growing Power of the Sun*, that Northern soldiers sang *Tenting Tonight*, that Beethoven was deaf and loved the country, and so on. These can amount to no more than sterile bits of information, and unfortunately they often do.

Then there is the risk of *superficiality*, for it can often happen that music introduced into a comprehensive unit is not in any way adequately realized as music. It may be, and sometimes is, casually presented, casually listened to, casually sung, and that is all. When this happens, its point and value are lost.

What, then, should we do? I will offer the following guiding suggestions.

A. When music is introduced in a comprehensive unit, it should always be realized as far as possible as music. It should not simply be brought in like a museum piece, noticed, and passed by. It should be enjoyed and understood for what it is. Its beauty and its possibilities should be realized in listening, in singing, in playing. For instance, if *Growing Power of the Sun* is brought into a unit on Indians, it should not, indeed, be used for a developed lesson. But the children should be guided and helped to feel it and to sing it so that it speaks to them of something, so that its expressiveness is revealed. This may mean spending a little time with the music of the unit. But if music is worth introducing at all, it is worth doing well. Here is one of the many points in the program at which the music specialist and the general teacher can work fruitfully together, each contributing his own valuable quota. To sum up so far, if you have anything to do with music used in comprehensive units, emphasize the musical quality of the experiences.

B. The choice of music is very important. It should be characteristic. It should be in the closest possible relationship to the unit. It should express the emotional side of the intellectual content of the unit. This is really the reason for having it at all. It is a good reason. One learns about Indian life, or South American life, or the life of one's own community by dint of understanding. But one also learns something about them in and through their artistic expressions, and what is so conveyed can be conveyed and learned in no other way. The intellect enables us to understand, but the arts enable us to feel.

So a casual choice of music will not do. Here again the music specialist and the general teacher can work fruitfully together. The classroom teacher knows her situation best; but she needs help in finding what will work best in her situation, and in using it to the best advantage when it is found.

Moreover, it is always very desirable to encourage the children to search for, find, and suggest music for any unit on which they

are at work. The reason is that this is one of the best ways for
them to realize that there is music everywhere, and that it says
many things that nothing else can say. But of course help and
guidance will be needed, or the children may get nowhere. They
must be shown where to look for suitable music, how to judge
what they find, how to decide on the best possible choices. It is
self-evident that experiences like this will tend to make music
a significant factor in the lives of the children. In other words,
such experiences make for integration.

Notice once again that the comprehensive unit, in itself, is not
identical with integration. It is simply a device or arrangement
by which certain influences can be brought to bear. It is a very
convenient, and indeed a very valuable, arrangement. But everything depends on how it is used.

5. If we want to make music a powerful, continuing influence
in children's lives, one of the most obvious things to do will be
to help them to realize the place and importance of *music in the
modern world*. So here is yet another valuable possibility for
integration.

A. We can make children aware of the many kinds of music
in today's world, how to enjoy them, how to evaluate them, how
and where to find them. This would certainly include jazz,
popular music so-called, and the music of contemporary composers, among very many other types. There is always an argument about whether or not one or other of these kinds of music
should be represented in the school music program. So far as I
know, there has never been any very solid or satisfactory answer.
Certainly it is not a point about which I would feel able to be
dogmatic, or even to speak with great assurance. All I can hon-
estly say is that I think we must keep in mind our purpose, which
is to get music into people's lives as a genuine and positive influence, and that we should beware of letting our own prepossessions stand in the way. One helpful suggestion might be to
present and use samples of as many kinds of music as we can,

and to employ readings, bulletin boards displays and notices, and discussions to stimulate children to explore the musical possibilities around them.

B. We can call attention to and feature present-day musical media, and musical opportunities. It will be important to be realistic about the phonograph, the radio, and television. Certainly it will be well in line with our purpose to give children some understanding of these devices, how they work, what their qualities and prices are, and what high-fidelity equipment has to offer. The possibility of starting one's own record collection may be worth suggesting. Also to arouse interest in and to give information about performing organizations, distinguished artists, concerts, opera performances, and radio programs will be appropriate for our program. Children should know where to find such opportunities, how to use them to the best advantage, how to evaluate them, (which latter might mean introducing them to current musical criticisms and reviews).

C. The issue of so-called classical music is often very baffling, as I have already said elsewhere. I do not think that there is any hard-and-fast and easy answer. One way toward a solution might be to set up a sequence—or, in secondary school general music, a unit—on kinds of music that people like. In any such unit or sequence, the standard repertoire, its extensive use, and its wide acceptance, would certainly have to be featured prominently. This might help to avoid hair-splitting distinctions about what is and what is not "classical" music, for as a matter of fact, classical music is not too far from being identical with the standard repertoire, with its legitimate extensions. To present it as music that people like might make a difference, particularly because the designation is perfectly true. And also one might be able to raise the question whether more music of the same kind cannot be found that, for one reason or another, is not widely known and accepted.

As you will see, I have discussed four practical possibilities for achieving integration through our music program. Undoubtedly there could be many more, for almost everything in this book bears on the subject in one way or another. However, the important thing is always to remember that when we talk about integration, we do not mean some particular type of curriculum organization or teaching procedure. The word refers to the effect produced by music on human beings and human lives. If you will keep this constantly in mind, you will find many opportunities for achieving integration in every part of the music program.

Integration and Musical Growth

The relationship between integration and musical growth raises a broader issue than any of the foregoing. Our eleventh principle says that a program *planned to promote musical growth* must seek to make music an integrating influence in people's lives. I now want to bring out the thought that musical growth is essential if such an integrating influence is to be exerted.

Perhaps it will be best if I begin by pointing out in general the relationship between musical growth and integration, and then follow up by discussing various special aspects of the relationship. When we say that a person grows musically, we mean that his realization of music and his response to music becomes steadily wider, deeper, more discriminating, and more exact.

In this last sentence there are two key words; one is the word "music," and the other is the word "grows." A person who grows musically is never out of touch with music itself. In all that he does, even including the most minute technical study, he is always experiencing music itself. To use what may seem like a crude expression, music is constantly "selling itself" to him, and, as it were, claiming a place in his life and interest. This, in itself, is an integrating effect of great power.

So much for the significance of the word "music" in the above summary sentence. Now for the word "grows." A person's musical growth may start with nothing more than a fairly mild liking; but when we say that he grows, we mean that he goes far beyond this. Music gives him an ever keener and subtler pleasure; he comes to see more and more in it; he comes to be able to do more and more with it. If this process of growth goes forward, music will tend to get a stronger and stronger grip upon him, will seem more and more worthwhile to him, and mean more and more in his life. But if there is no musical growth, or only a very little, music will remain a fairly trivial pleasure, and will never be one of the dynamic focal points, one of the important influences, in his living. So, as you will see, if music is to become an integrating influence in the present and future living of children, we must bring about musical growth. This is the general statement that I promised. Now let us go on to various details and consequences.

Musical growth certainly involves an increasing knowledge and understanding of the structure of music—of key and key relationships, or harmony and harmonic sequences, of phrase patterns, of rhythm patterns, and the like. But it involves something more than and different from a *mere* increase of knowledge. This something more is an increasingly deep and exact grasp of the expressive values, meanings, and possibilities of these structural elements. It is quite possible to get away from music itself in studying its structural content. On the other hand, such study can lead one to a deeper and deeper realization and appreciation of music.

Musical growth certainly involves an increase in technical skill in performance. But it involves something more than an increase in *mere* technical skill. This something more is an increasing ability to use voice or instrument to project an expressive intention. Technique can be studied simply as a matter of physical dexterity. But this kind of technical study takes one away from music. On the other hand, technique can be studied as the capacity to realize in the chosen medium a musical conception grasped by the mind and felt by the heart. Then once more, technical study leads straight to a deeper and deeper realization and appreciation of music.

Musical growth certainly involves an increasing capacity to read music. But this is not at all the same thing as an increasing capacity to spell out the score symbols quickly and accurately. Music reading so taught and so learned tends to take one away from music. Music reading should be developed as an increasing ability to perceive the intentions of the composer as conveyed in the notation, and, as skill and independence are gained, the ability to translate artistically and intelligently these intentions into sound.

Musical growth certainly involves an increasing acquaintance with composers, compositions, and the literature and tradition of music. But this should never be considered as the equivalent of mere factual knowledge. As before, the study of the history, literature, and tradition of music can be almost entirely divorced from music itself. What is required is an increasing ability to appreciate, to discriminate, to choose, to evaluate, to understand, to explore, to enjoy.

All this should make it abundantly clear why musical growth is our primary agency for integration, why musical growth is necessary if music is to exercise its integrating effect, why a developmental program, in and of itself, points straight to the integration of music with life. Music has its own power, its own appeal, its own magic. All we can ever do is to create the conditions under which that power can operate, and that appeal be effectively felt. A program of routine and mechanical learnings will not create these conditions, because it takes the learner away from music itself, and puts him out of touch with the one great and potent reality. Sporadic and superficial experiences will not create these conditions, because they leave musical response at a childish, an immature level. Musical growth is the only solution, the sufficient solution, and its promotion is the unavoidably indicated policy.

Let me return for a moment to some of our previous ideas, with the thought of making them more specific and more sharply pointed and defined. Integration requires something far more and something far different from merely "bringing in" some music in connection with this or that unit or topic. It may, of course, be interesting to learn that the Latter Day Saints, or the Boers, or the Chinese use music in their social doings, or that the music of Mozart seems to have affinities with the *rococo* style, and so on. But unless there is much more than this, the impressions will be superficial, and probably transitory and of small effect. Music must be studied, must be understood, must be emotionally realized in settings like these, and elsewhere too, if its full relationship to human life and experience is to be sensed and its full message caught. It cannot be treated as a sort or side-show, or something dragged in adventitiously and handled with scant respect. Otherwise there will be sham, not real integration, for there will be no musical growth.

Intregration and Basic Aims

The first two chapters of this book centered on the claim that we ought to think out the basic aims of our music program, and that these basic aims must consist of the desirable effects that music can produce on human nature and human living. This chapter has centered on the claim that the entire program must be a means of making music a significant influence in human life. What is the relationship between these two sets of ideas? Is there any inconsistency between them? Should one or the other be omitted?

To round out the present discussion I must answer these questions; and I can do so simply and briefly. The relationship is this. In the first two chapters, and in this chapter, we are looking at the same thing from different sides. Or if you will, in this chapter we are dealing with the general, and in the earlier chapters we are dealing with the particular.

The five aims proposed in chapter two are five ways in which music can and should influence living. It can give people lasting and rewarding pleasure. It can enrich life with the reassuring sense of achievement and success. It can involve exacting yet intriguing experiences of discipline. It can do much to foster fruitful and helpful social relationships. It can stimulate an expanding interest in the whole range of culture. These are determining aims, and the program can be geared to them. Also they are integrating influences—influences which can be foci of living. That, in brief, is the relationship.

As to the question of overlapping, it is always valuable to look at any problem or issue from more than one side. In this case, it is particularly valuable to do so. Integration, as I have already said, is a concept that is both widely discussed and greatly misunderstood. Very likely you may at some time be asked what you think about it, and what you believe ought to be done about it. Certainly you should be ready to make a good, well-considered answer. If you are wise, you will not argue the pros and cons of comprehensive units, for these are matters of detail, and if there is agreement on fundamentals, they will be easy to settle. You will point out that integration has to do with the effect of music on human beings, that it involves far more than any questions of procedure, that it goes right to the very root of the whole music program and is not a special aspect of that program. For a program that is planned and organized, from the ground up, to achieve clearly envisaged human values, and to make music a resource for better living, is a program that achieves integration in the only intelligible sense of the word.

Questions for Discussion, Thought, and Study

1. If a youngster becomes a fan for jazz, or "hot" music, or "popular" music, does this mean that music is an integrating influence in his life? If so, is it a good influence or a bad one? Does the tremendous popularity of this kind of music suggest anything for our music program?

2. It is often hard to get young people to accept "classical" music. Consider ways and means of getting them to accept it. No doubt there is no sure-fire way, but also you can certainly collect many helpful suggestions that will often work.

3. Are there any good reasons for getting young people to accept "classical" music if we want to make music an integrating influence in their lives?

4. Review very carefully the argument that the quality of musical experiences in school is more important than their quantity. Can you think of any actual illustrations, from your own personal experience or the experiences of others, that seem to bear this out?

5. It is very likely that music is an important integrating influence in your own life. What does this mean, specifically, and as a practical matter that affects your own choices and decisions?

6. How did you yourself first get interested in music? Do you find here any suggestions about how to present music effectively and convincingly to children.

7. Review what was said in Chapter 4 about the development of purpose as essential to musical growth. Is not this essentially the same argument as that set forth in the present chapter more fully, and in connection with integration?

8. Can we have "music integration" in a curriculum organized subject-wise?

9. Why is it easier to make music a genuine integrating influence if we have a unit-wise curriculum, or a centers-of-interest curriculum, or an activity curriculum, than it is with a subject curriculum.

10. Is there any danger that integration, as properly understood, may be neglected in a core curriculum or an activity curriculum,

and that we may have only the appearance and not the reality? What is this danger?

Readings

Paul R. Mathews, *You Can Teach Music*, New York, E. P. Dutton and Co., Inc., 1953. Chapter 9, "Music Doesn't Walk Alone."

Again, many good ideas.

James L. Mursell, *Music and the Classroom Teacher*. New York, Silver Burdett Company, 1951.

Look through this book for many instances of musical activities, and see how they relate to integration as here explained.

Paul R. Mort and Wm. S. Vincent, *Modern Educational Practice*. McGraw-Hill Book Company, Inc., 1950.

This is an immense collection of actual classroom practices and procedures, and has great practical interest. Look up "Music" and "Musical" in the index, and you will find many interesting items.

CHAPTER TWELVE

Creation

The Principle

In a program planned to promote musical growth, our constant endeavor must be to encourage and help children to respond creatively in all their dealings with music.

Creativeness! Creative experience! Creative response! How often one hears these magic words used, in connection with education in general, and with music education in particular! Yet very often they are misinterpreted, and their true and far-reaching meanings are misunderstood. The point of this twelfth principle is that it puts them in their proper setting.

It is often supposed that a music program has five main components, singing, playing instruments, listening, rhythmic activities, and creative activities. Our principle warns us that this way of thinking is wrong.

Creative response is not a separate subdivision of the program. It is not in the least confined to making up songs, and indeed it may even not include this particular activity at all. It is not something that happens sometimes but not at other times. If our program is to be what it should, and accomplish what it should, creative response must go on all the time. It must permeate the whole program. For it indicates the kind and quality of dealings with music that are necessary for musical growth.

Our principle speaks explicitly of the *children*. It says that the children should respond creatively in all their dealings with music. But the principle has something for the teacher too, although it does not mention him directly. To open the way for, to evoke, to encourage, to guide creative response in others is itself a creative act. So, by clear implication, though not directly, our principle indicates that a program planned to promote musical growth requires *creative teaching*.

All this will become clearer as we proceed. But before doing so, let me pause for a moment to mention the relationship of this principle and the topic of this chapter to the general plan of the book. In this third part we are dealing with the coordinating factors of our program. I am sure you will see already that creativeness is one of these coordinating, all-permeating factors, and not a special or segregated area of the program. I want to stress this because it helps to make the plan of the book clear. But still more I want to stress it because of the importance of the idea itself. To regard creation as a special type of work is a fatal mistake. To realize that it is all-pervading, all-permeating points straight to the kind of teaching that "blesseth him that gives, and him that takes."

What Is Creative Response?

What should you understand, what should you have in mind, by creative response? I ask you to face this question, because much of your planning, much of the work you do, will depend upon your answer.

1. The first and most obvious thing to say is that a creative response is one from which comes *something new*. A friend read Shakespeare's poem *Hark! Hark! The Lark!* aloud to Schubert, and instantly the lovely song flashed into his mind. A great novelist, Arnold Bennett, saw two old women eating together in a cheap Parisian restaurant, and the idea for his best novel

came to him. The novel took years to write, but the seed was planted there. On a stormy winter night, Longfellow was sitting before the fire in a seaside tavern, listening to the sound of wind and waves. As he sat there, *The Wreck of the Hesperus* took shape in his mind. Newton saw an apple fall from a tree, and the answer to many questionings and wonderings arrived, and the law of gravity came forth. All these are instances of creative response, for in all of them something new was born.

But you may find these instances discouraging, even though interesting. They are all the creative responses of great and gifted men, from which great works and great ideas emerged. Perhaps you think them far removed from anything that ordinary people can do—far removed from what is possible for you and for your children. Not at all! To be sure, they are great and striking creative acts. But what makes them creative is not their impressiveness or their wonder, but their quality. To see the point of a problem, to grasp the real meaning of a symbol, to awaken to hitherto unrealized beauty, to discover success in the performance of an act—these, too, are creative responses. They are creative responses because from them comes something new. So all creative response is discovery, and all discovery is creative response. That is the point to grasp.

A. The discovery of an unsuspected ability in oneself is a creative experience. A child whom you may have begun to consider unmusical suddenly finds that he can sing a descant part against a melody. To be sure, the descant may consist of no more than one or two notes. But he can do it! Finding this out is a creative act. And what of your own dealings with this child? You have tried this; you have tried that; and nothing seems to work. Then you think of the little descant. You make it very easy. You bring about a situation in which the child is encouraged to try. He tries. He succeeds. But you have succeeded also. You have brought something new into existence. You have succeeded *because you have taught creatively.*

B. The discovery of a new and better level of achievement is a creative experience. Yesterday a first-grade child couldn't "make up" any kind of a tune. Today he can sing some of his thoughts, such as "I have a pair of new shoes," or "My puppy followed me to school." This, in the most genuine sense, is a creative experience. And the act of helping this child, or indeed any learner, young or old, beginner or expert, to make such a discovery is an act of creative teaching.

C. The discovery of unrealized realms of experience is a creative experience. A child may not be able to sing very well, but he finds he can respond with his body to "How do you like to go up in the swing," and suchlike. A record is put on, and the voice of a great singer interprets a well-known Christmas song. For a few memorable moments, a spell is woven. These also are creative experiences, and evoking them and making them possible is creative teaching.

2. A creative response may come suddenly or gradually. Please be clear on this point. It can save you from many a mistake.

A creative response can come in a flash. With some of the great artists and writers whose work I mentioned above, it did come in that way. It can come in that way for your children, and also for you. Here is a child to whom the musical symbols in his book mean little or nothing. One day, encouraged by you, he is experimenting at the piano keyboard. He sweeps upward with his hand. Then he looks at the notes of the song, "Up the hill I go," which, partly by chance, partly by management, is right there. In a moment he sees what it is all about. Again, creative learning, and creative teaching.

But don't think that speed and promptness are of the essence, or that all responses must be instantaneous if they are to be creative. Creation may be slow, it may be difficult. That is why I mentioned the novelist who got the idea for his book, but took years to work it out. Fourth grade children have chosen some songs for an assembly program. These songs are already familiar to them. Under your guidance, the children come to feel quite strongly that the songs must be done as well as possible. There is discussion, self-criticism, reviewing, polishing up. You call attention to the notation, and the children are surprised to find how much it can help when properly used. A great deal of hard work is put in. Obstacles are overcome. The rhythm is clarified, the phrases are better brought out, the meaning of the words is better emphasized. The singing of the songs is greatly improved, and the children themselves know it. All this takes time. It does not come in a flash. But it is a genuine creative experience, and your guidance of it is an act of creative teaching.

Notice that hard work for a goal, hard work dominated by the sense that one can get somewhere and is getting somewhere, is quite different from hard work imposed as a drab, unmeaning task. It is utterly false that children do not like hard work. Never believe it for an instant! Children do not like hard work of the treadmill variety. But then, who does? Everyone feels that in such hard work there is no nourishment, and the feeling is correct. But hard work to achieve a desired goal, even though that goal, at first, is only dimly seen, is altogether different. Such hard work is a creative process. And the evocation and guidance of it is creative teaching.

3. Creative response must come from within. I make a separate point of this, because the thought may be helpful to you, so it is worth stating explicitly. But, in reality, it is just another way of saying what I have already said; and every illustration I have used illustrates this idea also.

Perhaps you may think that if a child's creative response comes from within him, all that you, as a teacher, can do, is to sit by and hope that it will happen. This is not so at all. You can organize situations such that what is in a child has the best possible chance to come out. When the child who was baffled by the notation made a discovery while experimenting at the piano keyboard, the discovery was *his* discovery. He saw something, learned something, in his own way. When the child who could hardly sing found that he could respond rhythmically with his body, that also was *his* discovery. He too saw something, learned something, in his own way. But these discoveries, these seeings, these learnings would probably never have happened, if the helpful situation had been lacking. This is always so. Newton saw the apple fall. Schubert heard the poem. The situation, in each case, sparked the discovery. That is what you also have to do. That is what creative teaching is. Creative teaching is not telling the children the answers in your own way, and then making them memorize those answers. Creative teaching is sparking a discovery that is the learner's own discovery.

4. Creative response needs help and guidance. This is an extension of the last point; but again I think you may find it helpful to have an explicit statement, and to follow up the idea into some little detail.

Even the greatest geniuses need help and guidance in their creative work. I imagine that no one would have dared to try to "teach" Mozart, in the formal and accepted sense, when he was at the height of his powers. But a great many people helped and guided him. We know that he talked about his work to his father and his sister, corresponded with them about it, heeded their advice. We know that he often took his work to other musicians, and he himself has said that he was interested and influenced by their reactions. All this was really teaching, in the true sense of the word—a thought which you might well turn over in your mind, and apply to your own work. Well then, if Mozart needed help and guidance in his creative work, you can be sure that everybody does.

A. Creative response can be helped and guided by revealing new possibilities. A child transferred into a third grade from a rigidly regimented school. He had never dreamed of being able to make his own choices, of taking part in expressive bodily activities, of even making up some music. All this was a revelation, and he blossomed out.

B. Creative response can be helped and guided by avoiding or removing needless frustrations. A child in the fifth grade would like very much to compose some music. But he has no notion how to set about it. If he tries all by himself he is almost sure to be blocked. But some suggestions and advice start him on his way, and although success does not come without hard work, he already sees its gleaming promise. A child is in the late second grade, and in spite of nearly two years of music he still cannot seem to carry a tune. One day the teacher suggests that some of the children, instead of singing one of the songs right through, might like to come in on just a little bit of it—a call, a yodel, the toot of a train, or suchlike. She herself comes in on this small motive, with much zest. The hesitating child forgets his self-consciousness, gets into the game, succeeds, and from then on sings with increasing confidence.

C. Example, enthusiasm, and cooperation can do wonders to help and guide creative response. A fourth-grade classroom teacher was using a song called *The Mill Wheel,* in which a recurrent *so-do* figure represents the steady turning of the wheel. This effect was explained in the teacher's manual, but the teacher had her doubts. Her training had made her allergic to syllables, and she felt she could do nothing with them. Still, this effect did seem interesting, and it looked as though it might add something to the song. Taking her courage in both hands, she decided to work it out with the children. She told them quite frankly that there was something here that she did not fully understand, but that it looked worth understanding. The whole group examined and discussed the little passage, saw how the syllables connected with it, saw what they meant and what effect they indicated. Before long these *so-do's* were being executed with zest

and precision. Everybody present, including the teacher, had
found something out about music; and the teacher's own dread
of the syllables was sensibly diminished.

D. Providing opportunities and outlets may often be a very
good way of helping and guiding creative response. When a
composer has created a musical work, he wants other people to
hear it. So do children. When an artist has polished a piece to
a fine point, he wants other people to hear it. So do children. Do
what you can to create such opportunities. Taking music home,
taking music to another class, taking music to the school assembly, or the P.T.A., or perhaps to the local hospital—there are
some suggestions. Remember that the provision of such opportunities is real teaching. It is, in fact, genuine creative teaching.

5. Creative response can be blocked and inhibited by meaningless routines and impositions.

Here is a third-grade group going to work on a song. It is a
reading-study song, made up entirely of quarter notes, in the key
of C major. The music is very simple, and also very dull, for the
song was put together simply to teach reading. The teacher gives
the starting tone, and the children sing without accompaniment. They use a neutral syllable, and point at each note as they
come to it. Then they sing it with the so-fa syllables. Then they
sing it with words. Nothing is said about the spirit and meaning
of the song. Nothing is done to make the singing musical or
artistic. No opportunity is given for any child to make a suggestion or even ask a question.

"Theirs not to reason why."

It is not a music-reading lesson. It is a music-spelling lesson, and
a pure routine.

A second grade child cannot carry a tune. He is told to sit in
the front row. He is almost—but perhaps not quite—told not to

sing while two songs are sung by the group. After the two songs, he is told to stand up. The teacher says she is going to sing a note, and that he must sing it after her. He tries, and fails. This is done three times, and he still fails. Then he is told to sit down. How does one evaluate all this? The teacher, doubtless with the best of intentions, has been trying to impose something on the child. She has not made one single move, one least attempt, to draw out of him anything that might be there. He must do everything in *her* way, not in *his* way. He is not given the vestige of a chance to discover singing for himself. This child is very lucky, because before he is ruined he gets into better hands. In the third grade, another teacher deals with him quite differently. He is drawn into rhythmic activities, and invited to express his own insights in terms of bodily movement. He finds many simple instruments available, and is helped to choose and decide upon their uses. One day he is helped to select and play autoharp chords to accompany a song, and does so with much delight. Before he knows it, he is singing; and everyone is surprised to find that he has a very nice voice.

In those two instances you can see very clearly what meaningless routines and impositions can do to creative response. And you can also see the difference between routine teaching and creative teaching.

6. Creative response is the essence of growth. I bring this emphatically to your attention, just in case you may have an idea that talk about creative response is only sentimentality. You, and I, and everybody, including children, grow through creative response, or we do not grow at all.

Growth is not the piling up of a store of information. It is not the acquisition of the stunts and manipulative dexterities that some people call skill. Growth is the attainment of new vistas, the achievement of new powers, the gaining of new precisions, the deepening and defining of insights and understandings, the widening of horizons. If you want to call this the process of learning, you have a perfect right to do so; for learning and growth mean almost the same thing. But, whatever you call it, this is the way we human beings get places, and the only way we ever get places. It calls for hard work; but this is the hard work of an explorer, not the hard work of a piler-up of stones.

It has been said that Beethoven's nine symphonies are the stages of his musical education, of his own growth as a composer and a musician. These nine symphonies were adventures in which Beethoven discovered music and discovered himself. That is what we mean by saying that they were creative adventures. It is through just such creative adventures that we all learn and grow. That is why, in a program planned to promote musical growth, our constant endeavor must be to help and encourage children to respond creatively in all their dealings with music.

Creative Response and the Music Program

I have said that creative experience, far from being one special kind of experience, must permeate and pervade the whole of our developmental program. You may find it interesting and helpful to check through the program item by item, with this thought in mind.

1. Children gain the ability to read music in and through creative response. The proposition is based directly on our previous discussion of music reading; but let us look at the matter from this new point of view.

A. To develop music-reading ability is to develop an ever deeper, clearer, more precise understanding of and insight into music itself. When music reading is so developed, the symbols are not mere items in an arbitrary code to be memorized. Nor are they abstract intellectual problems, which must be solved in terms of words and figures. They are indications which enable us to hear, sing, play, and enjoy music more adequately.

B. Again, all good procedures for teaching music reading are simply ways of helping children to discover musical meanings. Seeing what one hears enables one to grasp what one hears more perfectly. Noting symbolized distinctive effects makes these effects stand out clearly, and brings fresh insight into musical beauties. The reading process itself is essentially a process of discovering music, of reaching back to the composer's intention through its visual indications.

C. Once again, the specifics of the notation should never be in isolation. Always they should be taught and learned in such a way that they illuminate and, as it were, explain musical experiences and musical effects, so that these effects are better and more fully realized.

Clearly, this amounts to saying that music reading must be developed in and through creative experience and creative response.

2. Children come to sing, and to improve in singing, in and through creative response.

A. Singing, as we have seen, is a basic natural activity. But a child's own discovery that he can sing is an authentic creative realization. It is a discovery of a power within himself. And it is an unending discovery, as the possibilities of song unendingly unfold.

B. All legitimate procedures for teaching singing—that is to say, for developing this natural ability, are essentially ways of evoking and encouraging creative realization. At the beginning, and indeed throughout, we must have songs that evoke singing. Also we must set up situations that evoke singing, by example, by encouragement, by opening the way for choice and preference, by encouraging children to share in decisions as to interpretation. Beyond this, and more specifically, all the techniques of voice production should be considered as devices for breaking barriers, removing frustrations, dissolving obstacles. The full development of any singer takes much time and much work; but we have seen that a creative enterprise may continue through many a year.

C. A question which many teachers ask is, how to deal with the hesitant singer or the non-singer. Throughout these pages I have made many suggestions pointing to an answer. But ultimately they all come to this; we must try to evoke a creative response. Forcing is no good. Tone-matching drills are no good. Anything that humiliates the hesitant child, or that undermines his self-confidence, is sure to be harmful. As a matter of fact, there is no fixed formula. We must try to establish situations in which the "singing potential" that is in him comes out. Perhaps the child will get into singing through rhythmic activity, or through dramatization, or quite casually while instruments are being used. Perhaps he will just be carried into song by the contagious enthusiasm of a group who are singing happily and freely. Perhaps at some moment we may realize that he is singing quietly to himself, and an encouraging word may fan the spark. Perhaps some little turn of phrase in a song that we are presenting, or perhaps the interest of a child-made song will accomplish what we hope for. In any case, we must approach the problem creatively ourselves, and try to evoke a creative response in him.

3. Children should deal with and learn to use and play instruments in and through creative response.

A. The use of easy-to-play instruments opens up a whole range of new realizations and personal satisfactions. Music takes on a new precision. New realms of tonal interest open up. The musically diffident have inviting opportunities for success. The musically confident find new expressive avenues. Never dictate the use of easy-to-play instruments. Always arrange matters so that the children can explore, experiment, and decide how and when to use them. Your business is to open up possibilities, and to guide matters so that needless frustrations and failures will be avoided.

B. Essentially the same ideas apply to the study of standard instruments. Interest and desire are essential criteria for selecting children for this kind of work; and there should be enough musical maturity so that the instrument is accepted as a musical opportunity rather than merely a manipulative puzzle. To the beginner, his instrument should be a new interest, a new life concern, a source of pride and confidence. The acquisition of skill will call for hard work; but this work should be quite different from meaningless drudgery. In working for command of his instrument, the child should work for the achievement of new musical ambitions; and when he has reached any given level of attainment, his progress must depend on his seeing still unrealized musical possibilities beckoning. This is how technique should be acquired, for it is equivalent to the ability to say what one wishes to say musically, and it should be learned in a musical setting and for conscious musical goals. In a word, we do not *build* a technique—we *create* it.

4. Children develop a feeling for and a grasp of rhythm in and through creative response.

This, perhaps, is obvious when we remember that rhythm is essentially expressive rather than arithmetical. A better grasp of rhythm always means a better realization of something inwardly but imperfectly felt. When anyone, child or adult, gets hold of the rhythm of a piece of music, he should not feel that he has managed correctly to learn an imposed lesson. He should feel that this is how the music ought to be. Expressive movement is the essential medium in and through which rhythm is grasped and realized, and it should be chosen and developed by the initiative and choices of the children. Rhythm instruments, again, point up and define rhythm patterns, and their possibilities should be explored and their uses decided primarily by the children. Once more, an understanding of the symbols for rhythm brings new insight, precision, and generality into music. They should not be taught as abstract lessons, but always as means for wider and surer musical and expressive realizations.

You may think that I have gone to an extreme in stressing the initiatives and personal choices of the children, and that I have left nothing for the teacher to do but sit in the background and watch things happen. *If this is all the teacher does, nothing much will happen.* Possibilities must be opened up, suggestions must be made, dead ends must be avoided. As an instance, if a teacher just turns six or eight kinds of rhythm instruments over to the children, the best outcome to be hoped will be bewilderment. For the children must explore, experiment, realize possibilities one by one before they can make very much of these new opportunities. Creative response requires such guidance everywhere; and the giving of this guidance is creative teaching.

5. Listening, as we have come to understand it, is in the profoundest sense a creative experience. It may be a guide and revelation, opening vistas for one's own performance; and this can be so either with young children or mature artists. It may issue in interpretations, in which the listener tells in words or actions or choices, what the music means to him. It may be an essential means of reaching new understandings of the content of music itself. It may open up new and wider musical horizons. It may be a most intimate, incommunicable inner experience, which enriches life, and endures through the years.

To make listening serve such purposes is, again, creative teaching. It is very different from the cut-and-dried appreciation lesson, or the music memory contest.

As you will no doubt have noticed, all that I have said in this section, about reading, singing, playing, rhythm, and listening, is a backward look over what has been said before, and a re-interpretation of it. The program that has been described all through these pages is a program of creative experiences and of creative teaching. What I have tried to do here is, briefly, to bring together everything previously said, and consider it all in the light of this idea.

Creating Original Music

Here is this chapter on creativeness, already well along, and very little has yet been said about creating new music! Perhaps you think this strange and even wrong. I do not agree. You need to see this business of creating new music in its full and proper setting, if it is to be valuable. There are two things to be understood about it, by way of preliminaries.

First, remember that creative experience is far wider, far more extensive, than the creation of new music. If you are not clear about this, you will never understand the proper place of creative experience in the program—for its place is *everywhere*.

Second, the making of new music is easy and natural in a program saturated through and through with the creative spirit —a program of creative learning and creative teaching, which is the only kind of program that really makes for musical growth. Moreover, the making of new music is likely to be valuable and repaying only in the setting of such a program. When the making of songs is introduced as a special kind of project or lesson in a program of mechanical learning and routine teaching, it too becomes mechanical and routine. And when this happens, it loses all that makes it worth doing. Those are the reasons why the topic has been postponed.

I know that many teachers want advice and direction about how to get children to make up music; and I shall have many practical suggestions in a moment. But before coming to them, there are a few general ideas that you will find helpful.

First, begin early, right down in first grade or kindergarten. Do not wait for the third or fourth grade. Children should get used to the feeling that making up music is a natural thing to do.

Second, begin simply. Children should find out that they can make music themselves, and they should feel confident in their ability to do it before they undertake anything ambitious. Third, move on to more ambitious projects, when, in your judgment, the children can deal with them. Fourth, vary your procedures, for there is no one "best" way. Children can make music group-wise, and there are many plans and procedures for helping them to do so. But also encourage individual children to make music, either in school, or at home. Fifth, help children to find ways and means of writing down and preserving the music they have made; but never let the experience of creating new music slump into a music-writing lesson. Sixth, be sure to manage matters so that children have outlets for the music they have made, in their own classrooms, elsewhere in the school, at home, and so on. Having made these points I will now go on to tell you of various procedures which teachers have found successful in helping children to create original music.

In the early grades and kindergarten, encourage children to sing their thoughts and ideas, in addition to speaking them. "Telling-time" in kindergarten offers fine opportunities. "Grandmother is visiting us." "We have a new baby at our house." "Daddy has gone on a trip." "I'm going to the circus." And so on.

Children go for a walk around the school. Some building is going on. They return, and sing about some of the things they saw. "The steam shovel goes swish swish." "Men are carrying bricks." "There's a big hole in the ground."

Children may make up music for a well-loved poem, turning it into a song. If they do this, they will probably need help in getting started. Get them to read the words aloud, expressively, rhythmically. Then take the first line, and ask for suggestions for a tune. Several will probably be forthcoming. When one has been chosen, everyone should sing it. Then go on to the second line, and so on. But always go back over the previously chosen musical phrases before the new one is finally settled, for this will make the song hang together. I doubt if you should begin with the scansion of the poem, although with older children this might be all right.

The children can make up the poem, and set it to music as above. Or they can make up words to go with a tune.

The children can make up new words to a familiar song, or add a new verse to a song they have learned.

The children can make up a second part or a descant to a familiar one-part song. This is not so hard as it sounds, because the descant may consist of no more than a single note or a couple of notes; but things can become more elaborate with older children who are used to undertakings of this kind.

The children may take a story like *The Three Bears,* and make a song-story out of it. This can turn into quite an extensive undertaking. For such a story will take quite a number of short songs, and a good deal of incidental and background music. Some of this may be composed in class, some of it composed by individual children.

Here is a much more elaborate undertaking, successfully carried out by sixth graders. A wild west theme was chosen. A committee plan for working out the story and music was set up. The best points from several stories were chosen, and worked into the outline of a play by the story committee. This outline was given to the music committee, and they decided that music should be used four times during the play. It was to be used in the beginning to set the mood, at the point where the pioneers sing and dance, after the Indian massacre, and at the end to add to the climax. With the help of the music consultant the music was composed, of course in relationship to the words. Substantially the same theme was to be used throughout, with changes in key and rhythm. The entire project was cooperative. Even the teaching of the music was done by members of the committee.

Here is quite a collection of workable ideas. They are not

arranged in any particular order. But you ought to be able to sort them out, and get something out of them. As to writing down music that has been created by the children, which is quite an important matter, younger children may diagram the melody on the board. Older children will probably need to use either the standard notation or some simplified form of it. In any case, you will need to help them to use, and if need be to invent, a symbolism that will capture and preserve their musical thought. But again, never let such projects turn into lessons on the writing of music.

Creative Teaching

Again and again in this chapter I have mentioned creative teaching. I do not intend to go into this subject at length. But it seems to me well to gather together the thoughts about it that have come our way as we have dealt with creativeness, and its place in the program.

1. What is creative teaching? Creative teaching is teaching that enables learners to respond creatively, and that gives them the encouragement, stimulation, help, and guidance that makes creative response possible, and successful, and rewarding. This is a definition that may be useful to you. It sums up much of what we have been saying; and it gives you a taking-off place for your own thinking, and work, and planning.

2. For the teacher herself, creative teaching means discovery. It means the unending discovery of music, its resources, its possibilities, its uses. It means the self-discovery by the teacher herself of new powers and capacities. Many a classroom teacher doubts her ability to do anything much with music. But she should remember that the simplest things are often the most worth-while. If, with whatever help and collaboration from the music specialist she may need, she will adventure, even though timidly, she will almost surely be amazed to find how

much is possible, and how seeming impossibilities become possible achievements.

3. Creative teaching differs from routine teaching in two ways. First, it does not mean the imposition of tasks, but the stimulation and guidance of initiative, choice, and discovery. Second, for the teacher herself, it means the discovery of new resources, musical and personal, and not the set repetition of standardized lessons, term by term, and year by year.

4. The heart and soul of creative teaching is inspiration. To discover how new realizations may be brought forth from children, how beauty may be revealed to them, how unsuspected powers may be elicited, is an inspiration for the teacher. And this inspiration is conveyed to and shared by the children also. For teaching that is worth-while is a vital contact of living, growing personalities, not a routine covering of ground, or a dull grind on unmeaning tasks. The teaching whose heart and soul is inspiration is the teaching that really produces lasting and rewarding outcomes. It is the kind of teaching required everywhere in a program planned to promote musical growth.

Questions for Thought, Discussion, and Study

1. Could we say, on the basis of the ideas presented in this chapter that all learning is creative?
2. In what sense is growth a creative process?
3. It has been said that Beethoven's nine symphonies are nine stages in his education as a musician. Consider this statement carefully. What does it imply for anyone's education, including your own. If you want to go more deeply into the matter, decide as far as you can what some of the things were that Beethoven learned from his symphonies.
4. It has been said in this chapter that listening can and should be creative. Does this apply to all the types of listening previously presented and discussed? To be specific, would it apply to receptive listening?

5. In some music programs a special type of activity called a "creative lesson" is introduced from time to time. What do you think of this practice?
6. When children compose a piece of music, is the writing out of it an important part of the process? In dealing with this question, you may find it interesting to consider the work of great creative artists. Did they find the writing out of their work part of the creative process itself, or a mere "chore"?
7. We are sometimes inclined to think that only a few people are gifted with creativeness. Is there any truth in this? May one person be more creative than others? If so, in what sense?
8. Review what was previously said about the teaching of music reading, and bring it into relationship with the claim made in this chapter that learning to read music is a creative experience.
9. Would you say that musical creativeness is a special form of creativeness?
10. Enumerate, consider, and discuss as many forms and kinds of creative activity as possible that can and should go on in connection with music, in addition to the composition of music.

Readings

Lillian Mohr Fox and L. Thomas Hopkins, *Creative School Music*. New York, Silver Burdett Company, 1936. Chapter 2, "Creativeness—Its Nature": Chapter 3, "Creativeness—Its Nurture."

Beatrice Perham, *Music in the New School*. Chicago, Neil J. Kjos Music Co., 1937. Chapter 5, "Creative Learning."

CHAPTER THIRTEEN

Administration

The Principle

If the program is to be effective in achieving human values by means of musical growth, it must be administered as an adequate and coordinated sequence of learning experiences, cooperatively carried on under positive leadership.

This thirteenth and last principle pulls together all the thinking of this book and points it in a new direction, bringing it to bear on the problem of administration.

What is administration? What is its essential function? It is worth our while to ask these fundamental questions right at the start. When you think of administration, perhaps certain procedures come first to your mind—ordering supplies, checking up on equipment and keeping it in order, planning schedules, making requisitions and reports, setting up the budget, and so on. All these are important tasks, and they must be done efficiently if any enterprise is to go well. But they are the machinery of administration, not its essence. *The essential function of administration is to establish and maintain ways of working together.*

Right here is the great weakness of many music programs. Often the members of the music staff find themselves pulled in twenty different directions. No careful thought has been given to the true and proper nature of their work, and nobody is clear about it. Their relationships to classroom teachers, principals, and the school system generally, are not well defined. And while they may be busy beyond all reason, their essential functions and duties are not clear cut. Music specialists are very often able, devoted, and respected people. But under such conditions they cannot make their proper contribution. Not seldom they themselves are well aware that something is wrong. But it often happens that they do not see just what is wrong, or what must be done to set it right. Again and again the cause of trouble lies in faulty ways of working together—that is to say, in bad administration.

The very essence of good administration is the clear and proper assignment of responsibility. Without this, nobody can work to good advantage; and, what is more, distressing and disabling clashes are almost sure to take place. Should the music specialist do all the music teaching? Should he give demonstration lessons? Should he teach the technical aspects of music, and leave all the rest to other people? Should he visit classrooms to observe the work of classroom teachers? Should he consider himself a "resource person", and confine himself to consultant duties? Should he be expected to set up a uniform music program in all grades in all schools? Should he hold stated conferences and workshops with classroom teachers and other school officers? Should classroom teachers handle most of the music? Should they be expected to work closely with the music specialist, or should the relationship be entirely voluntary and "permissive"? These questions all have to do with ways of working together. They are the central questions of administration. Too often they are answered on the basis of mere prejudice, or on the basis of vague general ideas that are really a camouflage for prejudice. Or they are not clearly answered at all.

It is this at which our thirteenth principle hits. It says two things. First, it gives us a criterion for planning good working relationships. Second, it tells us what kind of relationships these should be.

What Determines Good Working Relationships?

When a job is to be done, the nature of the job determines the working relationships of the people who do it. One does not run a bank as one would run a regiment. One does not run a regiment as one would run a school. One does not run a symphony orchestra as one would run a department store. One does not run a glee club as one would run a football squad. Presumably there are universal principles of good administration, but they are very general indeed, and differences are at least as important as similarities. For instance, in managing a ship at sea, a strict system of command and subordination is necessary. But this would be a very bad way of managing a research institute. Good administration is shaped and determined by the nature of the enterprise itself. This is the basic assumption of our thirteenth principle. The working relationships required for the music program—i.e., its proper administration—depend on the nature of the work to be done.

This amounts to saying that it is bad practice to start with a set of pre-determined administrative ideas, and then to apply them indiscriminately to every situation, including the music program. Ideas and prepossessions of this kind will always fail to fit, will always cause weakness, will always make trouble, because they do not arise from a genuine understanding of the nature and needs of the enterprise. The nature and needs of the enterprise must always be the controlling consideration.

School music programs today are much bedeviled and seriously weakened by various pre-determined administrative ideas that are not suited to them, but that tend to be applied indiscriminately and wholesale. I shall discuss two of them be-

cause of their immediate prominence, although there are others.
These two are the conception of the self-contained classroom,
and the movement away from special supervision. Both these
developments are causing much heat and agitation and plenty
of hard words; so I think a careful analysis is in order.

1. *The self-contained classroom*

Briefly put, the plan known as the self-contained classroom is
for a teacher to be assigned to a group of children, to work and
live with them continuously, and to do practically all the teaching, including, of course, the teaching of music. Thus music in
the elementary school is almost entirely in the hands of the classroom teachers. What evaluation is to be made of this plan?

A. The very first thing to have in mind is that the expression,
"the self-contained classroom," has become a slogan or catch-
word. This in itself should be enough to alert your critical facul-
ties, just as a wild animal is alerted by a hint of movement in the
forest. There have been many educational slogans in the past,
and doubtless they will always be with us. All of them are very
dangerous, because they tend to substitute easy formulae for
the often painful effort of thinking. Such is the case here. "The
self-contained classroom"—what a tidy mouthful! What a neat,
convenient expression! That is just the trouble. It is too neat,
too tidy, too convenient. It suggests a ready-made solution, emerging full-panoplied like Minerva from the head of Jove, all prepared for action, and—as the deacon said about the Doxology—
suitable for every occasion. There is no doubt that many excellent people accept it in just such a sense, congratulating themselves on being up-to-date. But you can be absolutely certain
that no educational problem can possibly be solved as easily as
that. Unquestionably the slogan with which we are dealing, like
all such slogans, has in it a solid modicum of genuine sense.
But very often it gets mixed in with a varying and sometimes
a quite large modicum of nonsense. So we must try to separate
the sense from the nonsense, the wheat from the chaff, and

retain the former while consigning the latter to the winds of heaven.

B. The sense—and it is very good sense—in the plan known as the self-contained classroom is that it is an excellent idea for one teacher to be responsible for living and working with one group of children all day, every day, throughout the school year. A teacher so situated is in a uniquely favorable position to know and understand her children, and so to deal with, help, guide, and teach them to the best advantage. Since the vital nerve of education is personal contact, the idea is manifestly sound; and when a working plan for putting it into operation is forthcoming, we have reason to rejoice. So far we are on solid ground and can be confident that we have hold on something eminently right. But let us remain sane, sober, and not uncritical in our confidence, rather than blindly exuberant, for quagmires lurk nearby.

C. Some people, unfortunately, are not satisfied to stay on this good solid ground. They rush on to far shakier footing. They not only say that Miss X is in a preferred position to understand her children, and that she ought to be in such a position, which is true. They go on to intimate that she is almost bound to understand them better than anyone else, and in particular, better than the music specialist. Here is a distinct trace of that dangerous euphoria so easily produced by slogans. For while the claim may sometimes be true, it can also be disastrously false. Understanding a group of human beings is a complex and subtle business, and depends on far more than length of contact. A sympathetic and perceptive music specialist can often see Miss X's situation with new eyes, and recognize in it human possibilities to which she herself has been blind. Not for nothing has it been said that an outsider sometimes sees most of the game!

D. The ground grows shakier still when it is said (as it actually seems to be in some quarters), not only that Miss X is in a position to understand her children well, not only that she understands them better than anyone else can, but that she understands *children in general or children as such* uniquely well, and certainly far better than the music specialist. Here the patient becomes really feverish, and his slogan-euphoria begins to verge toward delirium. For the idea is not merely false, but actually preposterous. What is it that endows Miss X with this unique human insight, this monopoly of child-understanding? Nothing whatever! It is a mere figment of the slogan-intoxicated mind. Maybe Miss X does understand children in general well. Let us, at least, hope she does. But so do lots of other people, including many with a good musical training. That is the simple though perhaps unpalatable truth.

To sum up, what is sound in the self-contained-classroom plan is, like all sound educational ideas, very old. Socrates once exclaimed, "Whom can I teach except my friends?" Very true! This indicates that it is very valuable for children to have one person who knows them well, deals with them wisely, and is able to help and teach them. But it does not mean that this one person should be their only guide, philosopher, and friend, or that this one person needs no help and no guidance, and should proceed entirely on her own devices. The self-contained classroom as a working device has its uses. But like a long series of other educational devices, it also has its limitations, and is no cure-all. Taken as a wholesale administrative practice for indiscriminate application, it is dangerous and destructive. Any conscious educator who supports it as such must ask himself, as a very sharp-edged question, whether he is not accepting a nostrum at the expense of the welfare of the children. And he must also ask himself whether he is not giving Miss X an impossible assignment, for he should be concerned with her welfare also.

2. *The movement away from special supervision*

A. The movement is supported in the main by general arguments. These are often called "philosophical" arguments; but

I do not see how a conscientious educator can be quite happy about them, for they so easily merge into rationalization.

B. So far as I am aware, no one has ever attempted to demonstrate, on a basis of fact, that specialist aid in connection with many phases of the educational enterprise is not necessary or valuable. Indeed, one may be reasonably sure that this could not be proved. Many kinds of teaching, including music, obviously require the skills, insights, and trained discrimination and judgment of specially qualified personnel. No research is required to show this. Surely a few classroom visits would be enough. Time and again one finds teachers who are admirable and highly competent in handling material where the medium is the English language, but who are completely illiterate in such areas as music and art. How can it possibly be doubted that such teachers need specialist aid, or that, without such aid, the classroom offerings will be impoverished?

C. A question about the type of specialist needed may very properly be raised. Administrators sometimes say that there is no need for the specialist services of concert virtuosi. Of course they are quite right. But what classroom teachers and children do need are the specialist services of broadly trained, musically sensitive, musically knowledgeable persons. That such persons can play an invaluable, and indeed an essential role, seems beyond all question.

D. It may be said that, while the specialist is necessary, he should not function as a supervisor. There is probably a good deal of truth in this, although the argument often seems to turn on a mere matter of title. But if the specialist should not function as a supervisor, it is still necessary to say how he should function. This question calls for a definitive answer. Moreover, however the specialist should function, he *must function with official authority*. His relationship to the work cannot be merely permissive, or his whole status becomes impossible and his potential contribution is sabotaged from the start.

E. If it is said that specially trained persons in general, and musically trained persons in particular, are incapable of understanding children, and dealing with them fruitfully, then one has to reply that this is simply untrue. No doubt any music specialist may make plenty of human blunders. But they can be matched by equally bad blunders made by classroom teachers, guidance workers, and administrators. Human wisdom is not confined to general educators and eliminated by special training. I would be almost ashamed to say anything so obvious if contrary suggestions did not, from time to time, appear.

F. It is suggested that specialists have less opportunity to know children well and to deal with them fruitfully than classroom teachers and others, who live and work with them more intimately. The point calls for consideration, but it is not decisive. Often a specialist will see potentialities in children, and find ways of helping them, to which his colleagues are oblivious. He can do this precisely because he is a specialist, and approaches children with his own point of view. After all, in dealing with human beings we are all, to some degree, specialists —to some degree limited. None of us sees all that there is to see. All of us have a contribution to make, and we all need the understanding help of our associates in dealing wisely and constructively with the children whom we try to serve.

So to summarize, the trend toward the self-contained classroom, and away from special supervision are movements that have some real and valid reasons behind them. But, like the interminable array of educational devices and much-touted gadgets that have preceded them, they are by no means cure-alls. Pushed to extremes by enthusiasts who understand neither their real potentialities or their limitations, they can do great harm. As administrative devices, they should be used with discrimination, not applied wholesale, regardless of the type of work involved, and of what it really requires.

Summing up at this point, the pattern of working relationships required by the music program, which is the essence of its effective administration, must depend upon the nature of the work itself. It should not depend on pre-determined administrative plans which, although they have their values, also have their limitations, and which can become destructive when applied wholesale. This much our thirteenth principle has already told us.

But our principle says something more. It indicates, very briefly, the essential features of a developmental music program about which all administrative arrangements must turn. That program must be *adequate*; it must be *coordinated*; and it must consist of a *sequence* of learning experiences. I now go on to consider these three characteristics, and to show what they imply for sound administration.

I. Adequacy

Our program must consist of *adequate* learning experiences. Adequate for what? Obviously, for the effective promotion of musical growth. For this purpose, learning experiences must be adequate in *number and variety*, and also in *kind and quality*.

1. For the effective promotion of musical growth, children must have learning experiences that are adequate in number and variety. Of course no one can say exactly what the minimum necessary number of learning experiences is; but it is perfectly clear that in many music programs there are far too few of them. Perhaps the music specialist is able to visit every classroom once a week for twenty minutes, and even this would be a favorable situation. Except for his visit, there is virtually no music at all. Unquestionably such a contact with music is far too meager to have any very marked effect on musical growth.

This is where the classroom teacher is essential. She can introduce music frequently during the day, and in many different ways. She can use music for rest and relaxation, for sociability, for carrying on rhythmic activities and dramatizations, in connection with comprehensive units, and for sheer enjoyment. She can do much to reveal to children the possibilities of music, and stimulate them to undertake their own musical explorations. Even if she is not a good singer, present-day resources make it quite possible for her to have considerable singing. Simple instruments can be used. Listening experiences can be set up. Often she will be able to help children to make up music for themselves. Thus the classroom teacher can carry on a wide and varied range of really valuable learning experiences in music.

But she will do all this much better and more easily if she has help. She will need materials, and equipment, and suggestions about how to use them. To bring new ideas and procedures to her attention will also be helpful. And perhaps more than anything else, she needs encouragement, and the assurance that what she is able to do with music is worth doing. So collaboration with the music specialist is indicated.

However, there is no reason why the music specialist should remain in the background, and confine himself to the role of consultant. He too should come into the classroom from time to time. The main reason why this is important is that he should never lose touch with the children. He may never know a classroom teacher's children as well as she does; but some acquaintance is far better than none. First-hand contacts are always valuable; and if the music specialist can be a fairly frequent visitor to any teacher's classroom, he will be able to help her to the best advantage.

What the specialist should do on his visits will depend on circumstances. Sometimes he may follow up and reinforce what the classroom teacher is already doing, offering, perhaps, some helpful suggestions to her afterwards. Sometimes he may think it advisable to introduce something quite new and different. His contribution need not and should not follow a set pattern, but should depend upon his knowledge of the situation, the children, and the teacher. Usually his visit will establish a scheduled music period; but even on the days when he can not be present, stated time should be set aside for music, in addition to its more incidental and less planned use.

2. For the effective promotion of musical growth, children must have learning experiences that are adequate in quality and kind. Here again the classroom teacher makes a large and essential contribution. It would be a great pity if qualitatively excellent, or serious, or significant learning experiences in music were brought to the children only by the music specialist. Moreover, this is quite unnecessary.

Even the simplest musical experiences—the imitative singing of a very simple song, the use of easy-to-play instruments, the realization of rhythm through bodily movement, listening—should be qualitatively excellent, for music that has expressiveness and worth should always be used. Moreover there is nothing terribly formidable about helping children to understand music better by the use of gesture symbols, picture symbols, and so forth. And even the introduction of the notation or the syllables here and there for this purpose is far from an impossibility, and is within the scope of many classroom teachers. You may remember from the two chapters on music reading, how immensely the developmental point of view simplifies teaching procedures and problems. So the average classroom teacher is perfectly well able to carry on a great many musical experiences that are qualitatively excellent, and that have a substantial and serious content.

But in doing so, she will certainly need help. The choice of materials is a very essential matter, and the specialist's wider knowledge and trained judgment must be at the disposal of the classroom teacher. Moreover, she will need to be helped with procedures. Many a classroom teacher is afraid of the notation, and afraid of the syllables, and is convinced that she can do nothing with music reading, nothing to promote musical understanding. The business of the music specialist then becomes to show her how easily and naturally many worth-while things can be done. This is a point at which demonstration lessons can be helpful. Let us say that, in a third-grade room, the music specialist develops a song, and features one of its most intriguing and characteristic turns of phrase by using the syllables or the notation. Quite possibly the classroom teacher, who thought that the only proper way to use syllables or notes was in a formidably organized step-wise lesson, and that nobody not thoroughly familiar with all the "fundamentals" should even attempt such a thing, will be amazed at the ease with which it is done, and will feel much inclined to try to do likewise.

II. Coordination

When we say that an enterprise is properly coordinated, we mean that it is consistent within itself, and well adjusted to its wider institutional setting. This is the meaning of the word "coordination" as applied to the music program. There are several areas in which coordination is necessary, if the music program is to work well.

First, there needs to be coordination within the music staff itself. The chief problem here is a working agreement among the various sub-specialists. In particular, the teaching of instrumental music has procedures peculiar to itself. But the over-all approach should be the same as that of the program as a whole. The study of a standard instrument should be regarded as a specialization within the general process of musical growth, not as something that goes on semi-independently, and perhaps with an inconsistent viewpoint and emphasis. This affects both the recruitment of pupils for instrumental work, and also the type of teaching that is offered. Also, the group of elementary music specialists, in systems where there are a number of them, should work together consistently, as a coordinated group. The purpose of coordination within the program is to assure that the entire music staff will stand together, having a common viewpoint which expresses itself in common practices and common policies. The same *kind* of program must be conducted everywhere. The learning experiences considered desirable must everywhere be the same in *kind*. This is the outcome desired. It can be obtained only through joint agreement, through adequate coordination within the staff. And of course a music staff in substantial agreement has far more influence within the system as a whole than one whose members follow mutually inconsistent courses of action.

Then the music program and the music staff must achieve proper coordination with the system as a whole. The work of music specialists and classroom teachers must be coordinated, so that each can contribute toward an outcome desired and understood by both. The work of the various classroom teachers must be coordinated, so that even if identical learning experiences are not set up in different classrooms, at any rate these learning experiences will be consistent in purpose and general character. And the work of the music staff must be coordinated with the general administration of the school, for the sake of proper action on such matters as schedule, secondary school credit for music, equipment, housing, pupil guidance, and the like.

This, briefly, is the problem of coordination as it affects the music program. Any experienced music specialist can see at once that it is immensely important, and that it affects his work in many ways. The question that now arises is how to secure such coordination.

The conventional instrument for securing coordination is the course of study. In it the music program is outlined. It indicates when various learnings should be introduced, and usually makes suggestions about materials and procedures. Its effect is to inform all concerned what should be taught, when it should be taught, and, within limits, how it should be taught. Thus it is intended to secure coordination.

Unfortunately the ordinary course of study is open to the gravest objections. In the first place, it concerns the general music program only, and therefore does nothing for coordination among the sub-specialties within the program. In the second place, it usually, though not always, sets up a list of topics to be mastered one by one, so that it makes for an additive rather than a developmental program. In the third place, it is far too rigid. When the course of study is used and taken seriously (which does not always happen), there is a tendency for the music specialists to insist, above everything else, that all teachers adhere to the indicated calendar sequence. But many teachers, who may be able to do very good work in their own way, *cannot* follow the sequence. And there are sure to be many situations where the sequence *ought not* to be followed.

Clearly, the solution is to work for coordination in a very different way. First, we must work for coordination through a *common understanding of basic aims*. What is important here is not to come out with a list of carefully formulated aims which is regarded as the last word on the subject, but to draw everybody into the adventure of thinking about desirable aims. This thinking should originate in the music staff; but it should spread as widely as possible throughout the system. Of course not everybody—classroom teachers, administrative, curriculum and guidance officers—can be expected to work intensively on the problem. But if active and vital thinking is going on, a great many people can be put in touch with it, to a greater or lesser degree. If all members of the music staff are thinking earnestly about the aims of the program, if large numbers of classroom teachers are drawn into this thinking to an appreciable degree, and if members of the general administrative staff are in sufficient touch with it to understand what is going on, and to give their own reactions from time to time, we have a good basis for a type of coordination that is both intelligent and flexible.

Second, we must work for coordination through a *common understanding of desirable procedures.* As I have pointed out again and again, the decisive criterion, and indeed the only final criterion, for a good music teaching procedure is that it is demonstrably likely to promote musical growth. This very definitely excludes certain types of teaching. But it makes possible an enormous flexibility. Very simple procedures may often be very good. Teaching which hardly seems like teaching may very often be excellent. For what is indicated is not patterned, cut-and-dried, closed-circuit lessons, but significant learning experiences. All this can be made clear by the music staff, by means of demonstration teaching, by workshops, by suggestions, by conferences, by lectures, by discussions, and last and by no means least by informal conversations. The idea that there are almost endless good ways of teaching music, and that what makes any way of teaching good is its effect on musical growth, can permeate the entire school system. It can be understood by classroom teachers, who then find that they have very large liberty to do what they themselves can do best, and to try out new departures of their own. It can be understood by administrative officers, who can then realize the importance of suitable schedule arrangements, and the provision of proper equipment.

Suppose we look at a music program which has developed a high degree of coordination by means of a common understanding of basic aims and of desirable procedures. What shall we see? The program will be very various and diversified. Teachers will be teaching in many different ways. Practice will not be static, for teachers will constantly be reaching out for new and better procedures. Helpful curriculum materials will be published and distributed from time to time. But, instead of indicating certain things that *must* be done, they will suggest many valuable and interesting things that *may* be done. On the surface the program will look almost un-coordinated, almost heterogeneous. But as one comes to realize what is actually being done, one will recognize a very vital end effective coordination. For everyone concerned, each in his own way and according to his own opportunities, is contributing to the promotion of musical growth.

III. Sequence

The learning experiences which constitute the content of our program must be sequential; otherwise they will not promote musical growth.

The familiar course of study, once again, is the conventional instrument for administering a sequential music program. Learnings are laid out, grade by grade, in what seems to be a reasonable order, and the intention is that this order should control the work in the classrooms. But, as in the case of coordination, the course of study in its usual form is a very ineffective means of securing sequence. It is wrong in conception, for it sets up a series of masteries to be achieved one by one, with the assumption that their accumulation will insure the advance that is wanted. Moreover, it is almost certain to be spurious. It is a sequence on paper only, which may and usually does have very little relationship to what actually happens in the children's minds. So we must find some other means of achieving the sequence that is an essential feature of a developmental music program.

Let us bring together, briefly, the chief ideas about sequence that have emerged in the course of our discussion. This defines the problem; and then the administrative means of dealing with it can be considered intelligently.

(i) It is always necessary to think in terms of a sequence of musical growth. What this means I have pointed out many times, but it may be well to recapitulate here. Musical growth is a process in which a child's response to music becomes more accurate and precise, more discriminating, wider, and deeper, and his musical understanding more generalized and specific. This, broadly speaking, is what the program must be arranged to bring about.

(ii) The sequence must be one of evolution rather than addition. What is at first vague, takes shape and form. What is at first dimly felt and seen, becomes more and more clearly understood. Reactions that are at first crude, come to be more and more refined.

(iii) There is no fixed or pre-determined time at which any activity (such as part-singing) must be introduced, or at which any concept (such as key signatures or note lengths) must be taught. All one can say is that musical symbols and concepts should be taught at some time when they arise in musical contexts that are meaningful to the children.

(iv) The sequence will be cyclical. That is to say, a concept such as "whole note", or "key center", or "six-eight time", or "leading-tone-tonic", will not be presented once, and once for all, with the thought that it can be mastered and retained. All such concepts will occur again and again in many and varied musical settings. The thought will not be that they must be clearly and completely learned on first presentation, but that their meanings must be progressively clarified through a variety of experiences.

(v) The sequence will be a continuity. Instead of a reading-readiness stage, the early beginnings of reading will occur almost from the very first. Instead of introducing part-singing at a certain level as a new activity, there will be a long series of evolving experiences, out of which part-singing ability will emerge.

These points summarize fairly well the chief ideas about sequence that must be kept in mind in considering the administrative problem of managing a sequential program. At first sight they may seem to you exceedingly baffling, for you can see at once that no fixed course of study can possibly conform to them. Without some such instrumentality, you may ask, how can sequence be achieved at all? My answer is: *By intelligent understanding of what sequence really is on the part of all concerned.* Once you realize this you will find that our whole notion of proper sequence, instead of seeming baffling and impractical, is amazingly liberating.

The key to the whole situation is to get teachers, *including classroom* teachers, to understand what a sequence of musical growth really is, and what it requires in practice. One of the great defects of the plan of the self-contained classroom, in its extreme form, is that the teacher tends to see and think of nothing but her own level of work. It is the very gravest kind of limitation in general; for no teacher can work to the best effect on any level unless she sees the relationship of what she is doing here and now to the long process of the children's total growth. This is the limitation that we have to overcome specifically in the case of music. And it can be done.

Let us consider a teacher assigned to a second-grade group. She believes that music can be, in many ways, beneficial to her children. Partly on her own initiative, partly with the help of the music specialist, she uses it freely and with considerable resourcefulness. In her classroom there is singing, listening, rhythmic activity, dramatization, and so on. Together with the music specialist she is setting up experiences that may be considered adequate both in extent and kind. Moreover, these experiences are in harmony with most of what goes on in the music program as a whole, so there is good coordination.

But what about the sequential effect of these experiences? Are they merely pleasant, merely superficial? If so, there is a great lack. What else, if anything, must this teacher do if she is to promote the musical growth of the children, instead of merely pleasing them with music?

The first thought that may come to mind is that the children should be making a start on music reading, which is often begun in the second grade. But our teacher feels that she can do very little with music reading; and even though she might consent to have it introduced, she would do so under protest. In any case, she may probably think that if anything is to be done with music reading, the music specialist must do it.

In terms of an additive or mechanical sequence, she would be right in all this. If music reading were introduced, it would be intruded into the pattern of musical experiences she has set up. But in terms of a developmental sequence, her misgivings are entirely groundless.

Music reading is developed by establishing connections between ear, eye, and understanding. It begins with gesture symbols, picture symbols, diagram symbols, which are very easy and natural to use. By means of such symbols, children can see what they hear, see what they sing, and to some extent sing what they see. In other words, *they begin to understand music.* Once this has been made clear to the teacher by the music specialist, she finds no difficulty with it. Moreover, there is no clash with the musical experiences she is already providing. On the contrary, these experiences are made richer, more precise, more significant, more intriguing. The process of musical growth has begun.

The teacher may be astonished to think that these are the true beginnings of music reading. This is where she needs some understanding of the long sequence. But this understanding is not in the least difficult. She has already seen that musical experiences become more insightful through the use of simple visual symbols, and therefore more repaying. So it is not hard for her to see that the introduction of more specific and adequate symbols will lead to better and clearer insights and understandings.

Should she herself introduce any of these more specific and

adequate symbols? There is no compulsion on her to do so; and no final reason why she should not. But here again she feels some doubts, both of herself and of the children.

What about standard notation? Can any person who is not thoroughly familiar with it deal with it at all? If it is to be taught lesson-wise in a fixed order, the answer is probably no. But if it is to be introduced to pick out and highlight interesting musical effects, the problem is vastly easier. With some help and guidance, she rightly feels that she can do this.

What about the syllables? Very likely she feels that a person must be able to use them freely, fluently, and confidently in singing a song if they are to be used at all. Since this is beyond her, she much prefers to leave them alone. But again everything is changed when she is helped to realize that the syllables can very fruitfully be used here and there to feature and pick out tonal trends which everyone feels, but which add much to the interest and charm of music when they are consciously recognized.

So much for the teacher. But what of the children? Should second grade children be introduced to syllables and to notation? This depends on two things. It depends first on how the introduction is made, which has already been discussed. And it depends on the maturity of this particular group of children. Here is where the joint insights of the classroom teacher and the music specialist must be brought to bear. The classroom teacher knows the children better than anyone else. But the music specialist knows them well enough to be intelligent about the question that is being raised. Between them they reach the answer, which may very well be to experiment and see what happens.

Notice that the classroom teacher is able to accommodate her work to the sequential program (and in so doing to enrich her work on its own level), because she has an understanding of the nature of the sequence. She does not see her own year's activities and experiences and nothing else. She sees these activities and experiences in the long perspective of the children's growth.

It is the same in all grades, and in all areas of the program. Can a third-grade classroom teacher do anything about part-singing? Should she do anything about it? If one means the sudden, full blown teaching of part-singing, the answer to both questions is almost certainly no. But if the teacher realizes that part-singing evolves from very simple beginnings—from having the children hear a one-or-two-note instrumental descant against a sung melody, from playing the second part of a two-part round on tone bells, and so forth—then she will feel that there is much that she can do and should do about part-singing.

I hope you will now realize that I was speaking nothing but the truth when I said that our conception of a developmental sequence comes as a great liberation. It makes possible a sequence that is not spurious, but genuine—not something on paper, but something in the children's minds. It makes possible great flexibility. And it enables classroom teachers to contribute effectively to the whole sequence of the program. But always remember that everything depends on having teachers understand what the developmental sequence is, and what kind of experiences contribute to it.

Does this all mean that the music staff should not lay out any sort or kind of grade-wise allocation of learnings? Not necessarily so. Suggestions along this line can be helpful. For instance, it is quite proper to say that it is in the fourth grade that we usually find that cooperative discovery of music from the notes works out well. Suggestions of this kind can be pegs for thinking. That is their usefulness. But it is the thinking, the insight, the grasp of what the sequence means, that is decisive.

How much musical growth and competence can we expect by the end of the sixth grade, granted a plan of this kind? Frankly, there can be no definite answer. The decisive factor will be the amount of cooperative intelligence brought to bear in running the program. However, one can reasonably expect a very appreciable musical maturity to result. If this seems an indefinite statement, consider the following for a moment. The conventional course of study *seems* to indicate just what children will learn about music in the elementary school. But the catch is that they never really learn all or nearly all of it. So the course of study is a deceptive document, leaving things still in a state of vagueness. And we may be sure that a developmental sequence will get far further than an additive sequence.

IV. Cooperation

The developmental program needs the classroom teacher. It needs the music specialist. Above all, it needs intelligent cooperation between and among these people. A rigid, mechanical, additive program can be administered by the book of rules. But a developmental program cannot be so administered. *Intelligent cooperation is the administrative mainspring of the developmental program.*

But intelligent cooperation does not just happen. It is more than a matter of good intentions, though without good intentions it is impossible. It must be initiated, fostered, and guided. To initiate, foster, and guide cooperation, and to see that this cooperation is intelligent, is the central and essential responsibility of the music specialist.

Mr. Smith is an elementary-school music specialist, one of five, in a fairly large school system. The director of music assigns him to five elementary schools with a total of thirty-five classrooms. What does this assignment require? How should Mr. Smith work?

Mr. Smith's first duty is to get to know these thirty-five situations as well as he can. He acquaints himself with them by visits; by conferences with teachers, principals, and guidance workers; by study of the school records; in fact, by using every available avenue of information. These thirty-five classrooms are his baili-wick, and it is his duty to make the music in them as good as it can possibly be.

Mr. Smith soon finds that all these situations are different. One school is in an underprivileged neighborhood. Another has a clientele made up mainly of junior executives, substantial businessmen, and professional people. The children in these two schools are very different indeed. Moreover, there are great differences among the teachers. Some have considerable musical background, and are able to play the piano and to sing. Others are very willing to use as much music as they can, but are dif-fident, and feel that they can do little because of their lack of training. A few are hostile to the very idea of music in the class-room, and at the most will grudgingly allow Mr. Smith to present a lesson from time to time because the administration requires them to do so.

What is Mr. Smith to do? Clearly, it would be very unwise for him to try to set up identical musical experiences and learnings in all these classrooms. Perhaps he has enough admin-istrative backing so that he could do so if he thought fit. But he should not think fit. If he tried to set up any rewarding ex-periences in the classrooms of the hostile teachers, he would have to do almost all the teaching himself; and any little adequacy his work might have would be killed by the teachers, for attitudes can be very influential even if hardly a word is said. Moreover, if he worked simply for a minimum uniform program, he would be wasting the abilities of the well-trained teachers, and probably discouraging the willing but diffident ones still further. His rela-tionship to his thirty-five classrooms is essentially one of admin-istration or leadership; and like any wise administrator, he must take his situations as they are, and try to capitalize on their strong points, and, little by little, to eliminate their weak points. This will get him much further than trying to impose uniformity.

First of all, he must get acquainted with his thirty-five teachers, and come to understand their viewpoints, their capabilities, their limitations, the children with whom they deal, the problems each one faces. He must try to know and understand them as persons, which means that he should approach them, not as an official with something to enforce, but as far as possible as an interested, helpful, sympathetic friend. He should go long on observation, and short on criticism, for he should aim to establish a relationship of mutual confidence and good will.

He will not have a pre-established way of getting to know these teachers and their situations, for his approach will depend on the person concerned. Classroom visits will be very desirable, but even here he must not use too much urging or insisting; for if his visit is to do much good, he must come at least as a willingly received if not an enthusiastically welcomed guest. Everything, always, depends on the person and the situation. This determines what he does when he visits a classroom, for sometimes he may do some teaching, and sometimes simply watch. It determines the number of times he will visit any one classroom, which need not be the same for all. It determines whatever he may do about a conference with the teacher after a visit has been made. Always his purpose will be to establish and develop confidence and co-operation. There is no uniform way of doing this. In fact, uniformity can spoil everything. But it can be done.

Before too long he has established good relationships with most, if not with all the teachers. More and more he finds it possible to take a positive line, to make suggestions, to indicate improvements and new departures here and there, without causing either resentment or dismay. He can do this because he understands the person he is talking to, and the situation she faces. Now the time arrives when some group discussion might go well and be helpful. Probably it will be best to begin with sub-groups, rather than with the whole thirty-five.

What should be taken up at these group discussions? If you will look back into this chapter, you will see the answer I would make. In very general terms, the discussion will deal with adequacy, coordination, and sequence. The purpose will be to help these teachers to see, and to begin to understand, the nature of the program as a whole, with reference to themselves. Mr. Smith has been working for this from the start, and probably has begun to get somewhere. But his group meetings create new opportunities. Here is a teacher who has never heard of the autoharp, or of singalong records. She finds that other teachers are using them to excellent effect. Why should they be used? What good can they do? Mr. Smith will not answer such questions by a long disquisition on music education and musical growth. He will operate with hints, elicited from others and thrown out by himself—hints that start thinking in a certain direction. Here is a teacher who sourly refuses to have anything to do with music. There is a shocked pause, followed by quite a flood of testimony. Mr. Smith keeps his tongue between his teeth, and refrains from so much as a breath of criticism; and perhaps the ice begins to thaw.

You see, what Mr. Smith is trying to do is to get these teachers to think about their work, to think about their own contribution, to think what they can do, to see what significance their contribution can have, to see what kind of contribution they should endeavor to make. He himself does just as little "telling" as he can. But he constantly steers and stimulates this group and individual thinking.

As the whole situation matures, a larger and more ambitious group conference becomes possible. Very likely there arises a demand for an after-school music workshop, and other members of the music staff can be drawn in. The teachers are all coming to see more and more clearly how music can be handled, what they themselves can do, how what they are doing is related to what others are doing. A first-grade teacher realizes with surprise that in some very simple musical experiences she is planting the seed which blossoms into some quite impressive sixth-grade projects. A third-grade teacher in one school gets a whole bagful of suggestions from a third-grade teacher in another school, and realizes, without a word from Mr. Smith, that some of the things she has been doing may not be so good. A common understanding is being established. Common insights are being created. And these understandings and insights are all related to practical procedures, to actual situations, and to the capabilities and inclinations of individuals. The music program in all these classrooms will never be uniform. Indeed, it should never be uniform. But it will become more and more adequate, better and better coordinated, more and more evidently sequential. Adequacy, coordination, and sequence are developing from the intelligent cooperation that Mr. Smith has created.

Mr. Smith's own activities, too, will not be uniform. They will be determined by the particular classroom situation concerned. Sometimes he may teach a lesson of his own choosing. Sometimes he will put on what is, in effect, a demonstration, because a teacher has asked for it, or because, from his understanding of the situation, he considers it wise. Sometimes he may do no teaching at all, and confine himself to the role of observer and commentator. Sometimes—though only in a very few cases—he may stay away, make no overt move, and wait for the general build-up that is going on to lead the teacher to seek him out.

What official title should Mr. Smith have? I really do not know. He is not exactly a supervisor, for he does not lay down the law, or order anyone about, or see to it that everyone sticks to the rule book. He is a consultant, but he does not sit like a spider in his den, waiting for consultees. He is a coordinator, but a leader too. Should he be called an advisor? Certainly he advises, but he also acts. The title elementary music specialist is neutral, and inclusive, and perhaps fits him best. But it is the nature of his work, as a promoter of intelligent cooperation that is important, not the tag under which his name appears in the roster of school personnel.

One thing, however, needs to be made quite clear. The music specialist must have sufficient authority to do his work as it needs to be done. Although he should use tact, persuasion, and patience, it should not depend simply on free individual choice whether his wishes and suggestions are heeded or not. He should, for instance, be fully entitled to visit any classroom when he sees fit, to do there what he considers necessary, to confer with individual teachers when it seems advisable to him to do so, to call group conferences from time to time, and so on. He should use his official authority always to promote intelligent cooperation. But those with whom he works must be expected to respond, rather than to resist, or to be indifferent; and this is a matter, not of choice, but of designated duty.

V. Leadership

No enterprise can go well without strong, positive, unified leadership. This statement certainly applies to the music program. The work must head up in some one person, perhaps with the title, and certainly with the functions, of director of music.

What Mr. Smith does for his own sector of the program, the director of music does for the program as a whole. He initiates, promotes, and guides intelligent cooperation. Above all, he stimulates and guides the thinking and planning of the music staff. This is his central responsibility, and it is a most essential one.

It often happens that the director of music is loaded down with far too many duties. He may, for instance, be the leader of the performing organizations in the high school, and perhaps do a great deal of the teaching of applied music. These are important and conspicuous activities, but compared to the director's essential work, they are secondary. Then too, the director may find that he has on his hands a great deal of musical busy-work, which cannot be considered of even secondary importance.

The consequence tends to be that he attends only to the machinery of administration, such as signing requisitions, approving bills, arranging schedules, and has no time, energy, and above all leisure to give his mind intensively to the basic educational problems of the program as a whole. Many directors of music have very little continuous influence on large and important sectors of the program, and particularly on the work that goes on in the elementary schools. When this happens, the work suffers everywhere.

To repeat what I have already said, the first duty of the director of music is to stimulate and guide the cooperative thinking and planning of the music staff. The music staff is made up of men and women of very diversified backgrounds and interests. Many of them will have spent years in becoming competent in some musical specialty; and like all specialists, their thinking is apt to be geared to their specialties. This is all right, and even admirable, so long as they are able to see beyond their specialties; and if they cannot, it becomes the duty of the director of music to lead them to do so. Every musical specialist, every instrumentalist, or band man, or piano teacher, or vocal teacher, or teacher of theory—can work well in and for a developmental program, *if he has a real understanding of that program.* He may not be able to step into a third-grade classroom, or take on the junior high school course in general music, and do a good job immediately. But he must have enough insight into the problems of the third-grade classroom, and of the general music course, to be able to see their relationship to his work, and to contribute his quota of suggestions and help for their improvement. A fine woodwind teacher may not have the breadth of view to take on the work of director of music, but he can and should have sufficient understanding of the nature and needs of the program to be able to follow the leads of the director of music with intelligence and discrimination. If the developmental program is to go properly, the staff must be capable of intelligent educational thinking. It is the first duty of the director to develop such thinking, on the basis of which all the special abilities of individuals can form a harmonious whole.

He develops this thinking by getting to know his staff members personally and individually, by maintaining enough first-hand contact with their situations to be able to understand them, by inaugurating varying patterns of group thinking which seem likely to be fruitful. When, for instance, misunderstandings arise between the high school instrumental teachers and the elementary-school specialists, he arranges for a meeting of minds in conference, and he himself provides the leadership needed for a constructive outcome. The true solution of all such misunderstandings and disputes is hardly ever the victory of one side and the capitulation of the other. Almost always what is required is a better comprehension of what a developmental music program really is, and what it requires. This is what the director of music must always seek to evoke.

The essential, vital problems about which the director of music sets his staff to work to thinking are always those of adequacy, coordination, and sequence. How can wider and better musical experiences be organized? How can a great and varied range of musical experiences be effectively coordinated, so that all of them point in one direction. How can such experiences be chosen and arranged so that out of them emerges a genuine and vital process of musical growth? These questions will always be in the mind of the director of music; and they will always be on his agenda in his dealings with his staff, both as individuals and in groups.

But above all, the director of music will use his influence to lead his staff to think earnestly and constantly about basic aims; for a common understanding of basic aims is the root of all real cooperative action, and the only ultimate justification for a program planned to promote musical growth. The question of aims need not explicitly arise in every conversation, every discussion, every group session. But it will aways be in the background, and never very far in the background. Often it will come to the forefront, and be matter for explicit discussion and consideration. For once the staff can, in substance, agree about the basic aims of their work, they are on the way toward developing solutions for their specific practical problems.

A thinking and cooperating staff is a necessity for the developmental program. All administrative devices, such as conferences, workshops, study groups, and the preparation of curriculum materials, are means for the self-education of such a staff. A thinking and cooperating staff is able to work fruitfully together, for its differences become enrichments rather than impediments. It has an essentially united outlook, which tends to permeate throughout the school system, and to influence both teachers and administrators. It is the supreme responsibility and privilege of the director of music to develop such a staff, because only by its agency can the rich benefits of music be brought in full measure into the lives of boys and girls.

Some Suggestions for Thought and Discussion

1. As you read this chapter, does it seem to you that any of the suggestions it presents might bring about the musical growth of the classroom teacher?
2. Under what circumstances should a visiting music specialist do just about what the classroom teacher is already doing with music? Under what circumstances should he do something entirely different?
3. If you were a music specialist visiting a classroom, and the classroom teacher absented herself while you were there, what would you do about it?
4. Would it ever be right for a music specialist to visit a classroom entirely for the sake of teaching the notation and music reading, and nothing else?
5. Would it be a good idea for a classroom teacher who knows that

the music specialist will be coming on a certain day, to "build up" his visit with the children?

6. Make as complete a list as you can of the functions of the elementary music specialist. Do the same with the classroom teacher, so far as her work with music is concerned.

7. If you were director of music, and your instrumental teachers in high school criticized the work in the elementary school because children came to them unable to read music, what would you do about it?

8. Would you be inclined to summarize what is said in this chapter as in effect saying that the elementary music specialist should educate the classroom teachers with reference to music and its uses.

9. Would you say that the director of music should educate his staff?

10. Can you see any ways in which participation in a developmental music program might lead a classroom teacher to grow in general as a teacher?

Some Suggested Readings

Very little has been published about the administration of the school music program; and most of that little deals with matters of detail, procedure, and machinery. Of course the general literature of educational administration is enormous, and much of it is valuable and relevant. But often it is long, and rather heavy going. So I have only the two following items to suggest.

James L. Mursell, *Principles of Democratic Education*, W. W. Norton Company, New York, 1955. Chapter 14, "Educational Administration."

Clyde M. Campbell (editor), *Practical Applications of Democratic Administration*, Harper and Brothers, New York, 1952. Chapter 2, "Educational Leadership in a Free Society."

Index